THE BIBLE IN ITS WORLD
The Bible and Archaeology Today

THE BIBLE
IN ITS WORLD

The Bible and Archaeology Today

by

K. A. KITCHEN

Reader in Egyptian & Coptic,
School of Archaeology & Oriental Studies,
University of Liverpool

EXETER
THE PATERNOSTER PRESS

ISBN 0 85364 211 7
Copyright © The Paternoster Press Ltd., 1977

AUSTRALIA
Emu Book Agencies, Ltd.,
63 Berry Street, Granville, N.S.W., 2142

SOUTH AFRICA
Oxford University Press,
P.O. Box 1141, Oxford House,
11 Buitencingle Street, Cape Town

Typeset by Input Typesetting Ltd., London and printed in
Great Britain by Butler and Tanner for The Paternoster
Press Ltd., Paternoster House, 3 Mount Radford Crescent,
Exeter, Devon.

Contents

Preface

Archaeology and the Bible remains a theme of unending fascination. The ancient Near East teemed with the life of rich and complex civilizations that show both change and continuity in how people lived in that part of our planet across a span of several thousand years. The study of the physical remains and of the innumerable inscriptions from the ancient Near-Eastern world is itself a complex and many-sided task. Yet, as that world is the Bible's world, the attempt is a necessary venture in order to see the books of the Bible in their ancient context. The enduring central themes of the Bible stand out clearly enough of themselves; but a more detailed understanding of the biblical writings can be gained by viewing them in relation to their ancient context.

Biblical studies have long been hindered by the persistence of long-outdated philosophical and literary theories (especially of 19th-century stamp), and by wholly inadequate use of first-hand sources in appreciating the earlier periods of the Old Testament story in particular. Therefore, this little book makes direct use of first-hand evidence from the ancient biblical world, both archaeology and texts, and concentrates principally upon the earlier periods down to the end of Solomon's reign. Much is already available on later periods, and therefore the closing chapters are deliberately and progressively briefer. In the notes (kept to a minimum) and bibliography, English-language works are cited whenever possible.

It is always an author's pleasantest duty to thank those who have lightened his task. My thanks thus go to Mr. Alan Millard for valuable criticisms of the whole; to my mother for statistical checking of the MS; and to the publishers (who invited me to write this work), for their patience and helpfulness. The shortcomings, naturally, remain the author's property, and his alone.

Woolton, June 1977   *K. A. Kitchen*

1
Archaeology — a Key to the Past

Ever since Napoleon rallied his troops by the Egyptian Pyramids
with the clarion-call, "Fifty centuries look down upon you!", the
more spectacular discoveries of archaeology have repeatedly hit
the world's headlines. The Egyptian Rosetta Stone in Napoleon's
day, huge Assyrian palaces in Queen Victoria's time, the golden
splendours of Tutankhamun in Egypt and the royal tombs at Ur in
Iraq in the roaring twenties, the Dead Sea Scrolls during the post-
war years, and whole series of ancient royal archives on clay
tablets, most recently at Syrian Ebla in the seventies – the
cavalcade of great finds is almost endless.

But of course, archaeology is not all romance. Most of it is simply persistent, methodical hard work, dealing with everyday
materials, to reach results as solid and enlightening as possible on
all aspects of ancient life, not just the spectacular highlights.

THE SCOPE OF ARCHAEOLOGY

'Archaeology' is simply the recovery of man's past by
systematically discovering, recording and studying the surviving
material remains that he has left behind. In the fullest use of the
term, those remains include all kinds of ancient written documents
as well as the objects of everyday life, and epochs and cultures
without writing. In turn, that much maligned term 'biblical

archaeology' is a convenient synthetic label for the archaeology of the 'Bible lands' (the ancient Near or Middle East) as drawn upon to elucidate and illustrate the biblical writings.

THE MATERIALS OF ARCHAEOLOGY

Throughout the ancient biblical Near East, mud or clay was used to make bricks that dried in the warm sun. Such sun-dried mud bricks were by far the cheapest, handiest, most popular material from which people could build their homes, and even kings their palaces. In lands like Mesopotamia (Iraq) where stone was rare, even the greatest temples were of brick, if sometimes faced with kiln-burnt bricks. But in the cliff-lined Nile Valley, the pharaohs could build their temples and tombs of stone. In Palestine and Syria, buildings were commonly of brick on stone foundations. Townships were commonly walled-round for defence, there and elsewhere.

Such mud-brick buildings were highly convenient, but not too permanent, lasting about 25/30 years. Unseasonably wet winters, accidental fires, or demolition by invading enemies could quickly turn houses, palaces or whole towns into desolate ruins. Then if the inhabitants decided to rebuild, they often just levelled-off the debris and built on top. Thus, through the centuries, towns grew ever upwards upon their own former ruins, level by level, age by age. In this way, early Jericho reached a height of 70 feet before Joshua's time (by the 13th century BC) above its Neolithic beginnings some 8000 years earlier. Beth Shan and Megiddo reached similar elevations above their prehistoric foundations.

At periods when a town-site was deserted, driving wind, sand and rains would often erode away the uppermost levels of the abandoned houses and walls. Thus, at Ur, the town of Neo-Babylonian times was largely swept away (attested mainly by burials), while 20 feet depth of human occupation-remains had been lost from ancient Babylonian Eshnunna (Tell Asmar) before it was excavated. Likewise, in barely 150 years (c.1550–1400 BC), most of the Middle Bronze Age town of Jericho and of its defence-walls (with 20 feet of scarp below them) were similarly eroded away. Small wonder, then, that from the still higher Late Bronze levels (Joshua's time), scarcely any traces have survived the 400 years of scouring and denudation that followed their destruction.

Buildings are not all. Age by age, fashions and fads changed in life's everyday tools and furnishings, especially pottery which survives in quantity. So, in the successive ruin-levels of ancient towns, the pottery and other effects vary through the ages. Similar levels in other sites enable us to link up the sequences in whole regions. Links with written records (found in particular levels) enable us to tie in the archaeological sequences with the flow of known history.

THE METHODS AND LIMITS OF ARCHAEOLOGY

Therefore, to recover the material history and successive life-styles of the peoples of antiquity, the archaeologist excavates the town-mounds of the ancient Near East, beginning at the top levels, left by the last occupants, and working his way downward through ever-earlier periods of settlement to reach bedrock on which the first inhabitants had built. Several floor-levels (indicating 'rebuilds') might belong to one longer cultural epoch; he observes the changes in styles of pottery and other artifacts, buildings, etc., period by period. Then, he can write up the cultural history of the site in proper order, from its beginning to its final end. If written documents from the site or elsewhere make it possible to tie in destructions and 'rebuilds' with known history, then the archaeological and literary histories supplement each other. From prehistory following the last 'Ice Age' or 'Wet Period', down to Roman times, it has been possible to chart the rise and variations of some 10,000 years of human culture and civilization in the ancient Near East. To assist the archaeologist to extract the maximum amount of useful information from a 'dig', all manner of scientific techniques have been devised. Soil-analysis, pollen-grain analysis, tests on human and animal remains, etc., can give us some idea of the climate, natural vegetation, crops, wild and domestic animals, people's diet, at various periods. Carbon-14 counts (measuring the amount of radio-active carbon emission from organic matter) can help to assess an approximate date for the samples tested, although complications can arise from contamination of samples, and so on.

Needless to say, practical 'digging' is often far more tricky than this 'ideal' outline might suggest, and it requires considerable expertise. Decayed mud-brick walls can sometimes barely be distinguished at first from the mud in which they are buried. Styles of pottery sometimes changed only slowly, making precise dating difficult. Foundation-trenches, and storage or rubbish-pits cut from one level down into another can mix up the remains from two or more different levels. An undulating town-site can result in late levels in one part being physically lower down than early levels in another part. These and other pitfalls frequently beset the field archaeologist.

Problems of other kinds can affect the results reached by excavations. The gaps in the record caused by erosion were noted

above. And normally, only a minute area of an entire site can ever
be dug, especially if explored to any great depth. Thus, ancient
Ashdod comprises about 70 acres of lower city area and about 20
acres of acropolis, some 90 acres in all – but only $1\frac{1}{2}$ acres of this
surface (less than 2%) has been excavated. At Tell Beit Mirsim
(possibly ancient Debir) about one-quarter of the surface-area of
this much smaller site was excavated, but only parts of that quarter
down to bedrock. At Tell el-Areini (once thought to be Gath), the
excavated areas cover barely 4% of the whole site, and likewise in
the Early Bronze city at Arad. Only about a tenth of the area of Et-
Tell (often supposed to be Ai) has been dug, and similarly at Tell el-
Ajjul (Beth Eglayim). While surface-potsherds from the slopes of a
mound can give valuable indications of the periods during which a
former ancient town was inhabited, only full-scale excavation can
reveal the total occupation-history. But as even 'full-scale' excavations rarely touch more than a fraction of a site – as we have just
seen – important features can still be missed by accident. If levels
of a particular period occur in only one part of a site – a part not
dug – then the archaeologist's 'record' will appear to show a gap in
that town's history, much as when erosion has taken its toll. If one
digs 5% of a site, one must expect to miss 95% (and 100%, if it is
the wrong site!). Sometimes, adjoining cemeteries can point to the
artificiality of a 'gap'.

Therefore, the information we obtain by excavation can often be
very incomplete. Ancient Gibeon is a good example. Despite the
narration in Joshua (9:3 – 10:2) which presupposes a settlement
there in the Late Bronze Age, the first three seasons of a very successful excavation by Professor J. B. Pritchard yielded not a scrap
from that period other than a stray Cypriot sherd or two. Only in
the fourth season were found a handful of fine Late Bronze Age
tombs, refuting the supposed contradiction between Joshua and
'archaeology'. Moreover, those four busy seasons dealt with barely
a twentieth of Gibeon's surface area and thus could not possibly
claim to be exhaustive. Whether eroded beyond recall or still safely
buried, a Late Bronze township evidently once existed at Gibeon.[1]
Some may ask, why is so little dug on these ancient sites? The
answer is threefold. In the first place, the cost of excavating an entire site from top to bottom, complete, is prohibitive. Millionaires
do not exactly tumble over each other to make it otherwise! Secondly, it is often wise in any case to leave good-sized areas of a site
intact for later generations to tackle with the hindsight of better
knowledge or improved techniques. Thirdly, in some cases, the
results throughout an entire level are so uniform that total excavation would give only repetitive results not commensurate with the

cost and time involved. However, this can only be certainly determined by wide testing.

How unreliable such 'gaps' in the record can be may also be illustrated at a biblical site across the Jordan in the land of Moab. One of the most famous towns of ancient Moab was Dibon, now represented by the mounds at Dhiban, where the renowned inscription of King Mesha of Moab was found over a century ago. Excavations at Dhiban produced definite traces of the Early Bronze Age township (3rd millennium BC), then practically nothing for the entire 2nd millennium (Middle and Late Bronze Ages). From the 1st millennium (Iron Age), parts of the citadel of the dynasty of Mesha were unearthed, plus remains of later epochs. Now, from such a gap for (e.g.) the Late Bronze Age, the unwary might be led to conclude that biblical mentions of Dibon no later than the 13th century BC (Late Bronze Age) as in Numbers 21:30 and 32:3,34 or Joshua 13:9,17, were in fact errors or anachronisms. But they would be mistaken. Because, in that very period, the pharaoh Ramesses II conquered Dibon a few decades before the Israelites reached it, and celebrated his victory in sculptured reliefs in his temple at Luxor in Upper Egypt.[2] Thus, Dibon certainly existed in the Late Bronze Age according to first-hand inscriptional evidence, evidence which supplements and corrects the quite inadequate results obtained from digging at Dibon itself. Future diggers may do better.

Then, there is the phenomenon of 'site-shift'. The citizens of an ancient town sometimes could no longer live comfortably on the crest of their tall mound; or destruction made a new start desirable; or new prosperity led to expansion beyond the old citadel. In such cases a new town or suburb was built either adjoining the old mound or at some little distance from it. Such a development could occur more than once. At some later date, in harder times, a much-reduced population might seek security by reoccupying the top of the long-defunct high mound. For modern investigators, the practical result is that a site appears not to have been lived in at certain periods of history – whereas, in fact, people had simply 'moved down the road' and actually lived nearby during the supposedly 'missing' periods. Thus, Old Testament Jericho (now Tell es-Sultan) was abandoned from Hellenistic times, and settlement moved to near the springs of Ain-Sultan, onto the site which became modern Jericho (Er-Riha). But in Hellenistic/Roman times, palaces and residential villas were built at a third site nearby (Tulul Abu el-Alaiq). So, today, there are three 'Jerichos'.[3] Consequent shifts of the ancient name can thus be deceptive. A century ago, Umm Lakis seemed to be Lachish by its name – but was in fact not occupied in biblical times. The real Lachish of antiquity is represented by the massive early site at Tell ed-Duweir, confirmed by the Lachish ostraca found there. Much more recently, when Tell Hesban in Transjordan was excavated in hopes of finding ancient Heshbon, little but one wall and much pottery-fill from before the 7th century BC was found, and few buildings earlier than Hellenistic/Roman, in the areas dug. As the owners of the 7th/6th century pottery must have had homes of their own, it is clear that most of the Iron Age structures had long since been destroyed, or simply not located. In the case of the Late Bronze Age, the remains may be destroyed or buried (as at Dibon) – or the real Heshbon is actually to be sought elsewhere, at Tell Jalul or Tell el-Umeiri (both occupied in the Bronze Ages[4]), precisely as early Lachish is at Tell ed-Duweir, not Umm Lakis.

WHICH SITE IS WHICH?

How, then, does one identify an ancient site as having once been a particular town mentioned in antiquity? This brings us to the relationship between the evidence of written history (inscriptions, the Old Testament, etc.) and the material sequences of buildings and cultures unearthed on excavated sites.[5] In Egypt or Babylonia, it is commonplace for ancient cities to be readily identified by name from actual inscriptions discovered in their ruins or to be read on standing temples, etc. This is partly true in Syria also, as at Ugarit, Mari and Ebla for example. But such convenient identification by inscriptions is much rarer in Palestine: examples are Gezer, Gibeon, Hazor and Lachish.

Where inscriptions are lacking, we have to use a combination of different kinds of evidence. From the Bible and other ancient documents, the outline history of an ancient town may be sketched – prominent in some periods, not at others, and so on. These references can be combed through likewise for geographical information – what known places are reputed to be near the one being studied? How near? In what directions? Are there any special natural features mentioned? These may all help to pinpoint the district and location where the appropriate ruin-heap should be found. Sometimes the ancient name has survived in use from antiquity through into modern Arabic. But it may now be attached either to the ancient site, or to only one part of it, or simply to another location nearby, as we have seen already. Therefore this item of evidence has to be used with care. Thus, (El)-Jib reflects ancient Gib(eon), and in fact marks its site; likewise, Dhiban ancient Dibon. But in contrast, oldest Jericho is located at Tell es-Sultan, not Er-Riha, and Lachish at Tell ed-Duweir, not Khirbet Umm Lakis several miles to the west.

Finally, when one digs a site considered to fit the criteria, the question arises: does its archaeologically revealed occupation-history match the story told by historical and other written records? (Always allowing, of course, for the pitfalls of erosion, part-occupation, 'site-shift' locally, and the like.) If all the criteria agree, or the apparent 'gaps' in data can be reasonably accounted for, then the identification of the present-day site and the ancient name may be taken as either possible, probable, or near-certain, depending on the quality of the evidence available. In detail, however, limited problems can persist even in the archaeology of known and identified sites. Thus, there is no doubt whatever that ancient Israelite Samaria (later Roman Sebaste) is the site known in modern Arabic as Sebastiyeh. The remains, location, name, overall site-history (compared with written history) all agree. Yet, there has been controversy over precisely which individual levels or archaeological strata should correspond to particular reigns. Were the pottery and levels I-II of Omri and Ahab, or of a settlement before theirs? And consequently, was the pottery and level III from the period of Jehu and Jeroboam II, or did it include the preceding reigns of Omri and Ahab's dynasty? Only with additional data or more refined methods can such details be solved in the course of time.

Frequently both the written and archaeological records are incomplete. As we saw above, Dibon is attested in Egyptian texts for the 13th century BC but only later archaeologically. Conversely, Jericho enters history only from Joshua's time (13th century BC onwards), but excavation has taken its story as a town back through thousands of years beyond the 'Bronze Ages' to Chalcolithic and Neolithic phases of early prehistory. Therefore, we need always to use all the resources available, and to allow for the all too often defective state of the evidence – after all, we *are* dealing with 'the wrecks of time' usually several thousand years after they were live and new!

INSCRIPTIONS AND WRITING IN THE BIBLICAL WORLD

Writing – the expression of connected ideas and language by visible signs – was first invented in Mesopotamia, sometime before about 3100 BC, followed soon after by its appearance in Egypt. The first writing consisted of pictures – a bird for a bird, a head of grain for that object, and so on. Such pictorial records were all very well for keeping accounts – 6 fowls, 12 fishes, 100 ears of grain, etc. But to write sounds and express all the ideas of which words and language are capable, required that the pictures should become symbols for sounds (to spell out words), and not just stand for the objects they represented. In English, this would work as follows. A picture-sign of a bee could stand for the sound-group 'bee', 'be'; a picture-sign of a leaf could stand for the syllable(s) 'leaf', 'leef', 'lief'. By putting together the picture of the bee and that of the leaf, one can then spell in two syllables the quite different word 'be-lief' – and 'belief' is a concept which it would be very difficult to draw a picture of!

It was by such means, using their pictures both for things represented and for sounds derived from the names of things, that the early Sumerians began the long history of writing, drawing their pictures on small pads or tablets of clay. Very quickly, the signs drawn on clay became simply groups of wedges, equally distinctive (if less 'artistic') and more easily and quickly written with a reed or 'stylus'. This, from the Latin *cuneus*, 'wedge', is what we term *cuneiform* writing. But the Sumerians were not the only inhabitants of earliest Mesopotamia. During the 3rd millennium BC, the Semitic-speaking Akkadians took over the cuneiform word-signs and syllables to spell out their own, quite different language – Akkadian, from which came the twin dialects Babylonian and Assyrian, all relatives of Hebrew and Arabic with the other Semitic tongues. Rather as we today can use Latin words or word-groups as the equivalent of English phrases (*et cetera* = 'and so on'), so the Akkadians, Babylonians and Assyrians could use Sumerian word-signs and groups to stand for words in their own language. They might write the signs LUGAL GAL, king + great, 'great king', but read them in their own tongue as *sharru rabu*, with the same meaning.

In Egypt, the concept of writing, using pictures for things and the sound of their names, may have been taken over from Mesopotamia, by *c.*3100 BC at the very latest. But here, the signs came to represent only the consonants of words, leaving the vowels to be filled-in by the reader. The Egyptian picture-signs – the famous hieroglyphs – kept their picturesque forms to the end in monumental use. But from the beginning, when written with reed-pen and carbon ink upon papyrus, they were modified to a flowing, continuous script ('hieratic'), the signs running into each other as with our own long-hand handwriting. From the 7th century BC, this cursive script became even more abbreviated ('demotic').

From both of these great ancient civilisations, Egypt and Mesopotamia, we have a vast but fragmentary mass of written documents. In Egypt, on stone temples and in formal inscriptions, the pharaohs set out their high deeds before the gods – rituals, annual festivals, and historical matters for religious purposes. Their subjects sometimes included biographical details of their own careers in inscriptions in their tomb-chapels or on their statues. But the vast majority of day-to-day writing was in the flowing hieratic script, on papyrus (an early form of 'paper', made from strips of the papyrus-plant), or upon spare bits of smooth potsherd or slips of white limestone – known to the Egyptologists as ostraca (singular, ostracon). These were the note-pads and 'scrap paper' of the Egyptians, costing nothing. It was upon papyri that fine literature, religious texts (hymns, rites, etc.), and all administrative records were written. Thus, as 90% of Egyptian papyri are lost forever, our losses of knowledge here are enormous. However, budding schoolboy and student scribes did their homework on ostraca, and many lesser administrative jottings likewise were drafted out on these sherds and flakes – so we do recover quite a sampling of all classes of Egyptian writing by this means.

In Mesopotamia, the Sumerians and their Akkadian contemporaries and successors were equally prolific. As clay tablets survive far more frequently than papyri, we have masses of administrative documents, letters and so on, although *not* equally for all periods (depending on the chances of discovery and excavation). On the tablets, a rich and considerable literature had survived (sometimes rather fragmented, as in Egypt), as well as technical vocabularies of terms, magical compilations (for interpreting omens, etc.) and religious rituals. Monumentally, we have the palace-inscriptions of Assyrian kings, and formal inscriptions of many other rulers.

In the far north-west beyond Mesopotamia and Syria, the Hittite kingdom in Anatolia or Asia Minor (modern Turkey) took over the use of the cuneiform script. The Hittite kings employed it to write their annals and for religious hymns and rituals, literature, legal and administrative documents – largely in their own Indo-European language (cuneiform Hittite, Nesite), partly in related dialects (Luvian, Palaic), partly in Semitic Akkadian for international diplomacy, partly in Hurrian (Horite) for religious purposes, and Hattian likewise. (The last two languages are related neither to each other nor to any of the rest.) From about 1300 BC onwards, they began also to write Luvian in a special hieroglyphic script ('Hittite hieroglyphs') on stone monuments – a script used also on state seals.

In Syria, the spectacular finds at Ebla (cf. Chapter 3) show that, as early as 2300 BC, major city-states could use cuneiform script and the Sumerian language for a wide variety of documents, administrative, religious and literary. And at Ebla, the local West-Semitic language was also written in that script. Later, during the 2nd millennium, Syrian states normally used the Akkadian language and cuneiform script. The seaport of Ugarit also wrote its own local West-Semitic language in a cuneiform alphabet. Like the Ebla dialect, Ugaritic is quite closely related to Hebrew, Canaanite and Phoenician. Where Egyptian influence was particularly strong – as at Byblos – the local rulers sometimes set up inscriptions in Egyptian hieroglyphs and language.

But in south Syria and Palestine (Canaan), a still more important script came into use from the mid 2nd millennium BC onwards: the alphabet. This was a set of 26 or 30 simple signs to stand each for a single consonantal sound (perhaps originally, plus any vowel). With this limited set of simple signs to spell any word by its consonantal framework, literacy steadily became possible for a far greater number of people. From the 'Proto-Sinaitic' inscriptions and other fragments (c.1500 BC and perhaps even earlier) down through early Canaanite (to 1200/1100 BC), it is possible to chart the history and progress of the alphabet in Phoenicia (from where it reached the Greeks), in Hebrew, Aramaic, and the Transjordanian dialects of Moab, Edom and Ammon, contemporary with the Hebrew kingdoms, exile and return, to Graeco-Roman times. In this group of West-Semitic languages and dialects, the alphabetic inscriptions vary greatly in content. We have royal inscriptions (Byblos, Moab, Ammon; Cilicia), administrative documents and private letters (ostraca, Hebrew and Aramaic), some papyri (mainly Aramaic), and innumerable personal stamp-seals bearing the names of their owners (practically all dialects), use of which presupposes that many people could read enough to distinguish between them. There are inscribed arrow-heads, notations of person, place, or capacity on jar-handles – the list of everyday uses is quite varied. Thus, certainly from c.1100 BC (and probably rather earlier), writing in Canaan, then in Israel, Phoenicia and round about was clearly part of everyday life and not restricted solely to a special scribal elite.[6]

Thus, throughout the ancient biblical world, not one but several systems of writing were in use, often at the same time, and sometimes even in one place (as at Ugarit, or with the Hittites). Whenever writing occurs, we find it used for documents and literature of every conceivable kind. With the advent of the West-Semitic alphabet, the use of writing became possible for many more people during biblical times.

2

The Most Ancient World

The antiquity of civilisation on our planet has always been a source of fascination to ancients and moderns alike. One thinks of the little girl visiting a major museum with her parents, pausing (like most children) before the inevitable Egyptian mummy, and asking, 'Is he older than Granny?' Or, away back in antiquity itself, the reader of the Babylonian Epic of Gilgamesh is invited to admire the ancient walls of the hero's city of Uruk: 'the wall of girdled Uruk he built ..., climb upon the wall of Uruk, walk about on it, inspect the foundation-terrace, examine the brickwork – see, is it not of burnt brick, and did not the ancient Seven Sages lay its foundations?'

TIME-PERSPECTIVES IN DEPTH

Primeval antiquity going back into 'the night of time' is one of the themes that formed part of the cultural heritage treasured in the ancient Near East both inside and outside the Old Testament. In the opening chapters of Genesis (1–11), we see the Old Testament's principal vista of early antiquity, drawn in broad outline, before the focus changes sharply to centre upon Abraham and his family. In contrast to 1–11, the narratives from Genesis 12 onwards deal in varying detail with individuals, a family and a clan, and no longer with events of cosmic dimension or in terms of long series of generations. The picture that Genesis 1–11 presents to us has three episodes – creation, flood, origins of Abraham – linked by the thread of two long genealogies (Genesis 5 and 11). As we shall see later, other peoples of the biblical world also formulated traditions about early antiquity in similar fashion, using lists, genealogies, and accounts of primeval events such as creation, a flood, and earliest leaders. So in Mesopotamia among the Sumerians, and (in a different way) in Egypt, where the dynasty of the gods (with a destruction of mankind under Re) preceded the demi-gods and historic kings. But just as modern historical study fills out a history based on kings and queens of England and Scotland from 1066 to Queen Victoria (with episodes like the Black Death, Act of Union, etc.), so with the striking but necessarily circumscribed traditions in Genesis 1–11, early Sumer and Akkad, or ancient Egypt. Fresh dimensions are added to these traditions from the results of two lines of exploration – archaeological excavations, and the study of the body of ancient literary and religious written compositions.

TEN TO TWO THOUSAND YEARS BC

Barely fifty years ago, ancient Near Eastern (and world) history began about 3500/3000 BC (on today's dating) with the emergence of writing, and the prehistory that preceded it was of the vaguest practically everywhere except in Egypt and Mesopotamia. Following pioneer work in the thirties, widespread excavation throughout the Near East and intensive study in the last twenty-five years has transformed the whole picture. The newer methods of dating remains (Carbon–14, bristlecone pine ring-counts, etc.) have helped to provide a still-flexible outline of broad dates for well before 3000 BC.

Thus, before the earliest practicable date for an Abraham (about 2000 BC or so), there extends back through time an immense perspective of ancient cultures and civilisation for over 80 centuries back to about 10,000 BC or more. Of this long period, only the last 12 centuries (3200–2000 BC) – a little more than the 3rd millennium – stand increasingly in the full light of history because of the invention and use of writing. But the previous sixty eight centuries pulsate also with life and colour.

1. Foundations of Culture, c. 10,000–6000 BC

Before the tenth millennium BC, we know only of hunters, fishers, collectors of edible fruits and roots, of people living in caves and in temporary shelters – the so-called Palaeolithic ('Old Stone') and Mesolithic ('Middle Stone') Ages, But from roughly 9000 BC onwards, we find the first real settlements in the Near East, as people gradually became keepers of goats, sheep or cattle, and learned to cultivate grain-crops. From this Neolithic ('New Stone') phase, a series of ancient towns has come to light in Palestine, Syria, Anatolia and Mesopotamia. Oldest Jericho became in time a walled township ten acres in extent, with massive watchtowers and round houses, for a population of perhaps 2000 people. The sheer mass of the stone-built defences, the economy based partly on local cultivation of irrigated ground and partly on trade, and the general material layout and quality of life – all suggest a well-organised community under effective leadership able to muster the common resources for major undertakings – and fearing jealous foes against whom defence was thought needful. Still later, when the old was long gone, a new population built a new town of rectangular houses with fine plastered floors (and using reed mats). [1] But pottery was one convenience that had not yet come into use in Palestine. In Syria, along the middle Euphrates, comparable townships arose at sites such as those known today as Mureybet and Tell Abu Hureyra, the latter being almost a city.

Far north in Anatolia, remarkable towns grew up at this early epoch (7th millennium if not earlier), at Hacilar (old settlement) and especially Catal Huyuk – a town-site of 32 acres, thrice as large as Jericho. Life here was enlivened with some of the world's earliest pottery. However, the only entry/exit of the houses was up and down ladders through a roof-hatch, hence no doubt some nasty falls, probably reflected in broken bones in the skeletons of former inhabitants. The excavator notes also a good number of head-wounds that may well have resulted from family and neighbours' quarrels, with people living so closely together – sad testimony to human nature in all ages! And possibly life was both stimulated and shadowed by sinister-seeming religious cults. A series of shrines bore paintings that included vulture-figures pecking at headless human bodies, and had clay-plastered bulls' heads, before which were laid baskets containing human skulls (prior to later burial?).

Westward in Cyprus, the oldest settlements at Khirokitia had a paved street, and 'upstairs-downstairs' beehive-domed houses. Eastward, in Mesopotamia, arose villages in the Zagros foothills (as at Jarmo) and townships in the steppes and central plains (like Umm Dabaghiyah). Thus, across a vast area, from central Europe and over the entire Near East into Iran and beyond the Caucasus, there grew up a vast swathe of local cultures based on agriculture and animal husbandry, sometimes partly at least on trade, building villages and towns of mud-brick, worshipping deities that personified natural forces (e.g., reproduction), and using a considerable array of tools and furnishings, sometimes of a quality of finish or aesthetic appeal that still commands our admiration today.

2.   *The Flowering of Pre-literate High Cultures, c. 6000–3200 BC*

From about 6000 BC onwards, the use of pottery steadily became universal in the ancient Near East, in a great variety of styles, forms and decoration, in different regions and cultures, and with the passage of time. Thus it becomes the archaeologist's handiest material indicator to follow the spread of cultural influence and to trace sequences of cultures down through time. From at least 6000 BC onwards, copper came into use for tools alongside stone. It first was used as native metal, hammered cold, but smelting and casting techniques made possible a wide range of uses. Conventionally, archaeologists sometimes speaks of this as the Chalcolithic Age ('Copper/Stone' Age). With the full use of copper and other metals, c. 3200 BC onwards, the rather misleading term 'Early Bronze Age' is customary, despite the lack of bronze at that early epoch.

In Palestine, the Chalcolithic age (*c.* 4000–3200 BC) is most famed for its technical achievements and religious art. Across the Jordan at Ghassul, several buildings had coloured frescoes on their plastered walls, perhaps illustrating local mythology: an eight-pointed star, strange bird-like figures, as well as geometric patterns and a group of human figures. To a temple at En-Gedi may have belonged such a ritual treasure as that found at Nahal Mishmar with its remarkable copper sceptres and processional (?) standards.[2] Technologically astonishing was the great desert township at Jawa in Transjordan, totally dependent upon an elaborate water-conservation system of dam, channels and pools.[3]

In Syria, sites that are famous in later periods, like Byblos and Ugarit (Ras Shamra), show the impact of the Halaf and Ubaid cultures of Mesopotamia. The whole period *c.* 5000 to 3200 BC witnessed the emerging brilliance of Mesopotamian culture, whose influence radiated out to Syria and southern Anatolia, as marked by the successive spread of pottery styles, be it the brilliant painted vessels of Halaf or Ubaid, or the plainer wares of the Uruk period. Throughout Mesopotamia we see the rise of cities centred upon impressive temples displaying the most spectacular architecture, from Eridu and Uruk (biblical Erech) in the 'deep South' to Gawra in the far north. The Sumerians may already have been the leading element in the population. Direct Mesopotamian influence already reached far west, to the westernmost bend of the Euphrates in Syria where a huge, purely Mesopotamian fortress a thousand metres long was built (*c.* 3300 BC) at Habuba el-Kabira – perhaps by order of some precursor of that archetypal Sumerian adventurer Gilgamesh! However, rival city-states rather than far-flung empires were already probably the rule in Mesopotamia. Finally, the use of pictures on pads of clay to keep accounts began the history of writing - and likewise the era of written history. In Egypt, a distinct agricultural civilistion arose in Valley and Delta; arrival of the concept of writing stimulated the invention of the hieroglyphs just before a southern king conquered also the north to found the first dynasty of the pharaonic monarchy about 3200 BC.

3. *The Brilliant Third Millennium, c. 3200–2000 BC*

Such, then, in the very barest, simplest outline, runs the story of the rise of civilisation for some sixty eight centuries or so, down to a point (the start of written history) still well over a thousand years before Abraham. During this final thousand years and more before 2000 BC, the civilisations of Egypt and Sumer reached their first peak of maturity and brilliant achievement.

In Egypt, the Old Kingdom or 'Pyramid Age' witnessed splendid stone architecture: temples of the gods, vast pyramids as tombs of the kings, these being surrounded by veritable streets and cities of tomb-chapels of the principal officials of the realm. The growing number of inscriptions attests a complex administration under the pharaoh and his vizier. Superb craftsmanship appears in the fine arts, jewellery, sculpture and painting. Writing skills extended beyond administration to other, more literary spheres. Narrative is represented by biographical inscriptions of officials in their tomb-chapels. Spells, hymns, and a variety of long and elaborate rituals make up much of the so-called 'Pyramid Texts' that were inscribed within the later pyramids of the period. A series of wisdom-writings (related in form and matter to Proverbs) probably originated at this time, although preserved to us in later copies so far.

In Mesopotamia, the Sumerian city-states lacked the political unity of Egypt, but rivalled her in all the arts, in sophisticated administration, and in pioneering the beginnings of literature. Besides word-lists and sign-lists, we have – again – wisdom-books and hymns, as well as brief royal inscriptions. During about 2400–2200 BC, the Semitic-speaking dynasty of Sargon of Akkad established an empire that controlled all of Mesopotamia and disputed the rule of the Middle Euphrates region with the great North-Syrian kingdom of Ebla. Collapse of the Akkad empire led to foreign (Gutian) domination, until the Sumerian Third Dynasty of Ur (*c.* 2100–2000 BC) reunited Mesopotamia in the last flowering of Sumerian political power. Under the rule of both Akkad and Ur,

all the arts, crafts and skills flourished, and much new literature
was composed. It is mainly the hymnology that has so far survived
to us from this, plus some royal inscriptions. After the fall of Ur,
Mesopotamia split up into a series of rival city-states (Old-
Babylonian period), with Semitic dynasties, increasingly of West-
Semitic-speaking stock, called by the Babylonians 'Amurrites'
(Amorites) or 'Westerners'. In this period of ferment, a vast
amount of the most varied Sumerian literature was cultivated in the
scribal schools, and Akkadian (Babylonian, rather than its sister
Assyrian) gave birth to a vigorous literature in narrative (epic,
legend), wisdom, hymnody and so on. A common culture was
shared by Sumerians, Babylonians and Western Semites in
Mesopotamia.

In the Levant – Anatolia, Syria, Palestine – city-states were the
rule politically, with semi-nomadic pastoralists moving about in the
fringe areas of the sedentary, agriculture-based mini-states.
Mesopotamian cultural influence was felt in North Syria. This appears at Ebla, great rival of Akkad, whose vast archives used
Sumerian script and language, besides going on to use cuneiform to
write the local West-Semitic language. Those archives, too, include
religious, narrative and wisdom literature. Unlike most of her
neighbours, Ebla became a 'great power', able to challenge the
Mesopotamian kings, during about 2400–2250 BC. Neither the
Anatolian princedoms in the far north (among whom the Hittites
were beginning to appear) nor the petty Palestinian city-states
could match Ebla politically, but all had their own regional high
culture materially.

4. *The Perspective of Eighty Centuries*

These major civilisations, even when focused on urban centres,
were still directly based upon agriculture and animal husbandry –
upon the farmer and the pastoralist. In Palestine, Syria, and certainly Upper Mesopotamia, the cultivator and the herdsman were
the two interdependent parts of the food-producing economy. In
Syria and Mesopotamia, the cities were centres of political powers
– of royal dynasties – but their satellite villages were the real centres of food-production. There lived the farmers, and around them
(between winter and summer pastures) moved the herdsmen of
sheep and cattle. This background is reflected in ancient texts, such
as the Sumerian 'debates' between farmer and shepherd in friendly
rivalry.[4] It needs to be remembered as the real economic and social
background when reading the patriarchal and other narratives in
the Old Testament. The patriarchs, for example, moved from Ur to
Haran to Palestine, going from one pastoral/agricultural setting to

another. In the first two cases, from territory dependent on the cities of Ur and Har(r)an, in the third phase interacting with the local Palestinian city-states and communities.

What else from this vast epoch before 2000 BC is of significance for the beginnings of the biblical story? First, the sheer length of time – the many generations, century upon century. By 2000 BC, the civilised world was already *ancient*. Throughout the ancient Near East, cultures and civilisations rose and fell not once but many times over. Little wonder, then, that before Abraham the narratives in Genesis 1–11 look back through genealogies on repetitive patterns to 'in the beginning'.

Secondly, there was never a cultural vacuum in the ancient biblical East. Pastoralists and farmers lived in close contact, and both had intimate dealings with the central powers of their time and place, where and whenever that might be. The famous Mari archives of the early 2nd millennium BC merely illustrate at length conditions that were true there and widely elsewhere not only in the early 2nd millennium BC but also long centuries before and after. Those interconnections in everyday life, at local level and on several planes – governmental, personal, and so on – made it impossible for any ordinary pastoral group or farming community to life a life in isolation, hermetically sealed off from all influences and contacts with the immediate world around them. All were heirs to the 'precipitate' of what had gone before, and through continual contacts came to share in varying degrees in the cultural movements of their own places and times.

Back in the nineteenth century AD, Old Testament scholars (working themselves in a virtual vacuum) simply could not believe in figures like the patriarchs who seemed – to them – to belong in the night of prehistoric time. Or in a Moses who suddenly produced a series of institutions (laws, rituals, the tabernacle, etc.) as if from nowhere. For these and other reasons, such figures had to be devalued and treated as imaginary reflections from later times, say from *c.* 900 BC onwards. But this total lack of perspective-in-depth is now visibly and totally false. The night of prehistoric time faded not in 900 BC but nearer 9000 BC, culturally speaking. Thus someone in the position of a Moses did not have to pluck laws or a covenant out of thin air – such were formulated within the terms of the long and highly-developed modes of life already existing at the time; in the 13th century BC, that was eighty-seven centuries *after* those earliest experimental settlements at Jericho or elsewhere. As intimated above, even an Abraham in or after 2000 BC came also late in time, in a teeming, busy world with over eighty centuries of varied cultural experience behind it.

Thus, whether one lived as a pastoralist with regularly-moving flocks, as a farmer based on village and field, or in the city in their midst, one never lived in total isolation at any period during the full-blown cultures of the ancient Near East.

BACK TO THE BEGINNINGS

While archaeology by excavation of sites shows us the rich complexity of human life across innumerable generations, archaeology by the study of ancient literary texts brings us very much closer to the profile of remote antiquity offered in Genesis 1–11: creation of the world and of mankind, alienation of mankind from deity, flood, and renewal.

This series of topics, and in this sequence, finds its counterpart in early Mesopotamia, in a variety of literary works written by the Sumerians and Babylonians. Just over a century ago, George Smith aroused great excitement when he announced and published his *Chaldean Account of Genesis* (1876) and 'Chaldean account of the Deluge' (1872/73).[5] Thus began the modern recovery of two great Babylonian epics: *Enuma Elish* (completed by *c.* 1000 BC), recounting the triumph and creative work of Marduk god of Babylon, and the *Epic of Gilgamesh* (*c.* 17th century BC and later), whose hero Gilgamesh was told of the flood by its sole survivor. Both texts are available today, substantially complete, in modern translations.[6]

1. *The Creation*

In the early days, Old Testament scholars seized upon even trivial comparisons between Enuma Elish and Genesis 1–2. Thus, the Hebrew word *tehom*, 'the deep', was derived from *Ti'amat*, the goddess personifying the salt sea waters. However, this kind of support is much too fragile to sustain the theory of Hebrew dependence upon the Babylonian epic, a fact long since recognised. *Tehom/Ti'amat* are Common Semitic. Thus, *thm* occurs not only in Ugaritic in the 14th/13th centuries BC, but also now as *ti'amatum* in the archives of Ebla a thousand years earlier still [7] in both cases, simply as a common noun, 'deep', 'ocean abyss'.

Even the theme of creation itself appears differently in Enuma Elish and in Genesis 1–2. In the latter, it is the sole theme of any importance. In Enuma Elish, the great theme is the supremacy won by Marduk, and creation (if more than an afterthought) is but one feature of his activity. Otherwise the two texts share little else but the 'banalities' of creation: the order of heaven and earth before plants, creatures and mankind is essential, to have somewhere to put these latter! Plants, too, may be expected to be given before animals that eat them, and so forth. Light appears before named sources (e.g. sun, moon) in both accounts,[8] but otherwise the points of comparison turn out to be divergent or just commonplaces. Moreover, Enuma Elish itself is not *the* Babylonian account of creation, but merely a subsidiary offshoot of that tradition.[9] Other accounts exist in brief form. Hence, it is not surprising that Assyriological scholarship has by now largely rejected the old idea that Genesis 1–2 had any close relation at all with Enuma Elish. Such is essentially the verdict of Heidel, Kinnier-Wilson, Lambert, and Millard, for example.[10] Writers on the Old Testament who suggest the contrary are out-of-date.

The other principal Babylonian fragments concerned with creation are mainly of still later date (12th to 6th centuries BC in present copies), and diverge even more from what we find in Genesis. These include a bilingual (Sumerian/Babylonian) creation of man (*c.* 1200/800 BC) to be bondservant of the gods,[11] a fragment from Nineveh (7th century BC) mentioning the creation of two 'servants' (of the gods?),[12] another bilingual piece with Marduk as creator (6th century BC or earlier),[13] a brief prologue to an incantation against toothache (same date-range),[14] and finally a 'theogony' giving the generations of the gods (7th century BC, probably composed earlier).[15] None of these bears any but the slightest resemblance to the account in Genesis 1–2.

2. The Flood

Also long known is the Babylonian story of a great flood sent by the gods to wipe out a noisy and troublesome mankind, before which one god secretly warned his favourite to build a boat to save himself and his family from the impending deluge. From his vessel when marooned on Mt Nisir amid the watery wastes, the hero sent forth a dove, swallow and raven before being sure that the waters were receding. Once on *terra firma*, he then offered a sacrifice round which 'the gods gathered like flies', subsequently bestowing immortality upon him.

This is the story told by Ut-napishtim (in the Epic of Gilgamesh) to Gilgamesh, an ancient king of south-Babylonian Uruk in quest of immortality. The flood-story, thus, is only a secondary feature in this epic – and in fact only occurs (to date) in the 7th-century copies. Parallels between this Babylonian account, and Noah's flood in Genesis 6–8 are obvious to the eye. Thus, almost a century ago, it became commonplace to assume that the biblical account was simply copied or adapted from the Gilgamesh one, and that both in any case were purely folkloristic fiction. The only contrary evidence seemed to be Woolley's controversial claim to have found traces of the legendary flood in a layer of silt at Ur.

However, this too-simple picture and the old assumptions have alike been overtaken by fuller information. Thus, a variety of flood deposits have been found at Mesopotamian sites other than Ur, usually of different dates from both the Ur deposit and each other. That at Ur is impressive in thickness, but may have been relatively 'local' even so. Combined with further literary evidence (see below), this increased archaeological information has been subjected to lively discussion. Some archaeologists have attempted in fact to identify and date the flood of Mesopotamian tradition (with which Noah's may be associated), considering that a real if distant event is in question, not solely a fiction. [16]

The inscriptional material is now much richer than just Gilgamesh. The oldest mention is probably that in the Sumerian King List, possibly in the first line of its original edition (*c.* 2000 BC): 'after the flood had swept over, when kingship was lowered from heaven . . .', followed by the list of kings after the flood. [17] In its 'second edition', the List was prefaced by a forty-line account of kings before the flood, giving the full sequence: pre-flood kings, flood, kings after the flood.

Then, by the 17th century BC at latest, there was composed the Semitic Old-Babylonian Epic of Atrakhasis, which originally included the fullest Babylonian account of the flood. [18] To about 1600 BC is dated the Sumerian flood-story, covering the same ground at one-quarter of the length (about 300 lines instead of 1245 lines). [19] A Babylonian tablet about the flood and mentioning Atrakhasis was found at ancient Ugarit on the Syrian coast, dated to the period *c.* 1400–1200 BC. [20] Finally, there is the Babylonian Epic of Gilgamesh with which we began. Most of this epic is attested by copies of the early 2nd millennium BC, but for Tablet XI (the flood) only 7th-century copies are known as yet. Thus, ancient Mesopotamia has passed on to us not one, but several, flood-accounts, of which one was studied as far away as Ugarit on the Syrian coast. [21]

What may we learn from all this? First, we have a multiplicity of accounts from Mesopotamia, with some variety in their treatment of the flood theme. None is absolutely identical with any other, still less with the account in Genesis 6–8. As any reader of both the Mesopotamian and Genesis narratives can verify personally, there is a clear outline in common and much difference in detail. The common framework includes: 1. Divine decision to send a punishing flood; 2. One chosen man told to save self, family and creatures by building a boat; 3. A great flood destroys the rest of the people; 4. The boat grounds on a mountain; 5. Birds are sent forth to determine availability of habitable land; 6. The hero sacrifices to deity; 7. Renewal of mankind upon earth.

The differences in detail are many, but include the following:

1. Cause: The Mesopotamian gods tire of the noisiness (not the sins) of mankind, and arbitrarily decide to sweep all mankind away (just or unjust); but in Genesis, God sees the corruption and universal wickedness of mankind, hence decides to punish this.

2. The Mesopotamian assembly of gods is at pains to conceal their flood plan entirely from mankind – this is not evident in Genesis at all.

3. The saving of the hero is entirely by trickery, by the deceit of one god behind his colleagues' backs in the Mesopotamian epics, *against* the orders of the entire divine assembly. In Genesis, God from the first tells Noah plainly, without subterfuge, that judgement comes and he alone has been judged faithful and so must build a boat.

4. The size and type of craft differ entirely in the various versions. That in Gilgamesh has the proportions of a vast cube, perhaps even of a great floating ziggurat (temple-tower); that in Genesis has far more the proportions of a real craft – and less vast than Berossus's one.

5. The duration of the flood differs in the Mesopotamian and biblical accounts. Thus, Atrakhasis has seven days and seven nights of storm and tempest, as does the Sumerian version; Gilgamesh has six (or seven) days and nights, with subsidence of the waters beginning on the seventh day; none of the Mesopotamian narratives give any idea of how long the flood-waters took to subside thereafter. In contrast, Genesis has an entirely consistent, [22] more detailed time-scale. After seven days' warning, the storm and floods rage for 40 days, then the waters stay for 150 days before beginning to sink, and further intervals follow, until the earth was dry a year and ten days after the cataclysm began (Gen. 7:11; 8:14).

6. The inhabitants of the boat include (besides animals, the hero and his family) also a pilot and craftsman, etc., in the Mesopotamian versions; in Genesis we find (besides animals) [23] only Noah and his immediate family.

7. The details of sending out birds differ entirely, as between Gilgamesh, Berossus, and Genesis 8:7 ff.; this is lost in Atrakhasis (if ever present).

8. The Mesopotamian hero leaves the boat of his own accord, and then offers a sacrifice to win the acceptance of the gods. By contrast, Noah stays in the boat *until* God summons him forth, and then presents what is virtually a sacrifice of thanksgiving (he

being already accepted personally) following which divine blessing is expressed without regret (contrast Enlil's initial anger over man's survival).

9. Replenishment of the land or earth is partly through renewed divine activity in Mesopotamia (cf. in Atrakhasis), but simply and naturally through the survivors themselves (Noah and family) in Genesis.

Thus, it is fair to say that the Mesopotamians – Sumerians, Babylonians and Western Semites– had a flood-tradition in common, which existed and was transmitted in several versions. To talk of borrowing the Hebrew from the Babylonian (or Sumerian) or vice-versa seems excluded. Parallel traditions about some ancient event in common Mesopotamian memory would be a simpler and more satisfying answer. The Genesis account is in no way more 'evolved' than its neighbours, and often reads more simply. In terms of length, for example, its 60 verses (Gen. 6:9 – 8:22) might be roughly equal to 120 lines of Sumerian or Akkadian text. In contrast, the relevant parts of Atrakhasis (in Tablets II and III) were originally at least some 370 lines long, and that in Gilgamesh XI some 200 lines long; only the relatively brief Sumerian account was 120 lines long or originally a little more. In other words, Genesis 6–8 was probably the simplest and shortest of all the ancient versions, possibly originating as early as they, and was certainly not a secondary elaboration of them.

Secondly, the Sumerians and Babylonians of *c.* 2000/1800 BC believed so firmly in the former historical occurrence of such a flood – in a land plagued by floods until modern times – that they inserted it into the Sumerian King List, and not merely in their epic tales. In the second and final form of that list, the flood was a bench-mark between kings before, and kings after, the flood. [24] Thus, as already noted above, it is not surprising to find authorities in Mesopotamian archaeology and history such as Mallowan or Hallo seriously essaying to date the flood of tradition. Pure fiction hardly seems likely, as a solution.

Thirdly, an agnostic note. It is, of course, impossible to dogmatize on the extent of the flood of Mesopotamian or biblical tradition. In the latter case, the word *'eres* covers in usage so broad a field from 'land' (limited location) to 'earth' (the known world) that it is unwise to opt for any extreme solution. Again, it is a sheer waste of time looking for remains of the ark on modern Mt Ararat, because the biblical text does not locate it there – it clearly says 'the mountains (plural) of Ararat' in Gen. 8:4, which name covers a whole vast region. The ultimate reality behind the narrative does not rest on wild-goose-chases of that kind.

3. Primeval Proto-history

However, the background importance of the Mesopotamian traditions of creation and flood is not restricted to these topics just in isolation. Of equal interest is their part in the overall tradition about the 'most ancient past' in both Genesis and Mesopotamia. In Genesis 1–11, we find the sequence of creation (1–2), man's alienation from God (3–4), linked by a ten-generation genealogy (5) to the flood and renewal (6–9). With the spread of mankind (10–11:9), a further nine-generation genealogy from Noah's son Shem to Abram's father Terah (Gen. 11:10–25) provides the link with the 'founding father' Abraham.

A similar outline (creation linked to flood, linked to later times) appears also in the early Mesopotamian works, as a literary whole.

The oldest, the Sumerian King List, presupposes creation, beginning with 'When kingship was lowered from heaven', and continues with a line of eight (or ten) kings [25], until 'the flood swept over (all)'. Then kingship was again lowered from heaven, and the long line of royal dynasties continues down into well-known historical times, to *c.* 2000/1800 BC. But from *c.* 1700 BC at latest, it is the narrative Atrakhasis Epic which presents the closest analogy. [26] In a world already created, the gods fashion mankind to take over life's drudgery (cleaning canals, preparing food, etc.). Mankind becomes so numerous that Enlil the chief god decides to decimate them by plague, drought and famine – alienation had set in. Each time, the god Enki reveals to his favourite, Atrakhasis, a way to escape these blights. Likewise, when Enlil and the gods send the flood, Enki counsels Atrakhasis to build a boat. Afterwards, Enlil is reconciled to the survival of mankind, and arrangements are made for their continuance; the whole is comprised within an epic originally 1,245 lines long. Much shorter (about 300 lines) was the Sumerian 'flood story' (*c.* 1600BC), on a badly-damaged tablet. This shows the same basic outline as Atrakhasis: [created world], creation of mankind and five cities, [alienation], the pious hero told to save himself by boat, in the flood, and re-establishment of human life (the hero, immortalized). We may tabulate as follows:

Summerian King-L	Atrakhasis	Summerian Flood	Genesis 1-11
A: (Creation &) kingship —	(Creation &) mankind	[Creation &] mankind	Creation, incl. mankind
list: (8/10 names)	narrative: alienation	narrative: alienation	narrative: alienation, genealogy.
B: Flood new start,	Flood new start,	Flood new start,	Flood new start,

(Summerian King-L) kingship list:	(Atrakhasis) mankind	(Summerian Flood) mankind	(Genesis 1-11) mankind genealogy
	...	...	
C: Historic dynasties (c.2000/1800)	(Epic, c.17th ct.)	(Epic, c.17th ct.)	Abram's clan (c.2000/1700)

This table illustrates the comparisons and contrasts between the three traditions (King List, Mesopotamian epics, Genesis (W. Semitic) account). In effect, we find the common theme of protohistory (creation, crisis, continuance, of man) treated in several ways. In Sumerian, in both king list and narrative; in Akkadian, in narrative; and in West Semitic, in narratives linked by genealogies. Each component in the population of early 2nd-millennium Mesopotamia (Sumerians, Babylonians, Western Semites) contributed its formulation of inherited traditions, and it seems most probable that the West-Semitic version took shape in Mesopotamia[27] before being taken westward to Canaan by such as the early Hebrews like Terah and Abram. [28]

The King List and Genesis genealogies show instructive similarities and contrasts. Thus, before and after the flood, the Sumerian King List uses slightly different formulae to introduce and terminate successive dynasties. Likewise, there are differences in formula between the genealogies of Gen. 5 and 11 before and after the flood. It is interesting to recall that the pre-flood section of the King List was originally a distinct composition, prefaced to the List in its '2nd edition'; in Genesis, chapter 5 belongs to 'the document of the succession of Adam', while the genealogy in 11:10 ff. belongs to the 'succession of Shem' – the phrase 'these are the generations (or, succession) of X' is a well-known marker of successive sections in the present book of Genesis, almost like a series of tablets.[29] Again, both in the King List and in Genesis, one finds 'notes' included on some of the people listed. These indicate, not some kind of multiple authorship, but the compiler's wish to transmit traditions he valued, or which characterised the person named.

These affinities agree well with the thesis of a common literary heritage, formulated in each case in Mesopotamia in the early 2nd millennium BC. A West-Semitic tradition of such age can be no novelty now, in the light of still earlier West-Semitic writings at Ebla, *c.* 2300 BC. One may further notice the number of generations and kings, respectively, in Genesis 5 and the pre-flood section of the Sumerian King List, ten in the former and eight or ten in the latter. In either case, the eight or ten names represent a long time-lapse rather than literally that number.[30] The same applies to the nine generations after the flood (Gen. 11) and to the Sumerian post-flood dynasties, known to be incomplete. Some set in sequence were actually contemporary, while others (independently known) are not listed.[31] Proper caution in interpretation is called for in Genesis 5 and 11, where there is no guarantee that the phrase 'A begot B' always meant that A was literal father of B. Such a phrase can indicate simply that 'A begot (the lineage descending to) B', with the given names as representatives of a far longer series. Other biblical passages bear out such usage. Inside Genesis itself, 'the children that Zilpah bore to Jacob' (Gen. 46:18) actually include great-grandsons. The datum 'Joram begot Uzziah' (Matthew 1:8) summarises the fuller lineage whereby Joram actually fathered Ahaziah, father of Joash, father of Amaziah, father of Uzziah (cf. 2 Kings 8:25; 11:2; 14:1, 21), precisely as suggested may apply to Genesis 5 and 11.

Even so, where does that leave characters like Methuselah with 969 years to his credit (Gen. 5:27), or early Sumerian rulers whose reigns in the List range from a few hundred years back to some with 28,000 years or more? First impulse is to dismiss the lot; archaeological data, however, counsel patience and caution, not impulse.

Thus, for decades, no-one took the Sumerian King List at all seriously.[32] Then came Jacobsen's masterly edition of that list, plus Kramer's editions of the Sumerian Gilgamesh cycle of stories, and recovery of the Tummal Chronicle in which Gilgamesh appears amongst historical rulers of early Ur. Cuneiform historians came round to the view that early figures like Gilgamesh might have been real people after all, even if embellished by later legend.[33]

Proof positive came in 1959, when Edzard published an original inscription belonging to the reign of (En)mebaragisi[34], an early king of the city of Kish, and identified a second fragment of that reign.[35] *This* worthy was clearly an historical ruler, yet the Sumerian King List credits him with a reign of 900 years – a close rival to Methuselah! From this situation, one fact emerges with crystal clarity. Incredibly high numbers of years (whether reigns or lifespans) attached to a name in later documents do *not* prove that the person concerned was unhistorical. Whatever the origins of such numbers (which need study), this point on historicity has been clear to Sumerologists and Assyriologists for decades.[36] Thus, in Genesis too, the high numbers remain unaccountable at present, but likewise they constitute in themselves *no* adequate reason for rejecting the possible historicity of Abraham's remote ancestors. Methuselah and his kin may have been as real once as Enmebaragisi and Gilgamesh. Eber for example (Gen. 11:15–17) has been compared with Ebrum, king of Ebla (*c.* 2300 BC); the name is most likely identical (but for an archaic ending), but the individuals almost certainly were not.

While fruitful comparisons are thus possible between early Genesis and such documents as the Sumerian King List, yet both remain entirely independent documents with numerous basic differences which preclude any direct relationship beyond a common basic concept of protohistory. The Sumerian List is a list of unrelated, often non-successive, royal dynasties; early Genesis enshrines the linear genealogy of entirely private individuals.

At this point, we turn from the Sumerians and Akkadians (Babylonians) again to the third component in early Mesopotamia – the Western Semites, known to the Sumerians as Martu and to the Babylonians as Amurrites ('Amorites'), both terms meaning simply 'Westerners'. It has long been known that such people formed part of the population no later than the Third Dynasty of Ur (*c.* 2113–2006 BC), with whose fall the way was open for West Semitic or 'Amorite' leaders to establish themselves as local kings in several cities of Babylonia, founding new dynasties ruling rival city-states. To such a dynasty belonged the famous Hammurabi of Babylon. Of this king and his elder contemporary and rival, Shamshi-Adad I, King of Assyria, we possess remarkable and interlocking genealogies that reach back not less than 26 or 27 generations before these two kings – well over twice the number of named generations in Genesis 5 and 11 put together. The Babylonian document was composed for Hammurabi's great-grandson, to honour the latter's ancestors with funerary offerings to their memory.[37] The Assyrian document was incorporated into the later Assyrian King List, within which it appears in special sections,[38] and was linked to the first 17 kings of Assyria[39] 'who lived in tents'. The earliest sections have been regarded as artificial, and several names as merely corrupt or invented – e.g., Tudiya, who begins the Assyrian King List. However, this very same Tudiya is now known to be strictly historical, and to have lived *c.* 2350 BC when he made a treaty with the King of Ebla (see Chapter 3). Thus, with Hammurabi and Shamshi-Adad, we have a genealogical tradition parallel in form and concept with that in Gen. 11 and known to be historical at least at its beginning.

4. *Date of the Primeval Traditions*

One fact stands out especially clearly on dating. Nearly all of our principal sources and examples come from the early 2nd millennium BC (*c.* 2000–1600 BC). This is true of the Sumerian King List, the Sumerian 'flood story', the Epic of Atrakhasis, and the major part of Gilgamesh. It was an especially fruitful period for literature in Mesopotamia. Older Sumerian literature was being recorded in final written form, Semitic Babylonian literature was at the best of its creative brilliance, [40] and the Western Semites proudly retained record of their family traditions (cf. previous paragraph). Positively, one can conceive of no more fitting epoch for the original composition in literary form of most of the traditions now found in Genesis 1–11. Negatively, it is worth noticing the changed conditions, different interests, and even unsuitability, of later periods of ancient history. Thus, the creation-stories in Mesopotamia from *c.* 1100 BC onwards diverge from what we find in Genesis. And the grouped themes of creation, flood, primeval history, ceased to inspire new writers and new works. Alone, in the 7th century BC, the 'Dynastic Chronicle' retained the form of the Sumerian King List, adding-in some account of the flood, and continuing the long list of Babylonian dynasties to nearer its own time. [41] During the 1st millennium BC, other king-lists in Assyria and Babylonia never normally bothered to go back to either the flood or the creation. Generally, the 1st-millennium scribes were content to recopy and conserve the earlier works created in the 2nd millennium BC. Concerning the possible relation of early Genesis to Mesopotamian tradition, a leading cuneiform scholar long ago pointed out that [42] 'The [Babylonian] exile and the later part of the [Hebrew] monarchy are out of the question . . . That the matters spoken of were included in Genesis is proof that they were long established among the Hebrews'. [43] In short, the idea that the Hebrews in captivity in Nebuchadrezzar's Babylon (6th century BC) first 'borrowed' the content of early Genesis at that late date is a non-starter. By the time of the Babylonian exile and after, the forms of history-writing had changed. In a *real* post-exilic book like Chronicles, the whole of primeval antiquity down to Abraham's grandson Jacob/Israel is covered in just one initial chapter (1 Chron. 1:1–52), almost entirely of genealogies, in which neither the creation nor the flood are even mentioned, let alone any other 'primeval' details. The focus of interest of its author (*c.* 400 BC) lay in much later periods of biblical history. Thus, whenever it reached its present form within the entire book of Genesis, the unit Gen. 1–11 best finds its literary origins in the early 2nd millennium BC.

5. *Conclusions*

The earliest narratives in Genesis appear to be neither late concoctions nor mere bowdlerizations of Mesopotamian legend. They and their nearest Mesopotamian relatives almost certainly offer

lines of parallel and largely independent witness to ancient traditions held in common by the Sumerian, Akkadian and West-
Semitic population-elements in Mesopotamia from very early
epochs down to the early 2nd millennium BC, when those ancient
traditions were celebrated in a series of literary works, in Sumerian
(King List; flood), Akkadian (the epics), and West Semitic (first
version of Gen. 1–11; Ebla??). These peoples firmly believed in
divine creation, and in divine punishment expressed in a particular
flood as a distant historical event, distinct from the ordinary,
habitual inundations known in Mesopotamia. It is possible to prove
the historicity of some early figures (Enmebaragisi; Tudiya), and to
postulate it purely rationally for others (e.g., Gilgamesh), regardless of 'problem elements' such as long reigns or lifespans. The optimum date for the literary compositions in view (early second
millennium BC) agrees well with that general date for the Hebrew
patriarchs – Terah and Abram – shown as going westward from
Mesopotamia. They could well have carried such traditions
westward with them, hence their impress in the later book of
Genesis. They would not have been precocious in so doing. The
finds at Ebla of three to five centuries earlier show that Mesopotamian lore (including much literary and scholarly lore) had already
travelled west long since. The finds of cuneiform fragments in Middle Bronze Age Hazor in Canaan proper (as well as of a Gilgamesh
fragment in mid-2nd-millennium Megiddo) further illustrate the
westward movement of such written traditions, and their relatively
early currency among Semites in the 'westlands' of the Levant at
such a date.

3

Ebla – Queen of Ancient Syria

Like a brilliant mirage shimmering across the desert sands, the teeming ancient city of Ebla[1] has now emerged in something of its ancient splendour from the veil of sand and mud that entombs the huge ruin-mound known today as Tell Mardikh in North Syria, some 44 miles (70 km) south of Aleppo.

THE FIRST DECADE

However, the spectacular discoveries at Ebla are no mirage. Rather, they are the just reward of over ten years of systematic, dedicated work by the Italian archaeological expedition to Syria led by Professor Paolo Matthiae. Impressed by the huge size (140 acres) and prominent position of Tell Mardikh, Matthiae began a long-term 'dig'. For the first ten years (1964–1974), he successfully explored key areas of the then-unidentified ancient city. The lozenge-shaped mound had once been a walled town with four gateways, several temples, and large areas of private houses – all of mud brick – around a higher citadel or 'acropolis' in the centre. Here, in the 'city centre', he found remains of a palace on the north side, and of yet another temple towards the west side.

On the time-scale of antiquity, the history of the city could be traced level by level, beginning with a prehistoric settlement ('I') and a first town on the acropolis site ('IIA'), within about 3500–2400 BC. Then came two periods when the city first reached its full extent, with town-houses and temples around the acropolis crowned with its palace and main temple, *c.* 2400–2000 BC ('IIB', phases 1 & 2); each period ended with massive destruction, and then a rebuilding. Thus, from *c.* 2000–1600 BC, phoenix-like, the city again rose from its ashes, over its full area ('IIIA & B') before being devastated once more. Thereafter, it was a much humbler community that clung to the central acropolis through three more cultural periods for the next sixteen centuries ('IV', 1600–1200 BC; 'V', 1200–530 BC; 'VI', 530–60 BC). In Roman and Arabic times, the mound finally went to sleep, used only for a few poor burials ('VII', AD).

All this (with much valuable detail) was very welcome to archaeologists and ancient historians, although it hardly made headlines. Then in 1968 there was found a broken royal statue inscribed in Akkadian cuneiform, dedicated to the goddess Ishtar by Ibbit-Lim, king of Ebla. Did the huge mounds of Tell Mardikh conceal the ancient city of Ebla? The geographical range of Ebla as a North-Syrian city, so far known from inscriptions as far afield as Sumer and Egypt, was feasible. The history of Ebla as profiled in these sources also fitted the fortunes of Tell Mardikh: a great city subdued by the mighty Sargon of Akkad *c.* 2300 BC, destroyed by his grandson Naram-Sin *c.* 2250 BC, and much less important in later times. As the archaeological, inscriptional and geographical evidence all seemed to fit, Matthiae and his cuneiform colleague Pettinato favoured this identification of the site. Elsewhere in the world, scholars disagreed amongst themselves, some for, some against, as scholars will ...!

THE GREAT DISCOVERY

But the debate was stopped in its tracks in 1974/75. New excavations on the west side of the acropolis showed that the base of a large square tower was part of another royal palace. [2] The tower occupied the north-east corner of a great Court of Audience. A richly-decorated ceremonial staircase down the inside of the tower led to a throne-dais, sheltered by a colonnade along the north wall of the court. South from the tower ran the east wall of the court, also with a colonnade. Halfway along it, three steps through a doorway led into further buried rooms of the palace.

Discovery of this huge 'new' palace where once the kings of Ebla sat in state to hold audience was remarkable – but much more was to come. In 1974, a room (no. 2506) just north of the tower yielded 42 clay tablets and fragments inscribed in cuneiform. [3] By their script, all belonged to about 2300 BC, contemporary with the em-

pire of Akkad in Mesopotamia, far to the east. Forty-one of the
tablets were essentially administrative accounts for various
products, especially metals, textiles, wood and pottery. The real
surprise was the language used in the tablets. Alongside the
traditional Sumerian terminology borrowed from Mesopotamia,
the scribes also wrote entries in their own language – Eblaite. This
proved to be a North-West Semitic dialect, showing close links in
its grammar and vocabulary with later biblical Hebrew, Canaanite
and Phoenician. Dated at around 2300 BC, Eblaite is the oldest-
known language of this group, up to 1000 years before the tablets
of Ugarit, for example. In biblical terms, it is 500 years before the
patriarchs, 1000 years before Moses, 16 centuries before Isaiah, 20
centuries before Alexander the Great. For the present, therefore,
Professor Pettinato has classified the 'new' language (Eblaite) as
'Early Canaanite' or 'Palaeo-Canaanite'.

In 1975, the leads given by these finds were confirmed in
astonishing fashion. At the north end of the great court's eastern
colonnade, a small room yielded 1000 tablets and fragments, while
a second room nearer the south end contained up to another 14,-
000 tablets and fragments. These lay row upon row, just where
they had fallen from the burning wooden shelves when the palace
was destroyed by Naram-Sin's troops about 2250 BC.[4] This
overwhelming mass of written documents, some 15,000 all told,
was conveyed in 100 caseloads to the museum in Aleppo. From
preliminary reports on the first ten thousand or so tablets by Prof
Pettinato, and accounts of the archaeology of the site by Prof
Matthiae, it is possible to sketch an outline of Ebla and its 'empire'
at the height of its power and glory. What follows is based upon
their first-hand reports in Italian, French, German and English,
omitting the more dubious flourishes in secondary sources.

THE CITY AND SOCIETY OF EBLA (*c*. 2300 BC)

From about 2400 BC until about 1650/1600 BC, ancient Ebla
probably occupied the whole of its 140-acre site, the entire city being surrounded by strong walls, pierced by four great city gates of
varying size. Dominating the main area of the 'lower city' from its
higher position at the centre, there rose the 'acropolis' or citadel –
the nerve-centre of government where the royal palaces and administration were located. With the archaeological remains of
walls, gates and buildings can be combined data from the tablets.
One tablet in particular[5] permits us to see in outline the organization of this city which, at one period, had a population of 260,000
people.[6] The acropolis or 'governorate' contained four main cen-

tres. First was the *Palace of the King*. This doubtless comprised the
actual residence of the king, queen and royal family, besides the
central offices for Ebla's state administration and 'foreign office' –
as illustrated by the archives themselves, hard by the great court of
audience. To run this, we hear of 10 leading officials with 60 subordinates or 'dependants' – six aides per leader. Second was the
Palace of the City. This bureau probably ran the affairs of the city
of Ebla itself (as distinct from the wide-ranging territories beyond).
Its staff too had 10 leaders, but with just 55 subordinates. These
two corps of officials belonged to one common function whose role
has not yet been worked out. Third was the *Stables* – most likely
the focus of the immense commercial activity of Ebla, with
merchants and emissaries travelling to and fro, between Ebla and
innumerable foreign cities and kingdoms. This institution possessed
no fewer than 63 leaders, but these had only 60 aides between them
(one each, but for three without any). Fourth was the *Palace of
Service* (?) or *of Servants* (?) – possibly the offices that handled the
labour-supply for running the city and state administration. It had
20 leaders with 35 aides (2 each for 15 leaders, only one each for
the other 5). It is clear that the more numerous leaders in the
Stables and Services 'ministries' were of lesser status (only 1 or 2
aides each), concerned with more mundane affairs than the civil
service 'mandarins' in the Royal and Municipal 'palaces' with 5 or
6 aides each. Correspondingly, the leaders in the Stables and Services departments bore a title (Sumerian *ú-a*; Akkadian *zaninu*)
meaning 'providers' – they were responsible for supplies (food, income, etc.) for their 'ministries'. Thus, the royal citadel or acropolis
hummed with state affairs and bureaucratic activity – perhaps with
4,700 people working there according to one tablet. [7]

On the acropolis reigned the King, usually denoted by the
Sumerian term *en*, 'lord', corresponding to Eblaite *malik*, 'king' (cf.
Hebrew *melek*). By his side, the Queen (Eblaite *maliktum*, cf.
Hebrew *malka/maleket*) shared in state affairs, as did the crown
prince (home affairs) and the son second-in-succession (foreign
affairs). [8] In dealing with other rulers, the kings of Ebla used a two-
tier system. Kings who were their equals they called *en/malik*,
'sovereign', like themselves. Vassals or local kinglets of lesser
power and status they called *lugal* (Sumerian, 'chief man', 'king')
or *diku* ('judge').

So much for the 'upper crust' on the acropolis. What of the
'lower city'? This, too, was divided into four 'quarters' or city-
districts, each with a main city gate. Absolute certainty is not yet
possible in identifying the named gates and districts with those discovered archaeologically. However, the first or *City District* [9] with

the 'City Gate' (north-west one) and the *2nd District* with the 'Sipish Gate' [10] (north-east one) had each 20 leaders with 100 and 98 subordinates respectively (5 aides per leader, again), comparable in status with their chief colleagues on the acropolis. Smallest was the *3rd District*, having only 10 leaders and 30 aides (only 3 per leader), perhaps in the south-west quarter (? Dagan Gate). Of middle rank was the *4th District* (? and Reshep Gate; southeast area?), with 20 leaders and 50 aides. So, like any great city, Ebla probably had its favoured and lesser neighbourhoods – 'residential' and otherwise. The first three districts and their 50 leaders came under a separate (chief) inspector. The Eblaite word for these numerous sectional leaders or officers is *nase* – same as the Hebrew *nasi*, 'leader', 'ruler', in the Old Testament (cf. below). In the tablet that lists them, they are assigned grain-rations of half a measure each, using a term hitherto unknown.

This tablet is a representative of the first, and largest, group of documents in the Ebla archives: administrative and economic texts. These include many such 'ration-lists' for palace personnel, envoys to and from foreign parts, and offerings for the gods and their temples. Well represented is agriculture: grain-crops, vineyards, cattle-raising. Even more so, 'industry': metalworking (gold, silver, copper), gems, textiles, wood-working and pottery. Foreign trade in metalware and textiles was recorded on huge 'supertablets' over a foot square (35 × 30 cm), bearing up to 30 columns of text (up to 50 lines each) on each face of a tablet – some 6,000 lines of inscription per tablet! Business ledgers indeed, for the 'balance of payments'! [11]

Home affairs represent one side of a second class of tablets: historical and judicial texts. These include letters between high officials on matters of state, royal decrees, legal contracts of sale and purchase, and of division of property, plus collections of laws – centuries older than those of Ur-Nammu of Ur or of Hammurabi of Babylon. Politically important marriages and appointments to office also feature.

THE HISTORY AND WORLD HORIZONS OF EBLA
(c. 2400–1650 BC)

1. *The Clash of Empires: Ebla and Akkad (c. 2400–2250 BC)*

Until the great discoveries of 1975, no-one had even the slightest inkling of the former power of Ebla in the 24th/23rd centuries BC. In that epoch of ancient and world history, it was another power entirely that seemed to have the world stage to itself: the empire of Akkad. [12] During most of the third millennium BC, ancient

Mesopotamia saw the brilliant flowering of Sumerian civilization, divided politically among a series of rival city-states: Ur, Kish, Lagash, Uruk, and others. But after serving at the court of the king of Kish, a Semite (Akkadian) set himself up as a king – Sargon [13]– in a new city of his own: Akkad or Agade. Sargon of Akkad brought the whole of Mesopotamia under his sway, to the Persian or Arabian Gulf, and pushed north and west to Mari and the borders of Syria and Anatolia. He thus founded the first-ever Semitic empire, about 2350 BC. He briefly subdued Ebla, with other cities. At Sargon's death, two of his sons successively lost most of their father's empire, and it was his grandson Naram-Sin (*c.* 2250 BC) who restored the dominion of Akkad to its full extent, marching westward and destroying Ebla – which he hailed as a great victory. How great was not known in modern times until 1975 . . .

The archives of Ebla show now that the world stage was not monopolized by Akkad; the limelight was originally shared equally with Ebla. The following table may help in appreciating the revised history of the epoch. [14]

EBLA	MARI	ASSYRIA	AKKAD
(?Gumalum)			
Igrish-Halam			
Irkab-Damu	*Iblul-Il*		
Ar-Ennum [15]	*Enna-Dagan*		
	(of Ebla)		
			Sargon
Ebrum		*Tudiya*	
			Rimush
Ibbi-Sipish			
	Shura-Damu		*Manishtushu*
	(of Ebla)		
Dubuhu-Ada			
			Naram-Sin

Of the first Eblaite king named above – Gumalum – nothing is yet known, not even his proper date. [16] The first well-placed king, Igrish-Halam, reigned unchallenged over Ebla and north Syria while Sargon had not yet arisen to conquer either the Sumerian city-states or more distant lands. Irkab-Damu sought to build up a strong mercenary army, seeking to obtain good soldiers from Hamazi, far away to the east. [17] After a promising start, Ar-Ennum was less fortunate. Further east, on the middle Euphrates, King Iblul-Il of Mari had gained control over Assyria. But then Ar-Ennum of Ebla sent his general Enna-Dagan eastwards, who conquered the new-born 'empire' of Mari, compelling Iblul-Il to pay a massive tribute to Ebla of 11,000 lbs weight of silver and 880 lbs of gold. Enna-Dagan was then put in charge of Mari, as subject of Ar-Ennum of Ebla. But, by now, Sargon of Akkad had won control of all southern Mesopotamia, and was now looking northwestwards to Syria and Anatolia, sources of valuable timber and metal. He conquered Assyria, then Mari, northernmost Syria, and hammered on the gates of Ebla itself, whose submission and tribute he exacted,[18] perhaps before claiming sovereignty up to the Taurus Mountains and returning in triumph to Akkad.

The defeat of Ar-Ennum probably cost him his throne. Instead, the powerful dignitary Ebrum took over the rule of Ebla. Whether or not he was a son of Ar-Ennum, we do not know. However, the new king diligently restored the widespread rule of Ebla throughout north Syria and beyond. In due time, in Sargon's old age or after his death, Ebrum once more extended the sway of Ebla eastwards. He[19] again subdued Mari as his predecessor had done, installing his son Shura-Damu as vassal-king there. This time, the empire of Akkad under Sargon's son Rimush was powerless to reply − the new ruler of Akkad was too beset by revolts nearer home to worry about lands in the distant north-west. Going one step further, the ambitious Ebrum succeeded in imposing an international commercial treaty upon a new king of Assyria, Tudiya, who was definitely the lesser partner. Hitherto, Tudiya had been known to us only as the first name in the Assyrian King List, first of 'seventeen kings who lived in tents', so remote did he and they seem in later tradition. This treaty is but one of several international treaties found in the Ebla archives, heralds of seventeen centuries of ancient Near Eastern treaties. This one contains an introduction, listing the leading dignitaries of Ebla, then proceeds in twenty paragraphs of main text with the founding and regulation of a commercial centre (*karum*) and its merchants, and ends with a splendid curse-formula as sanction upon the Assyrian king, should he break the treaty − clearly making him virtually Ebla's vassal.[20] Such, now, was the triumph of Ebla that even Akkad itself paid tribute − perhaps not from the capital but from some northern province only, to buy off Ebla's encroachments. During the troubled reigns of Sargon's sons Rimush and Manishtushu, the eyes of Akkad looked south and east, leaving the north-west to Ebla's supremacy.

Now, in the relatively long reigns of Ebrum and his son and successor Ibbi-Sipish, was the golden age of the 'empire' of Ebla. From almost all quarters of the ancient Near East, messengers, merchants and tributaries formed the sinews of the influence and power of Ebla. Most of Syria west to the Mediterranean, south to

Hamath, north well beyond Aleppo,[21] and east to Mari and
Assyria, was ruled by the kings of Ebla, mainly through vassals.
But commercial and trading relations reached much further.
Northwards, Ebla's envoys climbed through the Taurus mountains
onto the Anatolian plateau to trade with the famous centre at
Kanesh and even to Hattu(sa)[22] – future Hittite capital seven cen-
turies into the future. Eastwards, along or within the upper and
middle Euphrates, we meet with cities like Carchemish, Urshu,
Nahur, Mari and Tuttul.[23] Southwards through Syria, via Hamath
inland and ports like Ugarit or Byblos or Tyre on the coast, Ebla's
commercial tentacles reached on into Palestine, already termed
'Canaan'.[24] Familiar names appear: Hazor, Megiddo, Dor, Joppa,
Lachish, Gaza, all the way south to Sinai itself. An Ashtarot is
perhaps the Ashteroth-Qarnaim located in Transjordan in Genesis
14:6. Salim (or rather, Urusalim) is almost certainly the Salim
(later, Jerusalem) of Genesis 14:18, some five or six centuries
before its next occurrence in the 'Execration Texts' from Egypt, *c.*
1800 BC.[25] Only Egypt, proud, aloof, and independent under the
Sixth-Dynasty pharaohs of the 'pyramid age', seems not yet to occur on Ebla's wide horizons. But, apart from Lebanese timber and
Sinai's minerals, the interest of the pharaohs was oftener directed
far south up the Nubian Nile.

The reign of Ibbi-Sipish's son, Dubuhu-Ada, may have been
short. By now, however, Sargon's grandson Naram-Sin ruled in
Akkad and sought to restore his ancestor's domains in full. At
home, Ebla's nearest vassal, the ruler of Armi (Aleppo), seemed
now more powerful than his lord. At length, when Naram-Sin
marched west, he defeated the hired levies of Ebla, ransacked and
destroyed the once great city, about 2250 BC. The great commercial network of Ebla collapsed completely under the blow, leaving
Naram-Sin 'king of the four quarters' of the known world, as his titles proudly proclaim him. However, in later years, Naram-Sin in
turn suffered eclipse as his unwieldy empire broke up around him,
and his son's reign ended in a chaos of usurpers, so that in a few
decades the empire of Akkad followed that of Ebla into oblivion.

2.   *The Later Ages of Ebla (c. 2250–1600 BC)*

Akkad was never to rise again, and its very site is lost to this
day. But after a brief interval, Ebla was rebuilt to its former extent
(level IIB, 2), and regained something of its former municipal splendour, but not its political power. The acropolis had a new palace on
the north side. On the west, a massive new ceremonial stairway led
up over the buried ruins of the former palace (with its 15,000
tablets . . .) to a restored main temple. In Syria, political supremacy

lay with other city-states (such as Aleppo). In Mesopotamia, the
Third Dynasty of Ur held sway, whose influence reached as far
west as Byblos,[26] but without the military pressure of the Akkad
conquerors.

About 2000 BC, Ebla was again sacked and again rebuilt (level
III). Massive brick fortifications crowned a smoothed-off mud,
sloping rampart all round (pierced as ever by the four gates), to de-
fend the city, its temples, and yet another new palace on the
acropolis. Of the kings of Ebla about 1900 BC, we know only the
names of Igrish-Khepa and his son Ibbit-Lim. The latter set up a
statue to the goddess Ishtar in her temple, in 'the 8th year of
Ishtar'. But Ebla now was a satellite of Aleppo, capital of the
strong kingdom of Yamkhad, often mentioned in the vast archives
of Mari in the 18th century BC (but Ebla, never). Finally, in the
17th century BC, the Hittite king Hattusil I reduced the power of
Aleppo, and his son Mursil I sacked it – and at the same time
probably Ebla as well, by about 1600 BC. Henceforth, Ebla was a
mere village on its acropolis down to Persian and Hellenistic times.

THE CULTURE OF THE GOLDEN AGE OF EBLA
(*c.* 2300 BC)

1. Schools and Scholars

To maintain the elaborate fabric of government and society, the
'empire' of Ebla needed skilled scribes. Thus, the royal archives
contained special works of reference, based on Sumerian models
current in Mesopotamia since at least 2500 BC. Besides paradigms
of verbs in Sumerian and Eblaite, these tablets included 'lexical'
texts: long classified lists of the Sumerian words for animals, birds,
fishes, terms for professions, types of personal names, geographical
names ('gazetteers'), and all manner of objects – 199 such tablets
have so far been found at Ebla. Among them are 32 (perhaps up to
56) *bilingual* vocabularies, having each Sumerian word translated
into Eblaite (i.e., early Canaanite). One superb example (with 18
duplicate copies!) contains 1000 words in both languages – an in-
estimable treasure for scholars today, as it was handy for scribes in
antiquity.[27] Aided also by the rest of the archives, these special
tablets will enable us to see the early history of many hundreds of
words familiar from biblical Hebrew and its relatives such as
Ugaritic and Phoenician.

2. Earliest Literature of the Levant

Hitherto, the world's oldest written literatures have been those of
the two great river-valley civilisations – Egypt on the Nile, and the

Sumerians and Akkadians of Mesopotamia. Now, we have a third 'world's earliest' centre, at Ebla, offering literature in the oldest-known West Semitic language (Eblaite) as well as in Sumerian. The *mythological stories* show this blend well; written in Eblaite, they celebrate Sumerian deities such as Enki, Enlil, Utu, and the goddess Inanna.[28] The *collections of proverbs* will rival those of Sumer and Egypt as representatives of the world's oldest wisdom literature. In the religious realm come some brief *hymns* to the gods, and *magical incantations*.[29]

3. *Religion*[30]

Ebla was populated by gods (about 500!) as well as by over a quarter-million human inhabitants. Naturally, in so large a pantheon, it is the leading figures that really mattered. Linked with Canaan, Mesopotamia and Anatolia, cosmopolitan Ebla drew its chief gods from three regions at least. Most at home were the West-Semitic deities. These included: *Il* or *El*, the 'senior god'; *Dagan* (OT, Dagon), god of grain; *Rasap* (OT, Resheph), god of plague and lightning-flash; the sun-god *Sipish* (cf. Babylonian Shamash; OT *shemesh*, 'sun'); the weather/storm god *Adad*; *Ashtar*, a male equivalent of Astarte (OT, Ashtoreth); the goddess *Ashera* (cf. OT Asherah); *Kashalu*, perhaps the same as Koshar, the artificer-god of later Ugarit; *Malik* (cf. Ammonite Milcom?); and Kemish, perhaps familiar 15 centuries later as Kemosh, god of the Moabites. Distinguished foreign members of Ebla's pantheon included such venerable Sumerian deities as *Enlil*, lord of the world order, and *Enki*, god of magic and wisdom. Even more exotic were gods of the Hurrians ('Horites') from the north and north-east; such were Ashtabi, a warrior-god, and the goddess Adammu.[31] Local forms of the great gods were popular, e.g. Dagan of Tuttul, Dagan of Canaan, and so on. The Sumerian-Eblaite vocabulary tablets show us how the theologians of Ebla equated Syrian deities with their Mesopotamian cousins. Thus Resheph = Sumerian Nergal, and Sipish = Utu, for example.

The ancient gods of Ebla had to be housed, fed and honoured as befitted their station in life. The administrative tablets mention the temples of Dagan, Ashtar, Resheph and Kemish. The regular cult of the gods required bread and drink offerings, plus animal sacrifices, especially on festival days – such as on the feasts of Ashtabi and Adammu, for example. The royal family were patrons of the state gods. Thus, in one month, the king (*en*) of Ebla gave as offerings '11 sheep to Adad', '12 sheep for Dagan', '10 sheep for Resheph'. The literary texts preserve brief hymns sung to the gods, probably on such occasions. The actual temples of the golden age of Ebla (*c.* 2300 BC) lie buried for the most part under later remains. However, the excavations have unearthed several temples of the later periods, *c.* 2200/2000 BC, and especially *c.* 2000/1650 BC.[32] The lower city boasted three in the south quarters (B1, B2, C) and one in the north districts (N). These sometimes had a large sanctuary within massive walls that once towered up to some height, with service-rooms around the outside. Most impressive of all was the great temple on the acropolis (site 'D'), with portico, vestibule and ample sanctuary, a distant forerunner in its layout of Late Bronze and Iron Age temples in Hazor and north Syria, and of the Tabernacle and Solomon's Temple. The furnishings of such a temple are illustrated by the fine stone libation-basin sculptured with scenes of the gods, doubtless used in the long, complex rituals of offering customary in all ancient Near-Eastern temples. From the tablets of *c.* 2300 BC, we learn also about the servants of the gods in such temples – priests, priestesses, and 'prophets'. For this latter group, two terms are used: *mahhu* (already known from later Akkadian), and *nabi'utum*, a word related to the Hebrew *nabi*, 'prophet'.

Naturally, the personal names of the people of Ebla often related to their gods, e.g. *Ebdu-Rasap*, 'servant of Resheph'; *Mi-ka-Il*, 'who is like El/God?' (cf. Hebrew *Mi-cha-el*). Some names end in the element *ya* or *a(w)*, as a seeming alternative to El. Prof Pettinato has questioned whether perhaps *El* and *Yaw* here alternate as names of god(s), somewhat as Elohim and YHWH in the Hebrew Bible.[33] If the form *Yaw* was actually an early form of YHWH, then of course the common misconception about Exodus 6:3, that the name YHWH was unkown before Moses, would be eliminated at a stroke, together with much of the 'critical' theories based in part upon such misconceptions. However, many West-Semitic names end in -*a* or -*ia*, a convenient abbreviation for the name of a deity (any deity) left unstated. Therefore, for the present, it is altogether more prudent to treat the -*ya* ending in Eblaite names as just such an abbreviation, rather than to base large assumptions upon it (however intriguing), until fuller and definite information becomes available.

EBLA AND THE OLD TESTAMENT

Ebla in 2300 BC is indeed a fascinating place – but how does it relate to the Old Testament? At first blush (and admittedly with a mischievous twinkle in the eye), one might just reply, 'Not at all!' No biblical characters or events feature in the vast archives from Ebla, and Ebla itself occurs nowhere in the Old Testament.

However, the overwhelming importance of most Near-Eastern discoveries for the Old Testament consists in the enlightening
background that they supply, rather than in specific mentions of
biblical people and happenings. On that score, Ebla certainly
deserves fullest consideration, even on the basis of the necessarily
limited information so far available.

1. *On General Approaches*
   Time and again in Old Testament studies, we are told that
'history knows of no such person' as, say, Abraham or Moses, or
'. . . of no such events' as the battles of Genesis 14, for example.
However such phrases are totally misleading. They simply cover
the ignorance not of 'history' personified but of the person making
this claim. Until 1975, Ebla was nothing more than a shadowy
name: a once-prominent north-Syrian city alongside many more,
such as Aleppo, Carchemish, Emar and the rest. If anyone *before*
1975 had stood up and dared proclaim that Ebla had been the centre of a vast economic empire, rival to that of Akkad, under a
dynasty of six kings, he or she would have been dismissed with
derision. History 'knew' of no such sweeping dominion, no such
line of kings, no such preeminence. But since 1975, of course, the
archives exhumed have changed all that!
   Therefore, one lesson that Ebla reinforces is that it is always extremely foolish to argue from a negative, especially in view of our
still very uneven and incomplete knowledge of the total history of
the ancient Near East. Many gaps *are* closed – many others, in
several regions, are not. As already mentioned, Akkad itself, the
very capital of Sargon and Naram-Sin, has so far never been found
in modern Iraq, even though its once-extensive remains must lie
buried somewhere in that land. But this negative fact has never im-
pelled any rational observer to doubt its former existence or importance. Therefore, it is entirely premature to dismiss on purely
negative grounds the possible existence of biblical characters such
as Abraham or Joseph, Moses or Solomon, for example.
   A good example from outside the Bible is that of the Assyrian
king Tudiya, already noted above for his treaty with Ebla. Until
1975, this shadowy name that heads the Assyrian King List (composed *c.* 1000 BC, in its first form) was treated with the greatest
scepticism along with his near fellows – his name was even dismissed as 'free invention, or a corruption'![34] Whereas in fact, the
name is real, the man is real, he was indeed Assyrian king as the
List records, and as such signed a treaty with Ebrum king of Ebla.
Thus, the genealogical tradition of the early part of the Assyrian
King List (linked as it is with Hammurabi's ancestral line back

from *c.* 1650 BC) is to this extent vindicated as preserving faithfully the memory of real early people who were Assyrian rulers. Not dissimilar material in the Old Testament, therefore, such as genealogical material in Genesis 11 or patriarchal traditions, should be treated with similar respect.

2. The Earliest Background for Biblical Hebrew

To the orientalist, it is commonplace to handle from Egypt three thousand years of documents written in successive forms of ancient Egyptian; or from Mesopotamia, Sumerian and East-Semitic (Akkadian) documents covering practically the same long timespan. But until now, this has not been so for the family group of West-Semitic dialects to which biblical Hebrew belongs. Before 1929, practically no West-Semitic texts were known from much earlier than about 900 BC, except for the obscure proto-Sinaitic fragments, and some Canaanite words and forms in the Amarna tablets of the 14th century BC (in Babylonian cuneiform). But during the 1930's, the twin discoveries at Ugarit and Mari drastically enlarged our knowledge of West Semitic in the 2nd millennium BC. At Ugarit, those tablets written in a local cuneiform alphabet used also a local Northwest Semitic language – Ugaritic – quite closely related to both Hebrew and Canaanite/Phoenician. All these tablets were written in the 14th/13th centuries BC prior to the fall of Ugarit in *c.* 1200 BC, while some compositions originated rather earlier. At Mari, the enormous archives of some 22,000 tablets (even bigger than Ebla) of about the 18th century BC contained many personal names expressed in a form of West Semitic often labelled 'Amorite', an early cousin of Ugaritic and El-Amarna Canaanite. But now, Ebla has taken our knowledge of West Semitic nearly half a millennium further back, to *c.* 2400 BC, almost to the mid-third millennium BC. West Semitic in its various forms now at last has an ancient history of two-and-a-half thousand years comparable in outline with Egyptian and Akkadian. A highly simplified table may serve to illustrate its successive phases set out in parallel with those of Egyptian and Akkadian for comparison.

EGYPTIAN	DATE	WEST SEMITIC	AKKADIAN
Old Egyptian	Mid-3rd mill-nm BC	Eblaite, or 'Palaeo-Canaanite'	Old Akkadian
Middle and Late Egyptian	Early-2nd mill-nm BC	'Amorite' (Mari)	Old-Babylonian & Old-Assyrian
	Later-2nd mill-nm BC	Canaanite, Ugaritic	Middle Babylonian & Middle Assyrian
Late-Eg.; Demotic	1st mill-nm BC	Hebrew, Phoenician, Aramaic; Moabite, etc.	Standard & Neo-Bab.; Neo-Assyr.; Late-Babyl.

Seventy or a hundred years ago, no such vast depth of perspective was possible; and to suit the purely theoretical reconstructions of Old Testament books and history by German Old Testament scholars in particular, many words in Hebrew were labelled 'late' – 600 BC and later, in effect. By this simple means, mere philosophical prejudices could be given the outward appearance of a 'scientific' linguistic foundation. This kind of manipulation is still a basic element in such reconstructions down to the present day.

However, the immense growth in our knowledge of the earlier history of words found in Old Testament Hebrew tends now to alter all this. If a given word is used in Ebla in 2300 BC, and in Ugarit in 1300 BC, then it *cannot* by any stretch of the imagination be a 'late' word (600 BC!), or an 'Aramaism' at periods when standard Aramaic had not yet evolved. It becomes instead an *early* word, a part of the ancestral inheritance of biblical Hebrew. More positively, the increased number of contexts that one gains for rarer words can provide useful confirmation – or correction – of our understanding of their meaning.[35]

Thus, to go back to the survey of city-officials at Ebla, the term used for those scores of 'leaders' was *nase*, the same word as *nasi*, a term in biblical Hebrew used for leaders of the tribes of Israel (e.g., Numbers 1:16, 44, etc.), and applied to other purely human rulers such as Solomon (1 Kings 11:34). Old-fashioned biblical criticism declared the word to be 'late', a mark of the hypothetical 'priestly code' for example.[36] The word *ketem*, 'gold', is in Hebrew a rare and poetic synonym for *zahab*, and is commonly dismissed as 'late'.[37] Unfortunately for this mis-dating, the word was borrowed into Egyptian from Canaanite back in the 12th century BC,[38] and now – over 1000 years earlier still – recurs as *kutim* in the Palaeo-Canaanite of Ebla, 2300 BC.[39] The rare word *sāgā* (two forms), 'be/grow great', is similarly neither an Aramaism nor 'late',[40] but is firmly attested in Ebla (2300 BC) in the personal name Shiga-Damu, 'Damu is great'.[41] The short relative form *she*, *sha*, may well be 'northern', but hardly 'late',[42] as it now occurs (as *shi*) in Eblaite – northern but very early![43] As remarked in Chapter 2, the Hebrew word *tehom*, 'deep', was not borrowed from Babylonian, seeing that it is attested not only in Ugaritic as *thmt* (13th century BC) but also at Ebla a thousand years earlier (*ti'amatum*).[44] The term is Common Semitic. As an example of a rare word confirmed in both existence and meaning, one may cite Hebrew *'ereshet*, 'desire', which occurs just once in the Bible, in Psalm 21:2 (Heb. 21:3). Besides being found in Ugaritic in the 13th century BC,[45] this word now appears a millennium earlier at Ebla as *irisatum* (Eblaite or Old-Akkadian) in the Sumerian/Eblaite vocabulary tablets. [46] Finally, the supposed 'late' verb *hadash/hiddesh*, 'be new'/'to renew' goes back – again – via Ugaritic (*hadath*) to Eblaite *(h)edash(u)*. [47] And so on, for many more besides.

The lessons here are – or should be – clear. Set against $2\frac{1}{2}$ thousand years of the history and development of the West Semitic dialects, the whole position of the dating of the vocabulary and usages in biblical Hebrew will need to be completely reexamined. The truth appears to be that early West Semitic in the 3rd and 2nd millennia BC had in common a vast and rich vocabulary, to which the later dialects such as Canaanite, Hebrew, Phoenician, Aramaic, etc., fell heirs – but in uneven measure. Words that remained in everyday prosaic use in one of these languages lingered on only in high-flown poetry or in traditional expressions in another of the group. Thus, not a few supposed 'late words' or 'Aramaisms' in Hebrew (especially in poetry) are nothing more than early West-Semitic words that have found less use in Hebrew but have stayed more alive in Aramaic. Conversely, supposed 'Hebraisms' in Aramaic are sometimes just words more alive in ordinary Hebrew, but inherited also in Aramaic as part of older, traditional usage. And, as illustrated above, the impact of this oldest West-Semitic language of Ebla – especially when allied with evidence from 'Amorite' and Ugaritic – promises to be drastic indeed upon the gross misuse of the 'late word argument' by Old Testament scholars intent on propping-up the long outdated 19th century reconstructions of Old Testament history and literature, based essentially on false philosophical presuppositions instead of upon verifiable facts.

3. *Lies, *** lies, and statistics!*

This saying is a child of our modern times, born of the welter of numbers that engulfs our lives, and of the uses and misuses to which they can be put. Numbers, however, can present great problems also in studying the ancient biblical Near East. Some – as today – represent the misuse of numbers, as when the court scribes of Sargon II of Assyria (*c.* 722–715 BC) deliberately inflated totals of booty claimed from one version of a text to another. Thus, 1235 sheep taken in one edition became 100,225 in a later one! [48] Other problems involved are quite different. In texts long transmitted by repeated recopying, the accurate transmission of numbers required particular care and was not always maintained. And sometimes the ancients provide us with first-hand statistics of indubitable authenticity that still surprise us.

Ebla illustrates this theme in several respects. Imperial Ebla at the height of its power must have had a vast income. From one defeated king of Mari alone, a tribute of 11,000 lbs of silver and 880 lbs of gold was exacted on one occasion.[49] This *ten tons* of silver and over *one third of a ton* of gold was no mean haul in itself. Yet it was simply one 'delectable extra' so far as the treasury-accounts of Ebla were concerned. In such an economic context, the 666 talents (about twenty tons) of gold as Solomon's basic income from his entire 'empire' some 15 centuries later (1 Kings 10:14; 2 Chronicles 9:13) loses its air of exaggeration and begins to look quite prosaic as just part of a wider picture of the considerable (if transient) wealth of major kingdoms of the ancient biblical world.[50] Again, the vast city and acropolis of Ebla with an area probably ten times that of Solomon's Jerusalem enjoyed a comparably larger administration. Where Solomon in Jerusalem had 12 officers in Israel to provide the royal supplies (1 Kings 4:7), the kings of Ebla had had 103 'leaders' (*nase*) and 210 'aides' to look after services for the four palaces of their acropolis already described above, not to mention the staff of 4,700 people employed there.

The comparisons just given do *not* prove that Solomon actually did receive 666 talents of gold, or that his kingdom was organised just as Kings describes. But they do indicate clearly (i) that the Old Testament data must be studied in the context of their world and *not* in isolation, and (ii) that the *scale* of activity portrayed in the Old Testament writings is neither impossible nor even improbable when measured by the relevant external standards.

4. *Personal Names*

Not a few of the proper names of inhabitants of Ebla have struck Pettinato and others by their obvious resemblances to a wide range of personal names of individuals in the Bible. Among the kings of Ebla, Pettinato has singled out Ebrum or Ebrium as possessing the same name as Eber of Genesis 11:14–16, a distant ancestor of Abraham, and as a possible equivalent of the term *ibri*, 'Hebrew'[51] (cf. 'Abram the Hebrew', in Genesis 14:13). That Ebrum is the same name as Eber (omitting the old ending -*um*) is quite probable – but there is no reason to suppose that they are the same person. Even inside Ebla, one finds quite a number of people, all different but bearing the same name – the 'John Smiths' of their time.[52] The Ebla example of Ebr(um) merely shows how early and how authentic Eber is, as a *real* personal name, not just a legendary invention, back in the 3rd millennium BC – which is as much as one might expect. The link with *ibri* (if correct) is of little consequence, except (again) to demonstrate the probable antiquity of the term.

Perhaps of greater interest are such names as Ishmail ('Ishmael'), Ishrail ('Israel')[53] – borne by ordinary flesh-and-blood citizens of Ebla, *c.* 2300 BC, five centuries or more before either the Ishmael and Israel of the biblical patriarchs (son and grandson of Abraham) or the well-known Yasmakh-El of Mari (*c.* 1800 BC) and Yisrail of Ugarit (*c.* 1300 BC), also real flesh-and-blood individuals. The most important contributions of the Ebla occurrences of these and other such names[54] are (i) to emphasize once more that these are names used by *real* human individuals (never by gods, or exclusively (if ever) by tribes, or by fairytale figures), and (ii) to indicate the immense antiquity of names of this type, and of these names in particular. It should occasion no surprise to find other Ishmaels and Israels in antiquity besides the biblical characters that bear these names. Many parents today have their own personal or special reasons for giving particular names to children – but the names so chosen are usually already-existing ones, not strange new ones invented for the occasion. So, too, in antiquity. Among the city 'leaders' of Ebla discussed already, we find three men all called Bedunum (Recto, III, 4, 6, 15), all in one section; three men called Ennaia (or 'Hanania'; Recto, IV, 5, V, 6; Verso, VI, 4); four men called Tilaia (Recto, IV, 3, 12; Verso, III, 12, V, 7), besides several pairs of men with each the same name. This feature of popularity of names is, of course, well known from many other sources besides Ebla in antiquity.

5. *Places*

Not a few towns of biblical interest appear in the Ebla tablets, which preserve (in most cases) the earliest-known mention of these in written records. Well east of Ebla, on or near the Khabur river, Nahur is mentioned – a centre familiar from the Mari archives – which might also be the 'city of Nahor' (Genesis 24:10). Nahor was a relatively common name, found also for the grandfather and the brother of Abraham (Genesis 11:24–26). However, if the 'city of Nahor' is to be taken as a personal reference to one of these men, then it may simply by a synonym for Haran where Terah died.

More useful, potentially, are the Eblaite mentions of familiar Palestinian place-names such as Hazor, Megiddo, Jerusalem, Lachish, Dor, Gaza, Ashtarot (-Qarnaim), etc. Several of these places are known archaeologically to have been inhabited towns in the 3rd millennium BC (Early Bronze Age III–IV), and these tablets confirm their early importance, possibly as local city-states. Finally, Canaan itself now appears as a geographical entity from the later 3rd millennium BC, long before any other dated external mention so far known to us – it will be interesting to learn what extent is accorded to Canaan in the Ebla texts.

6. *Religion*

Several of the West Semitic or 'Canaanite' gods familiar from the Old Testament and at Ugarit now have their histories extended some centuries back into the 3rd millennium BC – such include Dagan, El, Adad, Resheph, Ashera, Kemosh, etc.; as distinct from Adad, Baal has not been reported so far. As for the abodes of deity, the biggest temple at Ebla (acropolis, 'D', *c.* 1800 BC) shows a three-part plan that became one of the basic types of temple-plan in Syria-Palestine thenceforth. This comprised a portico, vestibule, and inner sanctuary or holy-of-holies. Over a millennium later, this scheme reappears in one of the temples at Hazor (area H) in the 13th century BC, as well as being reflected in Solomon's temple (as Matthiae has also noted[55]), besides other Syrian temples.

In matters like priests, cult and offerings the records from Ebla so far merely reinforce for Syria-Palestine what we already know for Egypt, Mesopotamia and Anatolia in the 3rd, 2nd and 1st millennia BC, and from the records of North-Syrian Qatna and Ugarit for the 2nd millennium BC. Namely, that well-organized temple cults, sacrifices, full rituals, etc., were a *constant* feature of ancient Near-Eastern religious life at *all* periods from prehistory down to Graeco-Roman times. They have nothing to do with baseless theories of the 19th century AD, whereby such features of religious life can only be a mark of 'late sophistication', virtually forbidden to the Hebrews until after the Babylonian exile – alone of *all* the peoples of the ancient East. There is simply no rational basis for the quaint idea that the simple rites of Moses' tabernacle (cf. Leviticus) or of Solomon's temple, both well over 1000 years later than the rituals practised in half-a-dozen Eblaite temples, must be the idle invention of idealising writers as late as the 5th century BC

The occurrence of *nabi'utum* (cf. Hebrew *nabi*) as a class of 'prophet' alongside the better-known *mahhu*[56] will add another chapter – the earliest yet – to the 'prehistory' of prophecy. It is certainly the oldest attestation of the term; knowledge of the function of such men at Ebla must await publication of the tablets.[57] The Eblaite *mahhu* may have had similar functions to those known from Mari in the 18th century BC. These men indeed delivered the 'message' of Dagan or other gods to the king of Mari – but always briefly, and purely in the king's political or military interests, sometimes with promise or threat, depending on the king's response. Never, however, do they adopt the stance of a Nathan, an Amos or a Hosea, or an Isaiah, to reprove and admonish on vital issues of personal morality, social justice, or obedience to God as man's due to him. Apart from the eloquent (but relatively 'secular') pleas for just conduct of affairs in Egyptian works such as the Eloquent Peasant or the Admonitions of Ipuwer, the moral and spiritual tone of the later Old Testament prophets remains without real parallel in the ancient world.

7. *In Conclusion*

From the foregoing, it should be evident that, in terms of background, Ebla has much to offer already to biblical studies, especially in relation to its early date, on West-Semitic languages, and a wide range of information on the most diverse topics. We may expect a very great deal more, when – eventually – the documents themselves are published in full and can be studied in depth.

4

Founding Fathers in Canaan and Egypt

Among the more memorable narratives in the Old Testament are those about Israel's ancestors, Abraham, Isaac and Jacob, culminating in the splendidly-told story of Joseph. In Genesis, these men are the recipients of promises for their descendants. Later in the Old Testament, from Moses onwards, it is in fulfilment of those promises that the Hebrews are brought out of Egypt, constituted a national community by covenant, and taken into Canaan. Thus, Abraham, Isaac and Jacob are the 'founding fathers' of ancient Israel, her natural ancestors going back beyond Moses and the Sinai covenant, in the biblical record.

A CENTURY OF CONTROVERSY – FOUNDERS OR FICTIONS?

During the later 19th century, rationalistic Old Testament scholarship in Germany decided that the Old Testament accounts of Hebrew history did not fit 'history' as it *'should'* have happened, according to their preconceived ideas. Therefore, its leading representatives rearranged the Old Testament writings (including imaginary divisions of these) until Old Testament history, religion and literature had been suitably manipulated to fit in with their philosophical preconceptions. Far and away the most accomplished advocate of this ultimately arbitrary method was Julius Wellhausen, brilliantly exemplified in his *Prolegomena to the*

History of Israel, first published in 1878 (in English, 1885), and in his article in the *Encyclopaedia Britannica* then.

According to these theories, the patriarchs were simply shadows, the vague stock of the 15th century BC (in 19th-century dating), from which sprang a few shepherds who made their way from south Palestine to Egypt and back again.[1] He claimed dogmatically that 'here [in Genesis] no historical knowledge about the patriarchs is to be gotten, but only about the period in which the stories about them arose among the Israelite people. This later period was simply to be projected back into hoary antiquity and reflected there like a glorified mirage.'[2] For Gunkel, the stories of the patriarchs were sagas or legends, in contrast to the history proper; the patriarchal figures he considered to be, not individual humans, but personified tribes and the like.[3]

From those distant days until now, therefore, German Old Testament scholarship has servilely adhered to the dogmas of Wellhausen and Gunkel, with minimal variation. This can be seen in Eissfeldt's words that the patriarchs 'have thus become representatives of the post-Mosaic people of Israel projected back into the pre-Mosaic age; what they do and endure . . . reveals indirectly the circumstances of an Israel settled in Canaan.'[4] Even Wellhausen's 15th-century date is kept, by misapplying the Nuzi data.[5]

Outside Germany, however, such unbelievable devotion to old-fashioned critical dogmas was left far behind during the 1930's onwards. At that time, W. F. Albright of Baltimore pioneered a new school of thought that sought to correlate the narratives of Genesis with the growing mass of inscriptional and archaeological evidence from the ancient biblical world, in particular setting the patriarchs in the first half of the 2nd millennium BC.[6] The archives from Mari (18th century BC) and Nuzi (15th century BC) were drawn upon to illustrate wide travel, semi-nomadism and West-Semitic personal names, and legal/social usages respectively. The classic modern outline of this view is that of Bright in his well-known history of ancient Israel.[7]

However, this relatively sane and moderate view of the patriarchs has in recent decades been clouded by treatments of very questionable value. C. H. Gordon opted for a 14th-century date on too-limited grounds,[8] as well as (with others) a highly-coloured view of Abraham as a merchant-prince. Others again made of Abraham a warrior-hero. And latterly, Albright himself advocated a view of Abraham as a 'donkey-caravaneer', a travelling trader rather than a pastoralist.[9] Speiser meantime had opted for a largely Hurrian (Horite) interpretation of the activities of the patriarchs, using principally the Nuzi archives as his resource.[10]

The founding fathers began to look more like Hurrians than Hebrews!

The view initiated by Albright and elaborated in these very varied ways by him and others held the field up to the beginning of the 1970's. During the current decade, however, and especially since the death of Albright (1971), reaction has – not too surprisingly – set in. Encouraged by old-style 'diehards' in both Germany and America, a small group of younger scholars have written at length to 'debunk' the views of the Albright school concerning the patriarchal age – and in fact, any view other than the negative attitude to early Hebrew tradition in the later 19th century.[11] Far from being 'radical' scholars, such writers are in truth 'reactionaries' who seek, in essence, to put the clock back by 100 years. And their highest role in reality is simply that of 'devil's advocate'. Thus, their works *do* perform the useful function of ruthlessly exposing sloppy argumentation by others, false or inadequate parallels, refuting the wilder excrescences of speculation, and emphasising the need to look at all periods (not only the 2nd millennium) in reviewing possible background to the patriarchal narratives. All this is salutary, and all to the good, in clearing the ground towards a more firmly based assessment.

However, these same advocates themselves then fail to match up to this selfsame standard of reviewing the patriarchal data against *all* periods. Instead, they neglect the 3rd millennium BC entirely, along with whole sections of relevant evidence from the early 2nd millennium, and give exaggerated attention to 1st-millennium materials. In the process, they fail, therefore, to distinguish between features attested at *all* periods (hence useless for dating), features attested in some periods, and features attested in only one period (early or late). In order to prop up the old 19th-century view of the patriarchs as late fictions dreamt up 1000 years after the 'patriarchal age', they are driven to produce arguments at times so tortuous and convoluted as to stand almost self-condemned as spurious and far from even remotely proving their case. For example, van Seters artificially excludes all patriarchal personal names from consideration other than Abraham on the excuse that they are tribal,[12] while in point of fact all external correlations show them to be personal! He makes the incredible suggestion that the detail of the patriarchs living in tents 'is more suggestive of the first millennium than of the second.'[13] Quite the contrary is the case. In the 20th century BC, the Egyptian Sinuhe who fled home to live in south Syria speaks easily and naturally of living in a tent, and (after single combat) of stripping his enemy's tent and camp.[14] In the Admonitions of Ipuwer (17th century BC at latest),[15] 'tents it is that are set up for them (displaced Egyptians) like the foreigners (do)'. [16] The foreigners envisaged would be Egypt's neighbours in Palestine. From the other end of the ancient Near East, the Sumerian 'Myth of the god Martu', eponym of the 'Amorites' of north Syria, dismisses the 'stereotype' Amorite in the words 'a tent-dweller [buffeted?] by wind and rain ... who in his lifetime does not have a house ...',[17] in a text of the early 2nd millennium BC. Later in the 2nd millennium, the Ugaritic epics mention tents (same word as Hebrew *'ohel*), as do Egyptian sources – the West-Semitic word recurs under Merenptah and Ramesses III (13th/12th centuries BC). And so on.[18] In other words, tents (not surprisingly) are to be expected at all periods and are useless for dating. And that camels as a *subordinate* item in the patriarchal narratives are anachronistic is flatly contradicted by the available evidence to the contrary.[19] Speculations by T. L. Thompson[20] in terms of 'Maccabean or post-Maccabean' (!) chronology imposed on the Hebrew text simply beggar belief as a species of cabbalistic gematria. Post-Maccabean is, in effect, the time of Herod and the Romans, the period of the Dead Sea Scrolls, when the text of such books as Genesis was already settled! And so one might continue the exposure of misconceptions, lop-sided presentations and downright special pleading.

TOWARDS A SOLUTION

From this welter of controversy, what – if anything – emerges? If we open the pages of Genesis, etc., what sort of patriarchs do we actually find? And of what use is the supposed ancient Near Eastern evidence? The answer to the first question depends on those to the latter two questions, to which we must briefly turn.

1. *The Patriarchs and Narratives themselves*

In Genesis 11:27 to 50:26, we have a series of narratives, punctuated by occasional genealogies and poems. An ordinary man, Terah, has three sons and a grandson in Ur. After the death of one son, the family moves off northwestwards to Har(r)an in Upper Mesopotamia, staying there until Terah's death. Leaving one branch of the family there, one son (Abraham) and his nephew travels west and south into Canaan, visiting Egypt briefly, then spending the rest of his days moving around Canaan, as a pastoralist,[21] and head of a growing clan of retainers.[22] Abraham desired offspring; his God gave him a covenant and promises. The adopted servant (Eliezer) and servant-girl's son (Ishmael) in due time made way for a true son (Isaac), whose marriage to a girl from the Haran branch of the family was arranged before Abraham's death. External events hardly touch the essentially 'family' narrative – the defeat of four eastern kings and the destruction of Sodom and Gomorrah (14;19) alone feature, because of Lot's involvement. Isaac (Genesis 26 ff.) followed quietly in his father's pastoral way of life, also growing occasional crops (Gen. 26:12, 14). Of his twin sons, Jacob took the lead, seeking refuge from Esau's wrath by living with the Haran branch of the family, marrying two of their girls. Later, he returned to Canaan and reconciliation soon before his father's death (Gen. 27–35). Then, in Gen. 37–50, we have essentially the story of Joseph (Jacob's eleventh son), magnificently told: a youngster sold into Egyptian bondage by jealous brothers, his godfearing integrity leading him to high position in Egypt, so that he is in due time enabled to sustain his family who come also to reside in the Egyptian east Delta.

Throughout these narratives, several features are apparent to any reader. They deal almost exclusively with *ordinary human beings*, men and women, who are born, marry, have children, tend sheep, goats, cattle, and grow a crop or two, who love, quarrel, die and are buried. They worship their God, building simple altars, and have dreams and visions. There is nothing here that is not within the range of known human experience. The narratives in Genesis are the *only* record available that mentions the patriarchs; like a myriad other private individuals in antiquity, they are not so far attested in any other ancient document. This has two consequences. First, this *is* our sole record – any attempt to amend it only substitutes guesswork (inherently of no authority) for the one definite record that we do have. Second, as this *is* the only record, a modern observer is initially free to take any of several conceivable views of the *nature* of these narratives. They could be pure fiction, precursor of the modern novel. They might be, quite in contrast, straight, factual narratives of historical people who actually lived precisely as described, from start to finish. Or, they might be something in between: e.g. narratives about people once real, about whom either (i) selected features were remembered or (ii) various stories clustered in the course of time. Various other possibilities have been canvassed.

Is there anything further in the narratives to guide us? At first sight, some might consider certain limited special features as giving a lead. First, the patriarchs speak with God and he with them. Second, the patriarchs tend to live rather long (Abraham: 175 years; Isaac: 180 years; Jacob: 147 years), even marrying later than many people do (e.g. Isaac marrying at 40; Gen. 25:20).

Third, other 'remarkable' points are few,[23] and in the Joseph narrative, nil; no 'miracles' disturb its even flow, for example. That real people can speak to deity – prayer! – proves nothing against their reality. Neither does deity speaking to man – as the Hebrew prophets later claimed, for example – witness Ramesses II at the Battle of Qadesh, who had Amun's reply to his prayer.[24] Thus, intercourse with deity has no bearing on historicity of the humans involved. Only very rarely are deity and humans shown confronted in these narratives: Hagar (Gen. 16:7–13), Abraham (Gen. 18–19), when humans appear as God's spokesmen, or a voice comes from heaven (Gen. 22:11, 15).[25] Likewise, concerning the long lifespans: far 'worse' than Abraham, Isaac or Jacob was Enmebaragisi king of Kish with 900 years' reign in the Sumerian King List – but who was indubitably historical nonetheless (cf. chapter 2 above). The transmission of numbers being a special issue on its own, these long spans have no direct bearing on the historicity or otherwise of the patriarchs.

2. Literary Background

In fact, one may go still further. We possess neither proof nor disproof, at first hand, of the historical existence of the patriarchs or of the narrations about them. But these same narratives can be compared with other ancient Near Eastern narrative works of several categories.[26]

In Egypt, we may distinguish between three categories of narratives (besides royal inscriptions and myths). *First*, 'autobiographies' and autobiographical narratives. The former are attested in the third, second and first millennia BC alike, from tombs, stelae and statues of officials. They are commonly expressed in the first person, often with an introduction in the third person; they are unquestionably historical.[27] Autobiographical narratives include Sinuhe (*c.* 1930 BC) and Wenamun (*c.* 1075 BC), known from papyri and recopied as literature. Wenamun is generally accepted as historical, and Sinuhe is most probably based on the tomb-text of a historical person. These too are in the first person, and share a vivid style with some of the autobiographies. Providential events do occur, and dealings with deity,[28] but no 'miracles'. *Second,* historical legends. In the second and first millennia, these are stories about known historical personalities – kings, princes, officials – but written at later periods, often long afterwards. Thus, the Tales of the Magicians (Papyrus Westcar), *c.* 1600 BC, tells of supposed magicians at the courts of known kings of a thousand years before; historical characters such as the sons of Kheops (builder of the Great Pyramid) appear. The acts of the

magicians are imaginary, and involve marvels: causing the severed
heads and bodies of decapitated animals to rejoin spontaneously,
etc.[29] *Third,* purely fictional stories. Such include adventures and
fantasies like the Shipwrecked Sailor (*c.* 1800 BC) with a magic
island, great talking serpent, etc.; or the Foredoomed Prince (thirteenth century BC) in which a king's only son (under three fates
from angry fairy godmothers) seeks his fortune incognito in distant
Syria, rescuing a princess from a tower, etc.; or the Tale of the Two
Brothers (thirteenth century BC) with the younger brother transforming himself from human form into a bull, then into two persea
trees, ultimately to reappear as the king's son. These usually [30] have
no named heroes or personalities, and none but the vaguest locales
in Egypt or abroad.[31]

  In Syria-Palestine, despite much more limited material (so far),
the situation is similar. *First,* 'autobiographies'. [32] The best known
example is that of king Idrimi of Alalakh (early fifteenth century
BC), telling of his life as a fugitive and how he regained his father's
throne, all in the first person. [33] *Second,* quasi-historical legends.
Here, the West-Semitic literary tablets from Ugarit (four-
teenth/thirteenth centuries BC) offer us two works probably of
this type. First and foremost is the Legend of King Keret, portrayed as ruler of a realm in the Habur region of Upper
Mesopotamia who (after losing first wife and offspring) seeks a new
wife with the god El's encouragement. By her, he raises a new
brood, falls ill, and is cured by a winged emissary from El. The
locations are probably real, and 'the assembly of Ditanu' probably
links up with historical tradition in Mesopotamia. [34] Apart from
El's ministering angel, there are no 'marvels'. However, the whole
text is set in a distinctive epic style, high-flown poetry rich in
standing clichés. It is clearly a legendary poetic epic whose chief
character was quite possibly a historical king of centuries before.
Secondly, there is the Legend of Danel and Aqhat. Danel is king of
Harnam in the Lebanese Beqa-region who, also, needs and is granted a son, Aqhat. This text, however, in similar poetic epic style, is
pure legend and mythology, as Danel, Aqhat and the various
Canaanite gods mingle freely in the action. If there ever was such a
king, his name, location and perhaps son are the sole conceivable
'historical' elements; the main thread of the epic lies elsewhere. [35]
Danel in fact is closer to Egypt's third class of narrative – purely
fictional tales – and is perhaps best so classified.

  In Mesopotamia, we find largely comparable literary groups.
First, as historical texts of kings preponderate, few 'non-royals'
have left biographical-type narratives. However, at a period of
relative weakness in Assyrian central government, the high official

Shamshi-ilu (eighth century BC) left monumental texts on his own account at Til Barsip, for example.[36] Two other officials show similar independence.[37] *Second*, historical legends. These occur in both the Sumerian and Akkadian literatures. In Sumerian (early second millennium BC), we possess a series of epic tales of early kings who lived in the early third millennium BC (nine hundred years earlier) – of Enmerkar and Lugalbanda (four works), and above all about Gilgamesh of Uruk (five separate legends). These three kings were all, originally, very early Sumerian city-state rulers whose fame became (literally!) legendary. Enmerkar and Lugalbanda are shown in negotiation and conflict with the distant land of Aratta (in Iran?). Gilgamesh fights with Agga king of Kish; goes on an expedition to the cedar-forests in the (Syrian) mountains; is involved with the goddess Inanna, etc. All these stories are set out in a high-flown, poetic style, and sometimes involve deities directly. In Akkadian (Babylonian) literature, the materials on Gilgamesh are woven into a single Epic of Gilgamesh, whose hero seeks immortal life after the loss of his friend. The great kings Sargon and Naram-Sin of Akkad (*c.* 2300 BC) were celebrated in legends of five hundred or more years later. These reflect in colourful form the imperial wars and battles of these known historical kings. In The King of Battle Legend, for example, Sargon marches to Anatolia to aid the merchants there, his route being encumbered by blocks of lapis-lazuli and gold as well as by forest and thorn-thickets![38] One of the five legends about Naram-Sin has demonic hordes invading his empire from the north-west.[39] The historical king of Assyria, Tukulti-Ninurta I (thirteenth century BC), was also commemorated by an epic composition, in this case composed in his reign.[40] *Third*, purely fictional tales, without historical content. Such are the Three Ox-Drivers of Adab and the Old Man and Young Girl (both Sumerian)[41] and the Poor Man of Nippur and At the Cleaner's (both Akkadian).[42] Specific detail of people and places is often minimal, and such stories are entertaining and generalized.

In Hittite Anatolia, further material is to be found. *First*, historical texts. These are almost all royal – the Deeds of Anittas from the dawn of Hittite history, the 'Annals' of Hattusil I, and the fuller records of the Empire kings. *Second*, historical legends. Here, the Hittites copied and translated Mesopotamian works about Gilgamesh and Sargon of Akkad, besides their own stories of (e.g.) King Anum-Khirbe and the City of Zalpa, and the Siege of Urshu. Here too, historical people and elements are set in later literary works. *Third*, stories of general, fictional type – stories of Appu, Keshshi and others.[43]

In summary, the ancient biblical world had a considerable (if un-evenly preserved) wealth of narratives varying from strictly historical/(auto)-biographical through historico-legendary (stories of former historical persons) to pure fiction, even fantasy. Where then, as West-Semitic narrations, do the patriarchal narratives stand in this wider literary context? First of all, as noted already, they are entirely concerned with a purely human family whose lifestyle is firmly tied to the everyday realities of herding livestock (pasture, wells), yearning for children, arranging suitable marriages, and so on. We never read (for example) of animals divided up that magically rejoin and live again, or of a patriarch's path barred by blocks of lapis or gold. Rather, bearing strictly real, human names, the patriarchs move in well-defined, specific loca-tions – Ur, Haran, Damascus, Shechem, Egypt, Shur, Hebron/Mamre, the Negeb, Gerar, etc. – and not in some vague, never-never land. By their names and characters, the patriarchs are a group of distinguishable individuals, neither ghosts nor stereo-types. Only two features seem other than purely mortal and 'secular', and neither is pertinent to deciding the question of historicity. As noticed above, long lifespans are no more contra-historical than the 900 years of an Enmebaragisi in Sumer. And the relations with deity are comparable in form with those attested of known historical people (e.g. Ramesses II), with the rarest excep-tions. Thus, even on a severely 'rationalistic' view, the scope for supposedly non-historical embellishments is very limited.

Secondly, therefore, on content and type, the patriarchal narratives of Genesis 11–50 can be seen to be wholly different from the third class of ancient Near-Eastern narratives, the vague fictions and fantasies of (e.g.) the Shipwrecked Sailor or the Tale of the Two Brothers. One need only read these and the Genesis narratives to see the striking differences. The latter, again, are also visibly different from the second class of ancient Near-Eastern narratives, the 'historical legends'. As remarked above, no 'animal magic' (cf. Tales of the Magicians), or gold and lapis outcrops or demonic hordes (Sargon, Naram-Sin.) And stylistically, the Genesis narratives are expressed in straightforward prose – not the stilted epic poetry of such as Keret and Danel at Ugarit. In both content and literary mould, the patriarchal narratives are visibly more 'realistic' and seemingly 'historical' than anything in most of the historical legends of the ancient Near East. How, then, do the patriarchal narratives compare with our first class of ancient Near-Eastern narratives (autobiographical, etc.)? The patriarchal narratives are neither royal inscriptions (formal texts for or by kings) nor autobiographical, first-person, accounts as transmitted to us. But they do share the straightforward narrative form of known autobiographical works. They are in the third person and set in the past; Genesis (50:26) ends with Joseph put in a coffin in Egypt. On type, therefore, our extant patriarchal narratives come *between* the first and second classes of ancient Near-Eastern narrative. In sober content and mode of expression, they are clearly closest to the first category, without being identical with it (not first person). They share their third person narrative form with occasional texts of the first category [44] and all texts of the second group — but entirely lack the fantasy-embellishments of the second group.

Hence, purely on literary type and content — as measured against the self-existent criteria of the biblical world — the patriarchal narratives stand closest to historically-founded narratives, sharing with 'legendary' narratives almost nothing but their 'posthumous' form. This by itself does *not*, of course, prove that the patriarchs are, or were, historical people. But these facts (based on external, tangible comparison) do favour understanding the patriarchs as having been historical persons within historically-based traditions, and equally clearly go against any arbitrary assumption that they 'must' have been simply a myth or legend. [45] In the latter case, we would have been entitled to expect a different type of narrative, more clearly of categories two or three. If the patriarchal narratives are not historical or quasi-historical, then they must be specimens of a type of imaginitive, 'realistic-fiction' novel not otherwise known to have been invented until several millennia later, in fact approaching modern times. That, in itself, would be more than passing strange.

An entirely separate issue from all of the foregoing is that of date. If the patriarchs indeed existed historically, the entire biblical tradition is unanimous in placing them long before the monarchy, and well before Moses, whose God was the God of the long-dead 'fathers', Abraham, Isaac and Jacob, and in fact some four centuries before the exodus on more than one statement. As any exodus from Egypt leading to settlement in Canaan must pre-date the fifth year of the pharaoh Merenptah, at *c.* 1220/1209 BC at the latest,[46] four centuries before the late thirteenth century BC gives the seventeenth century BC as the latest possible date (on explicit biblical data) for the patriarchs on entry to Egypt, and they may obviously go back rather earlier. A quite separate issue from this is that of the date of the narratives *about* the patriarchs. The 'minimalist' view promulgated late last century would be that — at most — vague traditions of distant founding fathers were much later woven into a whole cycle of 'patriarchal stories' during the Hebrew

monarchy (*c.* 1000–600 BC), stories that reflect only the late period
in which they were concocted.[47] However, this minimalist view is
subject to various difficulties, including: (i) it fails entirely to account for firm correlations between features in the patriarchal
narratives and relatively early phenomena (early second millennium), (ii) it entails acceptance of a 'modern novel' view of the
narratives already seen to be almost incredible (cf. just above), (iii)
the narratives do *not* take the proper, ancient Near-Eastern legendary forms that they should if the minimalist view were true.
Therefore, the late date and fictional nature of the narratives
favoured by this antiquated view do not fit the facts available today
– the date of the narratives should most probably be earlier, and
their nature be something stronger than fiction, nearer to historical.
If the patriarchs really had been early-second-millennium ancestors
of thirteenth-century Israel, then it is conceivable that traditions of
Abraham, Isaac, Jacob and their family-group were handed down
among the Hebrews in Egypt (in both oral and written forms). The
first formal one-document composition about them might have
been produced in the thirteenth century BC, or at the very latest by
the united monarchy (*c.* 1000 BC). In that case, the narratives
should preserve traces of early-second-millennium date plus
possibly traces of the time of final composition (thirteenth century
BC or later) and of any subsequent minor editing.

Before we turn to the question of possible correlations between
features of the patriarchal narratives and in the ancient Near East,
one other question must be considered – that of the *transmission* of
traditions across several centuries. Could traditions about the
patriarchs be reliably transmitted during, say, the 430 years from
Jacob and Joseph's time to Moses's day? Or even till later? In the
light of currently available knowledge, the answer in principle must
be 'yes'. Thus, the discoveries at Ebla (chapter 3, above) have
shown that the Assyrian King List of *c.* 1000 BC and after was perfectly correct in accurately retaining the name and the function of
Tudiya as its earliest-known king of Assyria, who reigned about
2300 BC. This is a case of reliable transmission across *thirteen centuries and more* – three times as long as the four centuries of
Genesis-Exodus, and half as long again as the spurious figure of
eight centuries that worried T. L. Thompson.[48] The Assyrian King
List tradition belonged to a West-Semitic family (that of Shamshi-
Adad I), as do the patriarchal traditions; and its original form
spanned a period of five centuries (*c.* 2300–1800 BC). Moreover,
this early Assyrian tradition had a close relative and part-parallel:
the less well transmitted list of ancestors of the great-grandson of
Hammurabi of Babylon, which ultimately went back seven cen-

turies to Tudiya. Furthermore, not all the ancestors in the twin lines of Shamshi-Adad and Hammurabi had actually been kings of Assyria or Babylon but had been nothing more than minor family chiefs – in effect, private people. Thus, quite apart from any theories about the Hebrew patriarchs, the phenomenon of several centuries' transmission of family memory is securely attested in the West Semitic world of the early second millennium BC.

Further north, in Anatolia, the Hittite archives of the four-teenth/thirteenth centuries BC preserved copies of an 'Annalistic Report' by a king Anittas of Kussara, who had supposedly reigned in an epoch (nineteenth/eighteenth century BC) before the founding of the Old-Hittite kingdom proper. The historical reality of Anittas was subsequently proven by archaeological discovery of tablets of his contemporaries naming him, and of a spear-head inscribed 'Palace of Anittas'. Even though the surviving copies are from about five centuries later, the authenticity of Anittas's 'Report' has been demonstrated on both linguistic and historical grounds: a case of reliable transmission across that span. [49]

Returning to Syria and West-Semitic tradition, we may glance at the King List of Ugarit. A ritual tablet from shortly before 1200 BC once contained a list of up to thirty-six consecutive kings of Ugarit, stretching back through over six centuries to the founder Yaqaru in the nineteenth century BC – royal ancestors of one of the last kings of Ugarit; another document may cite five protohistoric rulers back to 2000 BC or more. [50] Thus, the princes of a quite modest-sized city-state could retain records reaching back six, perhaps seven or eight centuries, BC. The reality of Yaqaru at least is essentially proven by his 'dynastic seal' – of a type from about the nineteenth century BC – used by later kings of Ugarit.

Finally, in Egypt, not only royal, but also private family records and memories could reach far back. Thus, a celebrated private law-suit concluded about Year 20 of Ramesses II (*c.* 1270/1260 BC) was fought for a century earlier by rival wings of one family, to gain control over a tract of land originally given to their ancestor Neshi some three hundred years before Ramesses II's time. [51] Only in recent years has Neshi himself turned up as a proven historical character, serving the pharaohs Kamose and Ahmose who expelled the Hyksos from Egypt, thus demonstrating the reliability of that family tradition. This family was of no great or exalted standing by Ramesses II's day, but zealously guarded its own traditions and knew how to consult official records to cite in law courts.

Thus, in all the principal cultural areas of the ancient biblical world, it was possible for the ancients to transmit family or other traditions across a span of several centuries; this is a matter of

observed fact, not merely of speculation, as the foregoing examples
should indicate.

3. *Cultural Backgrounds*

An ancient tradition reliably transmitted across several centuries
is all very well in principle. But what about practice? In the case of
the patriarchs, how far is it true that the narratives indeed reflect
early second millennium conditions? Or has recent reactionary
scholarship really won the day? A brief review is in order. [52]

(i) *Proper Names* The position here is that practically all the
patriarchal names find their best equivalents and analogues in the
early second millennium BC. Some names, elements and forms are
attested also in later centuries – and some from as early as the third
millennium BC. A point of particular importance is that all are
human names, names of individuals, in external sources as in
Genesis – *not* simply names of tribes, deities or other entities. Both
elements in the name Ab-ram, 'the father is exalted' or 'the exalted
one is father' occur in the Mari archives [53] and other early second
millennium sources, as well as in later centuries. Ab(u)-ram(a)
should not be confused with Abi-ram, 'my father is exalted'. The
extended form Ab-raham has its nearest relative in the name Abu-
rahan of the Egyptian Execration Texts (*c.* 1800 BC), *n* and *m* being
dialect-variants in some cases. [54] Ben-('son'-) names such as Benjamin are common at all periods. 'Amorite Imperfective' names
such as Jacob, Joseph, Isaac, Ishmael, Israel, are particularly
favoured in the early second millennium BC, go back to the third
millennium BC, and are in use in the later second millennium BC,
sometimes appearing later still. Thus, Ishmael is paralleled not only
by Yasmakh-El, etc., in the Mari archives (eigthteenth century BC)
but five hundred years earlier at Ebla, as Ishmail. Likewise, Israel
is paralleled not only by the thirteenth century Yisra-il of Ugarit
but also by the twenty-third century Ishrail of Ebla. Parallels for
Jacob are particularly well-known in the early to mid-second
millennium. [55] Zebulon is close to Old-Babylonian Zabilanu and the
Zabilu-Hadda of the Execration Texts, while Levi compares with
equally early second millennium names in Lawi-; and so on. [56] As
virtually the whole body of 'patriarchal' names has parallels from
the early second millennium BC (sometimes even from the third), it
is impossible to use later occurrences of some names or elements to
prove a late date. The names indicate a date either in or after the
early second millennium.

(ii) *Social and Legal Usages* Various of the social customs of
the patriarchs find no echo in the days of the Hebrew monarchy,
and practically none in the laws of Moses (Exodus-Deuteronomy).

But they do find analogy in the law-collections and usages of early second millennium Mesopotamia. These make it clear that the rights of children by more than one wife were to be safeguarded. Just as Jacob kept both Leah (whom he had not desired) and Rachel (whom he did), without divorcing the former, so in the Lipit-Ishtar laws (twentieth century BC), § 28, a man was to maintain his first as well as second wife.[57] Again, the children of more than one wife, including by slave-girls if acknowledged, all had rights of inheritance, as is clear from Lipit-Ishtar, § 24, and from Hammurabi's laws (eighteenth century BC), § 170. This too is admitted by Jacob, as all of his sons – by the handmaids Bilhah and Zilpah, as well as by Leah and Rachel – are included in his final blessing (Gen. 49); this usage did continue into at least the late second millennium, being recognised in Deuteronomy 21:15–17. Across the centuries, one may see a shift in emphasis in some details. Thus, in the twentieth century BC, Lipit-Ishtar's laws envisage (§ 24) equal shares among all the inheriting children. In the eighteenth century BC, Hammurabi's laws (§ 170) qualify this by giving a 'first choice' in the estate to the son(s) of the first wife. In the fifteenth century BC, various Nuzi adoption-tablets clearly accord a double share to a first-born natural son (in contrast to an adoptee).[58] In the thirteenth century BC, a double share is also the prerogative of the firstborn son in Deuteronomy 21:15–17. Several centuries later, in the sixth century BC, the Neo-Babylonian laws go a stage further, assigning two-thirds (i.e. double share) of the inheritance to the sons (plural; not solely the first-born) of the first wife, and one-third to the sons of the second wife.[59] As Jacob in Gen. 49 bestowed blessings upon all his sons, he stands closest to the oldest legal tradition here, not the latest.

However, the sons of wives of different status did not always fare analogously. The Lipit-Ishtar laws (§ 26) reserved the main inheritance to the children of a deceased first wife, excluding sons by a subsequent lesser (slave?) wife (separate provision). One may here compare Gen. 25:1–6, in which (correspondingly) Abraham 'gave all that he had to Isaac' his main heir, while giving parting gifts to lesser sons by the (lesser) wife Keturah and concubines.[60] In Hammurabi's laws, sons of slave-wives shared inheritance if acknowledged by their father (§ 170) but not if unacknowledged (§ 171). In this context, it is interesting to observe Abraham's evident desire to 'recognise' Ishmael (Gen. 17:18), and reluctance to dismiss Hagar and Ishmael from the family (Gen. 21:10–11). However, God's plan was for an heir (Isaac) by Abraham and Sarah, not Ishmael for whom a separate destiny was intended. Normally, if a slave-wife had borne children, she was not to be ex-

pelled or sold (so, Hammurabi's laws, § 146), thus Abraham's un-
willingness to do so (Gen. 21:10–11) was reinforced by binding
custom of the day; divine urging was needful to persuade him to
send Hagar and Ishmael away (Gen. 21:12–14). [61]

Before he had children at all, Abraham had adopted Eliezer, a
'son of his house' (cf. Gen. 15:3, RV) as his heir. Possibly a slave, [62]
probably simply a member of the household, the inheritance-rights
of such an adoptee were commonly guarded in Mesopotamian law,
even against the subsequent birth of offspring (natural heirs) to the
adoptor.[63] Such a position was explicitly accepted by Abraham
(Gen. 15:2, 3), until he was told and commanded otherwise (Gen.
15:4).

The whole of the foregoing sample of comparative legal material
gives some indication of how simply and straightforwardly the data
of the patriarchal narratives go along with evidence for prevailing
usage in the first half of the second millennium BC, especially the
early part. It will be noticed that Nuzi has hardly been drawn upon
– and when cited (in the notes) it essentially goes with the other
Mesopotamian evidence. Three lessons are to be learnt here. First,
patriarchal usage finds ample early context, well before, and independently of, Nuzi. Second, usages at Nuzi often belong to the
mainstream Mesopotamian tradition. Third, the thesis of a
specially Hurrian component in the legal/social usages at Nuzi
largely evaporates – and has no bearing on the patriarchs either.
Here, as in other things, the Hurrians largely assimilated to
Mesopotamian modes and culture; Nuzi is nearer the end of a
development than the beginning.

In contrast to the foregoing survey of 'positive' context, it is well
to note cases of alleged parallels that have not stood the test of
time, particularly from Nuzi. One such is the supposed Nuzi
parallels for Abraham calling his wife his 'sister' (Gen. 12:10–20;
20:2 ff.; cf. Isaac, 26:6–11) which are totally irrelevant. [64] The supposed role of the *teraphim* or 'household gods' (Gen. 31:19, 30–35)
as constituting the title-deeds to inheritance, inspired by Nuzi documents, seems also to be fallacious; [65] Rachel simply took them for
her own protection and blessing. Again, much has been made of
supposed sale of birthright, and of oral deathbed blessings, and
here too the Nuzi evidence is not what it was thought to be. [66]

Then there is the question of special pleading and misuse of data,
whether of first or second millennium BC. Thus, thrice over, van
Seters has tried to correlate a seventh-century Assyrian marriage-
conveyance with Sarah's giving of Hagar to Abraham to have a
son (Gen. 16:1 ff.), as well as an Egyptian text of the twelfth century BC.[67] The Egyptian text can be dismissed without further ado;

it consists solely of a remarkable series of adoptions (of a wife by a husband, of a brother by a sister, etc.), in which only one element is comparable with Sarah/Hagar – as direct background to Gen. 16 its value is virtually nil.[68] The Assyrian text is hardly in much better case. Van Seters overstresses the initiative of Sarah (Gen. 16:2), whereas it is Abraham to whom the matter of a son and heir is central concern (Gen. 15:2–6; 16:5; 17:2–6,16–17; 22). The Assyrian document contains the parallel of a servant-girl bearing sons in the childless wife's stead, but has no word about future inheritance, etc. Furthermore, it stipulates that the slave-girl may be sold off at will, in direct contrast to the position in Genesis (21:10–11) where – in harmony with most early second-millennium usage – Abraham did *not* expect to dispose of Hagar (whether by sale or simple expulsion). Hence, the Assyrian document is an inferior parallel to the second millennium data. And, as its latest editor makes clear,[69] this selfsame document is *not* a normative Neo-Assyrian marriage-contract, it is by its conditions 'without any parallel', 'out of the ordinary' for its epoch. Hence, this very imperfect, anomalous 'parallel' hardly links Genesis to the first millennium.

In the case of Genesis 23, two issues must be viewed separately. A question that remains open is the possible use of the Hittite Laws as background to that chapter. This would suggest that Abraham sought to buy only the Machpelah cave (carrying no land-dues), but – under the necessity of burying Sarah – had in fact to buy the entire holding inclusive of the cave (which meant paying also the dues).[70] Already, § 46 of the Hittite Laws has been rightly excluded, as it deals with gift, not sale.[71] However, the relation of § 47 (utilised above) turns on the status of Ephron (unknown!) and the meaning of particular terms in the laws.

But a question that can be considered closed is the attempted misuse of a class of first millennium documents to prove a late date for Gen. 23. These are so-called 'dialogue-documents' of Neo-Assyrian and Neo-Babylonian times, asserted to be the 'model' for Gen. 23.[72] However, there is not a scrap of evidence that Gen. 23 *is* a 'dialogue-document' – it is merely a narrative of negotiations and agreement; and the assertion that 'dialogue-documents' were only of the first millennium BC rested solely on negative evidence, notoriously unreliable.[73] And in fact erroneous, as this type of document *is* attested from the Old-Babylonian period, i.e. the early second millennium BC![74] At a stroke, the special pleading by Tucker and van Seters for a first millennium date must be dismissed. The type of document alleged is as likely to be early as late, and may not even be relevant.

(iii) *Patriarchal Religion* It remains true that by far the most cogent parallels and background for the concept of 'the God of the fathers' go back to the Old-Assyrian tablets of the nineteenth century BC, clearly superior to Nabatean and Safaitic part-parallels so late (virtually New Testament times!) as to have no bearing on the Genesis narratives.[75]

(iv) *Geopolitical* In Genesis 14 occur rival coalitions of kings from Mesopotamia and Transjordan. Petty kingdoms flourished in Canaan and Transjordan at most periods. By the thirteenth century BC onwards, city-states (Sodom, Gomorrah, etc.) were replaced by larger kingdoms in Transjordan (Moab, Edom; Sihon's realm, etc.). Hence, reports of city-state coalitions there must relate to the thirteenth century BC or earlier. But with coalitions of Mesopotamian and neighbouring kingdoms, the scope for dating seems to be still more limited. Between about 2000 BC (fall of the Third Dynasty of Ur) and roughly 1750 BC (triumph of Hammurabi of Babylon), such power-alliances were an outstanding feature of the politics of the day, reaching as far east as Elam, and far north-west to the borders of Anatolia. One famous Mari letter mentions alliances of ten, fifteen and even twenty kings. At least five other Mesopotamian-based coalitions are known from the nineteenth/eighteenth centuries BC, usually with four or five members per grouping.[76] Western expeditions by eastern kings are known from at least Sargon of Akkad onwards.[77] The phenomenon of Mesopotamian coalitions in the form found would not fit a date before 2000 BC (when the Third Dynasty of Ur dominated), and certainly not after Hammurabi's time (*c.* 1750 BC), when the twin kingdoms of Babylon and Assyria in due course became the *only* heartland Mesopotamian powers. Therefore, even though it is impractical to identify (and thus date) the individual kings of Gen. 14, the political framework in which they move is that of the early second millennium BC. Attempts to assign a late, still more a very late, date to Gen. 14 fail entirely to account for this situation. The comparison with late Mesopotamian chronicles[78] is spurious. The third-person narrative and brief speeches in Gen. 14 are no different to those elsewhere in Genesis; the subject-matter does not justify a 'chronicle' classification. With the rarest exceptions, the first-millennium Mesopotamian chronicles are altogether more stilted and staccato than Gen. 14, commonly with frequent regnal dates and month notations. In Gen. 14, we have no regnal dates, merely a period of twelve/fourteen years independent of any given reign. Just as it is no chronicle, so Gen. 14 is not a royal inscription, but it has more in common with the flowing narrative of a text like the early second millennium 'foundation-text' of Iahdun-Lim, King of Mari,[79] describing his

Syrian campaign, etc., than with any late chronicle.

(v) *Other Aspects* The preceding sections are in no way exhaustive; more could be said in each, and other topics added. The semi-settled status of the patriarchs, etc., is most easily comparable with the early second millennium data from Mari, when this is properly understood. The wide travel of the patriarchs is particularly in harmony with what we find in the early second millennium. The Canaan in which they circulate is a Canaan of petty, independent city-states and tribal groups – not one dominated by (e.g.) the Egyptian Empire, as was the case during *c.* 1540–1150 BC. Their Canaan is much more that of the Execration Texts of the nineteenth/eighteenth centuries BC. And so on.

So what, then do we end up with? Perhaps the following would be a fair summary. First, we have no external mentions of the patriarchs themselves beyond the pages of the Bible. Therefore, their historical existence remains unproven. In this, they stand on exactly the same level as (e.g.) Jezebel, Jeremiah, Zedekiah or Ezra – none of whom is named by name in any external, contemporary document, yet whose former existence is doubted by none. And so for many other characters of ancient history, high and low, famed or obscure. Negative evidence does not take one anywhere. Second, the patriarchs are figures of Israel's beginnings, from well before Moses, on the unanimous verdict of biblical tradition in its entirety. So, any real traditions surviving about the patriarchs should have their roots in the early second millennium, unless they have been totally changed; spurious 'traditions' first concocted in the first millennium BC cannot be expected to relate to second millennium conditions. Third, the actual narratives that we possess are clearly different from the 'legend' and 'fiction' groups of ancient Near-Eastern narratives. They are closest to the 'historical' class, differing from it only in past time-setting and third-person (which features *can* occur in that class); 'wonders' have remarkably little role. Thus, on literary-comparative grounds alone, essential historicity should be granted. Fourth, comparisons between the features of the narratives and external data show that the recent attempts to link the patriarchal narratives exclusively or predominantly with the mid-first millennium BC are artificial and mistaken. Some features are common to the second and first millennia, others more specifically belong to the early second millennium, and nearly all find their *optimum* place in the early second millennium, even when not exclusively.

ISRAEL INTO EGYPT: JOSEPH

Essentially, the Joseph-narrative is today in the same position as the rest of the patriarchal narratives. It is a straightforward account, without artificial flourishes. Some elements in the story suggest an early/mid second millennium origin.[81] Such features include the price paid for Joseph as a slave (20 shekels), the correct average price in the eighteenth century BC, and the use of the term *saris* in its earlier meaning of 'official', not its later meaning of 'eunuch', when applied to the (married) dignitary Potiphar.[82] Other features are not specifically tied to the earlier second millennium, but are well attested then. Asiatic slaves in Egypt, attached to the households of officials, are well-known in later Middle-Kingdom Egypt (*c.* 1850–1700 BC),[83] and Semites could rise to high position (even the throne, before the Hyksos period),[84] as did the chancellor Hur. Joseph's career would fall easily enough into the period of the late thirteenth and early fifteenth dynasties. The role of dreams is, of course, well-known at all periods. From Egypt, we have a dream-reader's textbook in a copy of *c.* 1300 BC, originating some centuries earlier; such works are known in first-millennium Assyria also.[85]

'Corn in Egypt' is a proverbial phrase, even in English. And as well as vivid tomb-paintings with fields of golden grain, Egyptian texts speak frequently of famine, and occasionally show its emaciated victims. The Delta was a favoured region for pasturing cattle, and the east Delta a favoured objective for herdsmen such as Joseph's family. Through becoming steward of a large Egyptian household (Gen. 39:4–6), and then as a chief official of pharaonic government (Gen. 41:39–45), anyone placed in Joseph's situation would willy-nilly be brought into close contact with writing and records. In about this period, the Middle Bronze Age, alphabetic writing seems first to have been invented. There is, therefore, the attractive (but totally unproven) possibility of patriarchal traditions being put into such script, in West-Semitic, from the seventeenth/sixteenth centuries BC onwards, as the basis of what later we now find in Genesis.

5

Birth of a Nation

When the biblical narrative reopens in the book of Exodus, we are
in a changed world from that in which the book of Genesis closed.
Long since dead, Joseph and his brothers are forgotten by all but
their own descendants. New pharaohs reign, and one arises for
whom Semitic pastoralists in the east Delta are simply a convenient
supply of additional forced labour. The change implies a distinct
lapse of time and change of regimes, as notable people were not
always so quickly forgotten.[1] Thus, the tradition of four centuries
gone by (cf. Exodus 12:40–41) should be taken seriously. These
are often dismissed as the four silent centuries, which is only partly
true. Negatively, their details evidently did not serve the purposes
of the writer of Exodus, and he therefore exercised an author's
right – then as now – to select what *he* deemed best for his requirements. Positively, from the period between entering Egypt (Jacob)
and settling in Canaan (Joshua and the judges), the Hebrews did in
fact retain some traditions, from which various genealogies survive,
preserved for us in 1 Chronicles 2 of the post-exilic age.[2]

OPPRESSION AND EXODUS

In Imperial Egypt of the fourteenth and thirteenth centuries BC,
the enormous building-projects of the pharaohs throughout Egypt
and Nubia required the deployment of a considerable amount of
manpower. For houses, offices, storerooms, barracks, and palaces,

myriads of mud bricks were needed. For the temples of the gods and similar enduring monuments, stone had to be cut, hauled from the quarries, shipped to the building-sites, and manoeuvred into position. The Eighteenth-Dynasty kings had expelled the alien Hyksos rulers, reunited Egypt, and established an empire in Syria-Palestine northwards as well as far south up the Nile into Nubia. For most of the Dynasty's two-and-a-half centuries of rule, the east Delta saw only limited royal works anywhere north of Bubastis and Athribis in the south part of that area. As base for their wars in Western Asia, the pharaohs had used Egypt's traditional capital, Memphis (not far south of modern Cairo, and across the river). Under Haremhab, this dynasty's last king, more interest began to be shown in the east Delta and in its principal town, Avaris, a former seat of the Hyksos rulers; this pharaoh refurbished the temple of the local god, Seth.

The land of Goshen, where the Hebrews lived, adjoined Avaris – now known to have been sited at Tell el-Dab'a (*not* at Tanis, as so many textbooks wrongly aver). Haremhab's interest in this locality perhaps stemmed from the fact that his second-in-command and official heir, the general and vizier Pramessu, hailed from this very region and possibly promoted the fortunes of his home district. Certainly, on economic and military grounds, Avaris was well suited to be a focus for communications between Canaan and Egypt proper. The need for labour in this region, therefore, probably began in Haremhab's time. Previously, there had been no such need beyond Bubastis (worked on by Amenophis III).

At Haremhab's death, the throne duly passed to his official heir Pramessu, known henceforth as Ramesses I, founder of the Nineteenth Dynasty of later historians. He reigned barely sixteen months leaving the throne to his vigorous son Sethos I. In a reign of ten or fifteen years, this bold ruler fought energetically to restore Egypt's diminished empire in Syria, and instituted massive building-projects in Egypt, such as the great hall of columns in the Karnak temple of Amun at Thebes. In the east Delta, just north of Avaris, he caused to be built a summer palace, nucleus of a new suburb. Sethos was first assisted, then succeeded, by his son, the irrepressible Ramesses II. One of the most remarkable pharaohs of all time, Ramesses reigned sixty six years, had eighty or ninety children, erected statues weighing up to one thousand tons, built temples the whole length of his empire. He too warred with the Hittites in Syria, eventually making peace with them and marriage-alliances. But one of his first acts was to proclaim the founding of a new capital city – Pi-Ramesse, 'Domain of Ramesses' – around his father's summer palace on the north of Avaris. This, the 'Delta

Residence' of the Ramesside kings, was the Ra'amses of Exodus 1:11. It was laid out on the grand scale. Great stone temples of the gods arose at each of the four cardinal points: of the sun-god Re on the east, of Theban Amun on the west, of the Memphite gods on the north, and of Seth of Avaris on the south, the royal palace being the central focus. The interconnected Nile branches, 'Waters of Re' and 'Waters of Avaris' led into a basin that afforded excellent port facilities. The great royal palace was of brick with stone-framed doorways, its staterooms brilliant with glazed tile decoration. The brick houses and villas of royal princes and high officials clustered nearby. Offices, barracks, stores and warehousing – and doubtless streets of lesser houses, shops or bazaars – made up the rest. All, now, is a levelled ruin-field, most of its stonework gone (reused) to other sites, dug only in part.[3] The once-splendid city has now to be reconstructed from mere fragments and descriptions. Like Solomon's Jerusalem, its golden splendours have entirely disappeared; its voluminous archives are likewise totally lost – a handful of standard wine-jar dockets and a series of stamp-seals alone survive. It is little wonder, therefore, that we have no Egyptian record of the Israelites in bondage near Pi-Ramesse; all such information, with near-absolute certainty, is irrevocably lost.

However, from both the Nineteenth Dynasty and its predecessor, we do have other background information on working conditions in imperial Egypt, data which (as any Egyptologist knows) would be applicable equally in the east Delta, Thebes, Memphis, Abydos or elsewhere. Long before, back in the Eighteenth Dynasty, the famous (and unique) brick-making scene in the Theban tomb-chapel of the vizier Rekhmire (*c.* 1460 BC) has frequently and justly been used to illustrate brickmaking in Egypt such as the Hebrews would have known it – the more so, as the labourers shown include Semites alongside Egyptians and others. Straw and chaff were included in the clay used for bricks, because experience showed that a better brick resulted. The same concern visible in Exodus 5 over use of straw and over maintaining brick production-quotas appears in thirteenth century Egyptian sources. Such are the well-known references in the Anastasi papyri from Memphis, to workmen 'making their quota of bricks daily', and another case where 'there are neither men to make bricks, nor straw in the neighbourhood.'[4] From Year 5 of Ramesses II (*c.* 1286/1275 BC), brick-accounts are recorded upon a leather scroll now in the Louvre Museum. Among other things, forty 'stablemasters' are each assigned a target-quota of 2000 bricks (i.e. 80,000 all told). The successive figures added after their names and 'target' show the progress of production, the target being rarely reached![5] These men by function correspond to the Egyptian taskmasters of Exodus 5:6, 10, 13–14, below whom come the workmen and their 'foremen'. In the work-rosters from the workmen's village at Deir elMedina in Western Thebes, people had days off for all sorts of reasons including 'offering to one's god' – just as Moses requested 'time off' for his people to go and worship in the wilderness (Ex. 5:1).[6]

Press-ganging of non-Egyptians into forced labour for building projects is also known in Ramesses II's reign. In the latter's Year 44 (*c.* 1247/1236 BC), far south in Nubia, the Viceroy Setau and his officers raided the western oases, rounding-up the luckless south Libyans in order to build at Ramesses II's temple at Wadi es-Sebua.[7] Back up north at Memphis, Papyrus Leiden 348 offers a long-known reference to 'the Apiru who drag stone for the great pylon (gateway) of the [building] "Ramesses II-Beloved-of-Truth" ...'.[8] We need not expect the east-Delta Hebrews to be any less strictly supervised than Egyptians making bricks for the stablemasters, or employed at Deir el-Medina, or to have been any less abruptly press-ganged than the South-Libyan oasis-dwellers.

The age-old answer to oppressive exploitation was flight. When the Hebrews left Egypt (Ex. 12:37), we read that the first stage of their journey went from Raamses to Succoth – in Egyptian terms, from Pi-Ramesse to Tjeku. This was precisely the route and first stage of flight adopted by two slaves some years later.[9] On the ground, they covered some 36 km (22 miles) from present-day Qantir, south then south-east, then east, to Tell el-Maskhuta; the Hebrews would have travelled a little less, if their living-quarters had been outside Pi-Ramesse (as the narratives imply). The next stage, to the Reed Sea, was less. Faced by the lakes and swamps (on the line of the present-day Suez canal), the Hebrews turned at right-angles to go along the edge, almost certainly northwards. Then came the pharaoh's pursuit, he sending 600 chariots after them (Ex. 14:7). This was a substantial force, but by no means disproportionate. For example, the Hittites had reputedly fielded 2,-500 chariots at the Battle of Qadesh, Tuthmosis III captured 924 Canaanite chariots on one campaign, and his son Amenophis II took 730 and 1,032 chariots on other campaigns; even Ahab of Israel was to provide 2,000 chariots against Assyria a few centuries later.[10] The phenomenon of the movement of the waters that brought escape is explained in the Hebrew text itself – 'the Lord sent a strong east wind' (Ex. 14:21). Such phenomena are independently attested, and are no fantasy. For example, the Egyptian engineer Ali Shafei Bey had an analogous (though not fatal!) experience in his car some decades ago, as a result of similar conditions elsewhere in the Delta.[11] Finally, after the overthrow of the Egyptian chariotry in the shifting waters, the Hebrews sang a hymn of deliverance and triumph (Ex. 15) – the counterpart to the triumph-hymns used in Egypt throughout the empire period during the fifteenth to twelfth centuries BC.

COVENANT AT SINAI AND IN MOAB

The central feature of the book of Exodus is the giving of the covenant-commandments, the law and the cult at Sinai. Exodus from chapter 19 onwards, and all of Leviticus, both centre upon Sinai, the founding-point of the Israelite nation in all later biblical tradition. After the time in the wilderness and Israel's arrival (as a new generation) in Moab before crossing the Jordan, there was a renewal of the covenant and its laws – enshrined in Deuteronomy.[12] The *form* of covenant found in Exodus-Leviticus and in Deuteronomy (plus Joshua 24) is neither arbitrary nor accidental. It is a form proper to the general period of the exodus, current in the 14th/13th centuries BC, and *neither earlier nor later* on the total available evidence.

In terms of Near-Eastern background, there are two components: law-collections and treaties. For the first, from *c.* 2100 to *c.* 1750 BC, Mesopotamia has yielded four law-collections ('codes'), two of them complete,[13] one damaged,[14] and one probably in 'extract' form.[15] The three originally given in full show a clear scheme with title, prologue, and the laws proper. The two complete documents then have a brief epilogue and, finally, brief blessings on those who respect the laws, and more extensive curses on such as would defy them. All this is as old as the patriarchs and before; Hammurabi's laws were recopied by scribes in the twelve centuries or so that followed his time. The 'laws' scheme may be diagrammed as follows:

(1) Title or Preamble
(2) Prologue
(3) Laws
(4) Epilogue
(5) *a/b*: Blessings, Curses

The second component is the treaties, particularly those between a sovereign and a vassal. Some forty different treaties[16] are known to us, covering seventeen centuries from the late third millennium BC well into the first millennium BC, excluding broken fragments, and now additional ones still to be published from Ebla. From this extensive series, an overall history of the changing forms of such treaties becomes plainly visible, and may be summarised as follows.

EARLY

1. In the late third millennium (*c.* 2300 BC), the treaties between Ebla and Tudiya of Assyria, and between Naram-Sin of Akkad and a king of Elam, each begin with witnesses, proceed with the stipulations, and end with other features – curses in the Ebla treaty, with oath, deposit and blessing in the Naram-Sin treaty. [17]

INTERMEDIATE

2. In the early second millennium BC, an Old-Babylonian treaty of Ilum-Gamil of Uruk is too damaged to show any features besides stipulations.

3a. In mid-second-millennium Syria, two treaties of kings Niqmepa and Idrimi of Alalakh with their contemporaries each have title, then stipulations, then curses as sanction against infringement.

3b. In the mid-second-millennium Hittite realm, the treaty of Arnuwandas and Ishmerikka-land has title, witnesses (as in the third millennium), stipulations. Then oath and curses (as in Syria), and perhaps a little more (now lost). Two other Hittite treaties have title and stipulations, but all else is lost. The Syrian and Hittite schemes for this period can be set out thus:

3a. Syria	*3b. Hatti*
(1) *Title/Preamble*	(1) *Title/Preamble*
(2) *Stipulations*	(2) Witnesses
(3) *Curses*	(3) *Stipulations*
	(4) Oath
	(5) *Curses*
	(6) Etc., lost

Features common to both regions are italicised.

MIDDLE

4. The twenty-one reasonably preserved treaties [18] of the late second millennium (fourteenth/thirteenth centuries BC) from the Hittite archives show a remarkable consistency of form which holds for almost the whole corpus, as follows: [19]

(1) Title/Preamble
(2) Historical Prologue
(3) Stipulations (basic; detailed)
(4) Depositing and regular reading of treaty
(5) Witnesses
(6) *a/b.* Curses, Blessings

To these could be added (7, 8, 9) oath, solemn ceremony, note of sanctions, but these were rarely put into writing within the formal framework. Leaving these minor flourishes aside, the basic scheme was remarkably constant. Item (4) is often missing, largely because it tends to come at the point where tablets have their lower obverse/upper reverse broken away. In just two treaties (with Anatolian population-groups), item (5) the witnesses is placed earlier in the scheme (as in older treaties), the rest conforming to pattern; other variations are minimal. The sheer consistency of such a body of texts cannot be mere coincidence.

LATE

5. From the first millennium BC, nine treaties out of a dozen can be used. Here, the basic pattern is entirely distinct from that of the late second millennium, and shows greater variation. Its two main forms on a regional basis can be set out as follows:

5a. Syria	*5b. Mesopotamia*
(1) Title/Preamble	(1) Title/Preamble
(2) Witnesses	(2) Witnesses
(3) Curses	(3) Stipulations
(4) Stipulations	(4) Curses

The principal difference between the two regions is in the mutually reversed order of stipulations and curses. The Mesopotamian scheme is directly reminiscent of the 'early' and 'intermediate' date treaties (third and early/mid-second millennium), while the Syrian placement of the curses is unparalleled. Both sets are totally different from the 'middle' date series of the later second millennium. Among minor variations in this group overall, one may note the occasional use of sub-titles before the stipulations, and (once) an 'epilogue' of blessing and curse for respect or disrespect shown, not to the contents, but to the physical *text* (monumentally inscribed) of a treaty.[20]

Such is the sum of the external evidence presented in basic outline. What, then, of the Old Testament covenant as reflected in Exodus-Leviticus, Deuteronomy and Joshua 24? How does it compare with the four successive historical phases, and with the laws series, surveyed above? It is important to remember that Exodus-Leviticus, Deuteronomy and Joshua 24 are not themselves actual covenant-documents; they describe the giving of the covenant and its renewals. Thus, our existing books of Exodus-Leviticus, Deuteronomy and Joshua 24 stand at one remove (but *only* one remove) from the actual covenant-documents, remaining very close to these and incorporating all their main features.

Within Ex.-Lev. (I), in Deut. (II), and in Josh. 24 (III), the following elements are clearly visible:[21]

		I		II	III
(1)	Title/Preamble:	Ex. 20:1	(1)	1:1–5	(1) 24:1–2
(2)	Historical Prologue:	20:2	(2)	1:6–3:29	(2) 24:2–13
(3)	Stipulations, basic & detailed:	Ex. 20:3–17, 22–26, plus 21–23, 25–31 (law), and Lev. 1–25 (ritual)	(3)	4; 5–11, plus 12–26	(3) 24:14–15, (& 16–25)
(4)	*a.* Deposit of Text:	Ex. 25:16, cf. 34:1, 28, 29[22]	(4)	*a.* 31:9, 24–26	(4) *a.* 24:26
	b. Public Reading:	–		*b.* 31:10–13	– (8:34)
(5)	Witnesses:	Ex. 24:4[23]	(5)	31:16–30, 26; 32:1–47	(5) 24:22
(6)	*a.* Blessing:	Lev. 26:3–13	(6)	*a.* 28:1–14	(6) *a.* implicit in
	b. Curses:	Lev. 26:14–33 (many)		*b.* 28:15–68 (many)	*b.* 24:19–20, (cf. 8:34)

To which may be added traces of (7, 8, 9), oath, solemn ceremony, and note of sanctions. For (7, 8), compare (I) Ex. 24:1–11 and (II) Deut. 27 (fulfilled, Josh. 8:30–35). Sanction for disobedience (9) finds its equivalent in the *rib* or 'controversy' motif in the Old Testament, which takes its starting-point from Deut. 32, with parallels going back into the second millennium BC. [24]

From comparison between the above analysis and those of the laws and treaties on preceding pages, several points stand out with crystal clarity, as follows.

First, the full series of observable elements in the Sinai covenant and its two renewals (either side of the Jordan) corresponds only and solely to the range and general order of elements found in the 'middle' series of treaties, those of the later second millennium, and *neither* to later treaties (first millennium) *nor* to earlier treaties (third to mid-second millennium). All six major elements in the 'middle' series recur in the Old Testament covenant. Significantly, too, item (4) which is least seen in the Old Testament is also the least-attested in that middle series.

Second, the *order* of blessings then curses, and the *proportion* of few blessings to distinctly more curses, are both features which correspond directly to those observable in the early second millennium law-collections, just as the stipulations of the covenant are law rather than treaty. Nothing parallel to this is so far known from the copies of later law-collections (e.g., Hittite, Middle-Assyrian, or Neo-Babylonian).

Third, we may now see here the real literary origins of the Sinai covenant's formulation: it is the happy *confluence* of law and treaty in their most developed second millennium forms. Both law and treaty begin with title or preamble, continue with a prologue (historical in treaties) and then pass on to laws/stipulations. Likewise does the Sinai covenant. Law-collections have blessing then curse, while treaties have curse then blessing. Here, covenant goes with law, including with the disproportion of few blessings and many curses. Law has an epilogue, with which one may compare the recapitulation in covenant (Deut. 29–30). On deposit and reading of the terms, covenant goes with treaty; also in having witnesses.

Fourth, the Sinai covenant and its renewals preserve not only the full number of elements found also in second millennium laws and treaties, but substantially also their *order* of elements. Thus, in Exodus-Leviticus, elements (1), (2), (3), (6*a/b*) all follow in sequence. (5) comes neatly between the civil and religious commands, with (4) included in the latter. In Deuteronomy, the entire sequence is present and in order, except that the group epilogue plus (4), (5), are placed at the end instead of before (6*a/b*). In Joshua 24, again, all follows in order except that (4) and (5) are mentioned in reverse order. These minor departures from treaty-order are no greater than those observable in some treaties of the 'middle' group, and stem from factors which have to be borne in mind. Such factors include: (i) Elements (4) deposit/reading and (5) witnesses are only present in one source of covenant-formulation – the treaty; not in the law-collections. Hence, in covenant, a confluence of law and treaty, their place is not bound to be that of the treaties. (ii) One must remember the *nature* of Exodus-Leviticus, Deuteronomy, and Joshua 24: a record of the acts of giving and of renewing the covenant, but (as noted above) *not* the actual, formal covenant-documents (and indeed, occasionally mentioning the writing-down of such documents, cf. Ex. 24:4, 7; Deut. 31:24; Josh. 24:25, 26).

Fifth, we have, therefore, no warrant factually to date the basic Sinai covenant and its two renewals any later than the time of the data to which they are most closely related, i.e. to the thirteenth century down to *c.* 1200 BC at the very latest. The present books of Exodus, Leviticus, Deuteronomy and the data of Joshua 24 would necessarily stem from about 1200 BC or not long afterwards, on the same basic criterion.

Sixth, the content of the covenant. The fundamental heart of the Sinai covenant (its stipulations) are the basic norms (the ten commandments) and the specific laws and customs for the Israelites, reafirmed in the renewals. In this, the covenant – regulating the life of a people – is closely related in nature to the law-collections of the ancient biblical world. For the last seventy or eighty years, analogies between laws in (e.g.) the 'code' of Hammurabi of Babylon and in Exodus-Deuteronomy in various matters of every-day life have been common knowledge. As Hammurabi reigned four or five centuries before Moses was at Sinai, those correspon-dences illustrate forcibly the *antiquity* and *continuity* of legal and social usage in the ancient Semitic world of the second millennium BC.[25] The terms of reference of the Sinai covenant – a Sovereign enters into a formal relationship with his subjects the people – are close to those of a treaty between suzerain and vassal. But here, in the covenant at Sinai, distinctive use is made of this framework. The Sovereign concerned is not simply a human 'great king', but Deity. Hence, in turn, the covenant possesses both moral and religious aspects not to be found in purely political state treaties. No service or tribute is requested here for the palace of a 'great king'. Instead, we have the Tabernacle instituted (Deity's audience room on earth with the people's representatives), and the rituals of the cult as service due to the divine Sovereign. Hence, the arrange-ments planned and executed in the latter part of the book of Ex-odus, and the rituals of Leviticus.

All this makes excellent sense. But the reaction of some Old Testament scholars, imprisoned within 19th-century theory, makes a fascinating study. In 1954, the close analogy between the late-second-millennium treaties and elements in Exodus and Joshua 24 was first pointed out by Mendenhall,[26] but omitting Deuteronomy, studied in this regard by others,[27] e.g. M. G. Kline.[28] The result of Mendenhall's study was a flood of papers and studies upon the theme of 'covenant' touching upon all sides of Old Testament study, and sometimes going to fanciful and therefore unjustified lengths.

Mendenhall's original point gained some initial acceptance from Old Testament scholars, but of course this result directly con-tradicted established theory – e.g., the late origin and use of 'cove-nant', both in word (*berit*, etc.) and in concept, the dogma that Deuteronomy could not be divorced from the reforms in Judah of 621 BC, and so on. So in 1963, D. J. McCarthy endeavoured to gloss over the clear distinctions visible between late second and first millennium treaties, despite being forced to admit the existence of what he called 'sub-groups'.[29] Far from being 'sub', these groups actually exhibit major distinctions as the data used above clearly show. In 1964, J. A. Thompson in turn sought to avoid recognition of the second/first millennium distinction, claiming that perhaps the historical prologues had been lost in the first millennium examples.[30] This idea is sufficiently invalidated by the existence of a title/preamble to some of the less-damaged first millennium examples, first item in any text. Even if it were not, it would be astonishing indeed, if all of that group of texts had lost *only* the prologues every time by an incredible freak of preservation and destruction![31] In 1965, E. Gerstenberger[32] attempted to reduce the covenant to just three elements, but to do so he evaded all consideration of the *full written form* of covenant, laws and treaties alike. R. Frankena and M. Weinfeld compared the curses in Deuteronomy with those in first millennium treaties,[33] drawing the conclusion that Deuteronomy was dependent on the Assyrian treaties, hence was itself of the seventh or sixth century BC. But the Assyrian treaties and Deuteronomy alike draw their repertoire of curses from a long pre-existent range of curses (even, groups of curses) going right back into the second millennium BC, centuries before either Deuteronomy or the first millennium treaties![34] And their erroneous view in any case failed to account for the clear late second millennium features present in Deuteronomy. And so, until in 1972 Weinfeld averred that no distinction of the kind existed, all treaties were in effect alike.[35]

Yet the facts themselves will *not* go away. The very words used for the covenant in Hebrew are old, not 'late'. *Berit* occurs in West-Semitic in Ugaritic (fourteenth/thirteenth century BC) and as a loanword in Egyptian (early and late thirteenth century BC), likewise the term *'edut* in *c.* 1160 BC in a secondary meaning indicating that it goes back earlier.[36] Neither the words nor the concept of 'covenant' can therefore possibly be treated as 'late' (i.e. first millennium BC only). The clear distinctions in form between treaties of different periods – and especially between late second and the first millennium BC – as outlined above remain fully and immoveably valid, established as they are by the texts of forty treaties in fifty-four 'editions',[37] not counting merest fragments. This evidence is here to stay. The correlations between the Sinai covenant and renewals and the second millennium treaties and law-collections also stand out with crystal clarity, are also here to stay.

ANCIENT HEBREW WORSHIP

Far from being some elaborate priestly pipe-dream of the Babylonian exile or later, the Tabernacle was essentially a modest structure (about 60 by 20 feet) compared with the larger shrines enjoyed by Canaanite gods (as at Ugarit or Hazor), not to mention with coverings – were those used for 'prefab' structures (religious and otherwise) in Egypt for up to fifteen centuries before Moses. [38] Its permanent staff of five (Ex. 28:1) is primitively minute compared with (e.g.) some 150 priests on regular duty in each of the personal temples of Ramesses II or III in Western Thebes. The Tabernacle's daily offering of two lambs with a few pints of oil, flour and wine is as nothing compared with (e.g.) the *daily* offering of 5,500 loaves, 54 cakes, 204 jugs of beer, up to 50 geese, an ox, and a variety of other items all regularly presented at either of the two Ramesside temples just mentioned. The dozen feasts of the Hebrew calendar are pitifully few when compared with the fifty or sixty religious festivals of ancient Thebes, for example.

In short, viewed against the proper background and perspective, the provisions of Exodus-Leviticus are neither 'advanced' for the thirteenth century BC, nor over-elaborate, nor inherently 'late'. Quite the contrary – they are extremely modest, and that to a primitive degree! Nor in concept (in the rituals, for example) is there anything very 'late'. Already in the fourteenth/thirteenth centuries BC, acts of consecration for a new shrine (cf. Lev. 8–9) were more elaborate elsewhere – witness the Hittite ritual of Ulippi. The principle of symbolical substitution by enacting transfer of sins (laying hands on a scapegoat) is also clearly attested in the fourteenth/thirteenth centuries BC, in the Hittite rituals of Uhhamuwa and Ashkhella (cf. Lev. 16:20–27) [39] – it was a gesture clearly understood in those times, not an invention of eight centuries later. And many other incidental details, such as the physical geography of Sinai, the Arabah and Transjordan, subjects like the itineraries, use of silver trumpets, of ox-wagons, etc., can be correlated with knowledge available to us from outside sources, particularly in the second millennium BC. [40]

CONQUEST AND SETTLEMENT

1. *The Negeb and Transjordan*

About to leave Kadesh in north-east Sinai with his people, Moses vainly sought permission from the king of Edom to lead them through Edom or Seir. Recently, the whole tradition about the exodus and journey of the Hebrews by Seir has been doubted merely because the Edomite centre of Bozrah (now Buseirah) was seemingly not occupied until the eighth century BC onwards, to judge from four seasons of assiduous excavation. [41] However, these doubts rest upon entirely false reasoning. No biblical text makes Bozrah the capital of Edom until the eighth century BC (period of Amos and Isaiah), [42] and Bozrah never appears in Numbers 20:14–21 or Judges 11:17! Edom possessed various centres, in-

cluding Sela, Teman, Bozrah and others. As Seir, it is frequently
mentioned in the inscriptions of Ramesses II in the thirteenth century BC, a clear indication that Seir/Edom then had some form of
stable population and organization, whatever its economic basis –
perhaps pastoral, mining and some limited cultivation. [43] The discovery of definite traces of Late Bronze/Early Iron I sites can only
be a matter of time.

Similarly, the current confusion over the relation of
archaeological sites in the Negeb (or 'southland' of Palestine) to
biblical place-names in Genesis, Numbers and Joshua-Judges rests,
ultimately, upon the still-inadequate scope of discovery to date. In
Genesis, the patriarchs pause at Beer-Sheba merely for the wells,
undoubtedly along the main wadi (Gen. 21:25 ff.; 26:23). Only
once here is Beer-Sheba actually called 'city', i.e. a full settlement,
in Gen. 26:33 – which in fact is an 'editorial note' ('to this day'),
and has nothing to do with the patriarchs. In Joshua 15:28 and
19:2, Beer-Sheba is merely one very minor place-name among
many others. Therefore, we have no reason to suppose any major
settlement there until *c.* 1200 BC at the earliest. The place's main
fame is as a traditional limit ('from Dan to Beer-Sheba'), not as a
great centre in itself. Therefore, we must dismiss as mistaken, the
late Prof Aharoni's interpretation of an Iron Age well up near the
later Israelite citadel as 'proof' that the Genesis narratives date to *c.*
1100 BC.[44] This well, he admits, was cut in the 12th century BC by
the new Israelite settlers – how, then, could they possibly be so
stupid as to imagine that the work of their own hands (for their
own settlement) was that of Abraham? As pastoralists living in
tents, the patriarchs could not be expected to leave any trace to be
found of their encampment at Beer-Sheba; nor of soon-obliterated
temporary altars (earth and rough stones?) and a tamarisk long
dead.

The excavations at Tell Arad, Tell Milh (Malhata) and Tell
Masos have similarly been used as basis for a theory putting the
Israelite conquests of *c.* 1230/1180 BC back to patriarchal times, [45]
hence to produce the artificial image of a 'conquest' that took centuries. However, this particular mirage depends simply on the lack
of discovery (so far) of Late Bronze Age settlements on or near the
Middle Bronze/Early Iron Age sites dug with such success. Such a
negative basis, however, is wholly unsatisfactory[46] as can be seen
from the situation in Transjordan (chapter 1, and below). Furthermore, site-shift was particularly prevalent in the Negeb – Tell
Masos has three distinct sub-sites, and Tell Ira is a fourth. [47] Beer-
Sheba itself has two main sites (Bir es-Saba, Tell Beersheba),
besides its Chalcolithic sites.

We now turn to the Hebrews in Transjordan. Skirting round
Edom and Moab, the Israelites were finally compelled to fight
against, and to defeat, Sihon, an Amorite ruler who had taken
Heshbon from the Moabites and now lost it to Israel with the rest
of his realm (Numbers 21:21–31). As we saw in chapter 1, it had
been customary to identify ancient Heshbon with Tell Hesban, but
excavations there failed to produce many buildings before Roman
age, or anything much but pottery-fill before the seventh century BC
at all.[48] Thus, unless the earlier levels had been missed or totally
obliterated, it is altogether more likely that Bronze-Age Heshbon
was at either Tell el-Umeiri or Tell Jalul nearby, both of which
show abundant occupation in the Bronze Age, Late and earlier, as
well as later.[49] Site-shift is the obvious answer, just as it was at
Jericho, Lachish and elsewhere.

In Moab proper Dibon offers an equally instructive example,
again noted in chapter 1. Here, the excavations found virtually
nothing of Late Bronze Age date,[50] even though Dibon is mentioned in Numbers (21:30; 32:3, 34, 45–46, etc.), precisely like the
'gap' at the Negeb sites. However, in this case, we have independent written evidence at first hand to prove the existence of Dibon
in the thirteenth century BC: the war-reliefs of Ramesses II
depicting his conquest of Batora and of Dibon 'in the land of
Moab',[51] these being shown as fortresses. Moab was then a state
with fortified strongpoints during the first half of the thirteenth century BC; the archaeological data from Dibon (Dhiban) are clearly
inadequate, as is so often the case with mute, uninscribed, time-
worn, incompletely-dug, archaeological sites. Such evidence is a
very unsatisfactory basis from which to pass judgement upon the
biblical or any other literary source.

From Tell Deir Alla in the Jordan valley, however, has come an
archaeological and inscriptional curiosity of a very different stamp.
A Dutch expedition found the fragmentary remains of an Aramaic
inscription upon plaster, perhaps originally applied to a stone
monument (stela).[52] Datable to roughly 700 BC (eighth/seventh
centuries overall) this text (or texts) exhibit(s) several remarkable
features. In the text, the title and beginnings of important
paragraphs or sections are written in red ink – 'rubrics' – precisely
as in good literary papyri in Egypt, where this usage was invented.
The language is Aramaic with features that are in some cases old,
in other cases analogous with its sister-language Hebrew. But most
remarkable of all is the content. When the Israelites were in Moab,
about to cross the Jordan, the king of Moab hired a foreign prophet
from north Syria, Balaam son of Beor, to curse the Hebrews (cf.
Numbers 22–24) – but Balaam was constrained to bless them. In

these badly-broken texts of some five centuries later occur mentions of Balaam as a 'seer of the gods' with fragments of colourful visions, interchanges with bystanders, and possibly curses. It is evident that Balaam had remained a prominent figure in local religious tradition and, as Hoftijzer remarks, it is quite possible that former oracles of his (or deemed to be his) were kept at the Deir Alla shrine and recopied as religious literature – as happened to the Old Testament prophets in Israel. As we have seen already (chapter 4), longevity of tradition about early historical characters is nothing untoward in the biblical world.

2. *Into Canaan*

As noted repeatedly by past observers, the sudden stoppage of the Jordan (Joshua 3:13–17) is a phenomenon well-known at intervals in the river's history, because of the nature of its clay banks. [53] Once across the Jordan, Israel's first challenge and first victory was at Jericho. The site of Old Testament Jericho is generally accepted to be the mound of Tell es-Sultan, just west of the modern settlement of Er-Riha that still preserves the name. Jericho has had a chequered career archaeologically as well as anciently. The more recent excavations by Dame Kathleen Kenyon (1952–58) showed clearly that the walls formerly attributed to the Late Bronze Age by Professor Garstang (1930–36) really belonged to a much earlier day (late third millennium BC). In the Middle Bronze Age (patriarchal period), Jericho had been a flourishing town, as the rich burials in abundant tombs have shown. However, once that town was destroyed, the Middle-Bronze remains lay fallow for some two hundred years, during which time severe erosion weathered away nearly all traces of the Middle Bronze township except low down on the east side. As already remarked in chapter 1, the very walls were largely swept away together with some twenty feet of scarp below them. [54] Thus, it is scarcely surprising to find that the Late Bronze Age settlement at Jericho hardly survives at all[55] (house-wall, hearth, a few tombs, *c.* 1380 BC onwards) – eroded not in two hundred, but for a whole four hundred, years (double the span) between the Hebrew conquest and the time of Ahab. Jericho is a classic example of incompleteness in the archaeological record caused by the depredations of man and nature combined, where – as at Dibon – the literary record (here, the Old Testament) retains phases of history lost to the excavator.

The other famous 'problem-site' is Ai. For many decades, Et-Tell has been the most popular candidate for identification as ancient Ai. However, excavations at Et-Tell, [56] as at nearby Khirbet Haiyan and Khirbet Khudriya, have totally failed to yield anything

of the Late Bronze Age, or in fact anything at all between the end
of the Early Bronze Age (late third millennium) and the Early Iron
Age (*c.* 1200 BC). The same moral may still apply to Et-Tell as to
Dibon or Jericho – or in fact, Et-Tell may never have been Ai in
the first place.[57] The verdict must be left to future discovery.

Quite different is the position at other sites. Perhaps Hazor (now
Tell el-Qedah) offers the greatest contrast, where an extensive Late
Bronze city and citadel was totally destroyed in the late thirteenth
century BC, seemingly in good agreement with Joshua 11:10–11.[58]
Again, Tell Beit Mirsim (probably Old Testament Debir,[59] despite
carping by some) and Bethel (Beitin[60]) were also destroyed in the
later thirteenth century BC. So also Lachish (Tell ed-Duweir) where
an Egyptian ostracon dated to a 'Year 4' in Ramesside hieratic
script may suggest that this town fell in that year of the pharaoh
Merenptah or of a later king.[61] It should, of course, be said that
some sites show multiple destructions,[62] and identification of particular destruction-levels as being those caused by the marauding
Israelites remains a matter of inference, even if the inference seems
highly probable. Once more, the severe limitations of 'dirt-
archaeology' bereft of inscriptions or related written evidence show
themselves all too clearly. Without such evidence in adequate form,
sites cannot so certainly be identified by former ancient name, nor
destructions be assigned without cavil to either Israelites or
Philistines from without, or to accident or revolt from within. Thus,
the series of destructions visible in Late-Bronze-Age Canaan in the
later thirteenth century BC may probably be assigned to the
Israelite invasion in good measure, but other factors must also be
allowed for.

In any case, a modicum of common sense needs to be applied, as
well as more careful study of the biblical text itself. The southern
campaign of Joshua 10 was indeed a dramatic sweep through
southern Canaan, cutting off kings and their principal forces,
besides any caught without having fled from the seven or eight
cities attacked. But beyond inflicting immediate loss, this campaign
achieved little else by itself – it was a sweep, not an occupation:
'Joshua *returned*, and all Israel with him, to the camp, to Gilgal'
(Joshua 10:15, 43). *Occupation* of the land, to live in it, keep
livestock and cultivate crops in it, etc., was a far slower process,
visible in part later in Joshua and in Judges. The error of con-
trasting Joshua's rapid campaigns (misread as permanent conquest) with the slower occupation in Judges 1 misses the point
entirely.[63] And how often the proponents of this theory omit even
to read Joshua 13! Thirty-one dead kinglets (Joshua 12) were not a
conquest in depth, merely a cropping of the leadership. At the end

of Joshua's career, there still remained 'very much land to be possessed' (13:1) – both the areas listed (13:2–6) largely unreached by Joshua's vigour, as well as the in-depth settlement of most of the districts already raided. That process was more painfully slow, even in Joshua's lifetime; cf. the remarks in Joshua 18:2–3 (Joshua's rebuke), besides the frustrated efforts recorded here and there (Josh. 15:63; 16:10; 17:12, 16). Moreover, careful comparison between Joshua and Judges 1 shows that *not* everything noted in Judges 1 is to be classed within 1:1–9, 16–19, as 'after the death of Joshua'. Some verses contain 'flashbacks' (1:10–15, 20) to Joshua's time (Jos. 14:13–15 and 15:13–19). Other sections are, strictly, undated (Judg. 1:21, 22–26, 27 ff.). Therefore, shallow contrasts between Joshua and Judges remain unjustified on the basis of the biblical narratives themselves. The absolute bottom date for Israel's presence in Western Palestine is clearly indicated by the mention of Israel as a people on the so-called 'Israel Stela' of the 5th year (*c.* 1220/1209 BC) of the pharaoh Merenptah, in the closing verses of his victory-hymn over the defeated Libyans mentioning also his supremacy in Canaan.

3. *Judges and Philistines*

The two centuries (twelfth and eleventh) from the end of the Late Bronze Age to the emergence of kings in Israel were a period of change and confusion in the ancient Near East. From the north-west (Aegean and Western Anatolia), the 'sea peoples' shared in the fall of the Hittite Empire and largely destroyed the old city-states of Syria and Canaan, being halted only on the borders of Egypt by Ramesses III (*c.* 1180/1170 BC). From the north-east, central Syria and Canaan were subjected also to a growing influx of Arameans. From the south-east, as we have seen, the Israelites passed through Transjordan, across the Jordan, and so into Canaan too. Both Egypt and the Mesopotamian powers (Assyria and Babylon) had lost their political and military power, leaving Syria and Palestine to be a cockpit for the struggles between these competing groups and the Canaanites and Amorites already there. Cultural standards nosedived; settlements, pottery, etc., of Early Iron Age I period (twelfth-eleventh centuries BC) are often poor compared with earlier times, regardless of whether settled by Israelites or others. War and literacy can be found combined in this age, in a series of inscribed arrowheads, 'arrow of so-and-so'. [64] Art is best represented by the exotic pottery of the Philistines, whose growing pressure on Israel forced her into a new age – the age of kings.

6

Kings and Poets

SAMUEL AND SAUL

As a group of often disunited tribes, oppressed by Philistines and others, often low in morale and without ongoing spiritual impetus, the Israelites looked for some tangible, permanent institution to deliver them out of their troubles. The kingship of their divine Sovereign had been expressed through deliverers or 'judges' raised up on occasion to meet the need, the greatest being Samuel. Samuel's sons however, were not of their father's calibre, but corrupt. So, at length, Israel's elders determined to have a king 'like all the (other) nations' (1 Samuel 8:1–5). This, they were granted – but not without a plain warning that desertion of their divine Sovereign for a fallible, bureaucratic, exploitative human ruler (conformed to this imperfect world) would mean a price to pay.

Thus, in his address, Samuel spelled out that price to Israel (1 Samuel 8:10–18). A worldly king would conscript free men's sons to serve as his attendants and in his armies, to till crown lands, to work in state workshops, and their daughters to give service also. State requisitioning of, and tax on, land and property, forced labour, etc., would in time cool the Israelites' enthusiasm for the new order. This passage has often been dismissed as a late and jaundiced view of the monarchy, written up centuries after Samuel's time, in the light of later experience. However, such a view is needless. From the archives of Alalakh and Ugarit comes abundant evidence on levantine kingship from long before Samuel's time, illustrating the whole gamut of such burdens on people and property. These were the normal 'cost' of such a monarchy, not simply abuses (except when pushed beyond reason), [1] long before and after Samuel.

Saul was Israel's first king, his reign marked by both triumphs and tragedy (1 Samuel 9–31). From his troubled times, archaeology has little to show directly. Saul's citadel at Gibeah (Tell el-Ful) has been excavated, with results that illustrate well the value and limitations of much archaeology for biblical study. The earliest main level (I) was an Early Iron Age settlement of the twelfth century BC. Some time after its destruction (*c.* 1100 BC), during the eleventh century, there was built a rectangular fortress with corner towers and 'casemate' walls [2] (level IIA). Later, this fortress was revamped, with masonry of better workmanship (level IIb). This fort was certainly Saul's abode in 'Gibeah of Saul' – but during which phase, IIA or IIB? The excavators and their colleagues considered that the first fort was Saul's work, later reconstructed under David. Others (e.g., Alt, Mazar) have queried whether it was the Philistines who built the first fort (as strongpoint against the Hebrews), which later Saul took over and rebuilt to be his centre of rule (second fort). The first view is perhaps, still preferable, but uncertainty still haunts the matter. [3] Initially, Saul was able to maintain a successful defence of his kingdom against foes from the north (Zobah), east (Ammon, Moab, Edom) and south (Amalek), as well as against the Philistines – but ultimately, the Philistines proved too much, bringing about the deaths of Saul and his principal sons, together with the seeming collapse of Israel as a state (1 Samuel 31; 2 Samuel 1).

DAVID: RESTORER OF THE KINGDOM, BUILDER OF AN EMPIRE

From modest origins, David ultimately became the greatest and archetypal Hebrew king. Within a decade of Saul's death, the tribes of Israel saw in him their sole effective leader. Capturing Jerusalem, he ruled from there over a reunited people. The new monarch found himself beset by foes, but not wholly without friends. First and foremost, the Philistines sought to crush the new ruler, but were thoroughly repulsed (2 Samuel 5:17 ff.; 8:1). Eastward, swayed by suspicion, the new king of Ammon insulted David's envoys, therefore hired allies from the north, but was vanquished (2 Samuel 10–12), as were Moab (2 Samuel 8:2) and

Edom (2 Samuel 11:14 ff., cf. 8:14). Then, in the north, David conquered the Aramean kingdom of Zobah and Damascus whence
Ammon had obtained aid (2 Samuel 8:3 ff., cf. 10:6, 8, 16–19).
This northern victory brought David two friends: the rulers of
Hamath inland and of Tyre on the coast. Toi king of Hamath had
already struggled with Hadadezer of Zobah for mastery of the
routes north-east to the Euphrates (cf. 2 Sa. 8:3, 10b). So, when
David eliminated the power of Zobah, that problem was solved,
and Toi sent his son south with rich gifts to seek alliance with the
new power, gifts accepted but not reciprocated (2 Sa. 8:9–11).
Thus, Toi probably became David's subject-ally. As pointed out
long since,[4] David's empire thus contained three political elements:
the home nucleus of Judah and Israel, the conquered territories to
east (Ammon, Moab, Edom) and centre-north, and Toi as subject-
ally further north and east to the Euphrates. On the evidence of
later Hittite hieroglyphic inscriptions, it is possible to determine
that the kingdom of Hamath did extend to the Euphrates, opposite
Laqe and Naharaim whence it could draw labour for work on
buildings in Hamath. The northern centre of Luash was also a
regular part of the kingdom.

David's other friend was Hiram I, king of Tyre, who was quick
to perceive the new star in the ascendant in the Levant, and to ally
himself with it – putting Phoenician craftsmanship and materials at
David's disposition (2 Sa. 5:11–12). This alliance continued under
Solomon, being renewed from time to time by the northern
successor-kingdom of Israel in later centuries. David wished to
build a temple for the God of Israel, but through Nathan the
prophet came the message that not he, but his son, should build it.
This 'hope deferred' did not deter him from welcoming the Ark of
the Covenant into Jerusalem, or from taking interest in the
associated worship, in music as well as with offerings. A persistent
and undoubtedly ancient tradition makes of David 'the sweet
psalmist of Israel' (2 Sa. 23:1). Long before his attention to music
in Jerusalem, he had been the youthful lyre-player who calmed
Saul (1 Sa. 16:18, 23; 18:10). The narratives of his life include his
lament over Saul and Jonathan (2 Sa. 1:17–27), his hymn of
praise at the time of his greatness (2 Sa. 22), and his parting psalm
(2 Sa. 23:1–7), quite apart from the persistent headings in the
Psalter itself.

DAVID AND THE ANTIQUITY OF POETRY

The tradition of poetry and hymnody in ancient Israel went far
back beyond David's day. The blessings pronounced by the

patriarchs were set in poetic form (Isaac, Gen. 27:27–29, 39–40; Jacob, Gen. 49:1–27). After the exodus, the 'Song of the Sea' uttered by Moses and Israel (Ex. 15) was a veritable triumph-hymn, as was the later Song of Deborah and Barak (Judges 5). The use of such poetic song in Saul's time is reflected in the refrain of the maidens that aroused Saul's jealousy of David (1 Sa. 18:7):

'Saul has slain his thousands,
    And David, his ten-thousands.'

From 1000 BC onwards, therefore, even within the Old Testament, poetry and psalmody were by no means a novelty. In fact, by that date, David and others were heirs to two thousand years of ancient Near Eastern poetic tradition. Hymns and psalms, even of considerable length, were commonplace for the thousand years before David, including in West Semitic to which Hebrew belongs.

Thus, the whole development of poetry in the ancient biblical world can be followed through in outline for its entire history. That majestic chronicle of ancient literary wealth cannot be presented here, so vast is it. Here, we must take but a brief glimpse.

In the third millennium BC, both Egypt and Mesopotamia pioneered poetic style, with converging results. In Egypt, a stone memorial palette from the very dawn of her history (*c.* 3200 BC) appears to honour a victory by either the first pharaoh or his local predecessor. It would be the earliest-known triumph-hymn. [5] The poetic unit is the single line. Every line has the same form, each one varying from the others only in the divine epithet used for the king and in the term used for the conquered city, at start and finish of each line:

'Horus has destroyed the City of the Owl,
[Seth] has destroyed the City of the Heron (?),
Vulture has destroyed the City of the Wrestlers, . . .'

and so on for seven lines all told, giving the effect of a solemn, monotonous litany.

During the third millennium BC, a long series of religious texts was composed to protect the pharaoh and his pyramid for the afterlife. From the late 5th Dynasty onwards (*c.* 2350 BC), they were actually inscribed within the royal pyramids – hence their modern name, the 'Pyramid Texts'. Besides rituals, spells, etc., they include also hymns, and show already a great variety of poetic usages.

First, the two-line 'couplet' that was to dominate ancient Near Eastern poetry for most of the rest of the pre-Christian era. Oldest is perhaps the 'non-parallel' couplet, where an idea is expressed not in one line or unit, but in two lines together. By varying one or

more elements in one line or both, a series of matching couplets
gives a poetic form to the whole. About 2300 BC, the official Uni
conducted campaigns in Palestine for Pepi I. His victory-hymn has
seven two-line verses all constructed thus:[6]

'This army has returned in peace,
   It has hacked up the land of the Sand-dwellers.
This army has returned in peace,
   It has crushed the land of the Sand-dwellers.
This army has returned in peace,
   It has demolished its forts . . .',

and so on. The other form of couplet which became favourite is the
'parallel' couplet. Here, the two lines can express the same basic
thought in different words ('synthetic parallelism'), or a concept
and its opposite ('antithetic parallelism'), or a thought in one line is
further developed in the second line ('expanded parallelism').
Already, these three forms can all be found as early as the Pyramid
Texts – for example, in the famous 'Cannibal Hymn':[7]

Synthetic: 'The lifetime of the King is eternity,
                His duration is everlasting.'
              'Their souls are in the King's stomach,
                Their spirits are in the King's possession.'
Antithetic: 'Lo, their souls are with the King,
                Their shades are gone from their owners.'
Expanded: 'The King feeds on the lungs of the Wise ones,
              He enjoys living on hearts and also on their magic.'

Besides the single line (still in use) and the ubiquitous couplet,
more elaborate forms came into use. Such included three-line units
(triplets or tricola), four-line units (of either four distinct lines, or
two linked couplets), and five, six, and longer line units, up to eight,
ten or eleven lines eventually. Some contain parallelism, some do
not, just as with couplets. For a triple parallelism unit from the
Pyramid texts, one may instance:

'The Nurse-Canal is opened,
   The Winding Waterway is flooded,
      The Fields of Rushes are filled with water.'

In Mesopotamia, Sumerian poets quickly attained an equal
mastery of these forms of poetic diction, also from the third millennium BC onwards. At random, one may turn to the long and hym-
nic building-inscription of Gudea, prince of Lagash *c.* 2100 BC. The
poetic art of his scribe runs from the simplest parallel couplet,

'Gudea arose, (it was from) sleep,
   He trembled, (it was) a vision',[9]

to elaborate and involved poetic devices such as chiasmus:

'*By night*, the moonlight will shine for you,
  By day, the bright(?) sunlight will shine for you,
  The house will be built for you *by day*,
It will be raised high for you *by night*.'[10]

Here, the poet has combined two parallel couplets into a four-line unit, and has 'enclosed' the whole within the sequence NIGHT/-DAY and the symmetrically reversed pair DAY/NIGHT, the pattern AB–BA often termed chiasmus.

What bearing do these poetic achievements in third-millennium Egypt and Mesopotamia have on the Levant? The answer lies in the close contacts between Syria-Palestine and both of these great civilizations from the third millennium onwards. From the height of the Pyramid Age (*c.* 2600 BC) until its end (*c.* 2200), Egypt had continuous contact with such seaports as Byblos. In North Syria, at Ebla, Mesopotamian literary influence is even more directly visible (see chapter 3, above). There, Sumerian literature was both copied and adapted, and local Palaeo-Canaanite texts written in cuneiform. Hymns were included in such activities. Hence, within the third millennium, Sumerian influence on the norms and forms of early Levantine and specifically West-Semitic literature is virtually certain. Therefore, in the Levant from that time on, we should expect the rise of a vigorous literary tradition with a good range of poetic forms.

During the early second millennium BC, such development is certain, and ancient Near Eastern literatures grew apace. In Middle-Kingdom Egypt there flowered a brilliant classical literature, including poetry. The Old-Babylonian schools canonized the older Sumerian literature, and adapted and continued composing Neo-Sumerian hymns and other works. Semitic Akkadian (Assyro-Babylonian) literature at this time probably enjoyed its greatest period of creative writing in all fields of endeavour.[11] In distant Anatolia, Hittite narrative art began with Anittas. In Syria-Palestine, both Egyptian and Mesopotamian stimulus continued. The latter is illustrated by the finding of Sumerian word-lists at Alalakh. The former, by the princes of Byblos actually putting up inscriptions in Egyptian language and hieroglyphs, well composed but barbarously carved, adapted to their own needs. By about 1700 BC or soon after, the Semitic linear alphabet was probably first born. The great West-Semitic epics known from Ugarit (copies of fourteenth/thirteenth centuries BC) were probably orally composed in the nineteenth to sixteenth centuries BC.[12]

In the later second millennium BC, cosmopolitan trends in the an-

cient Near East reached a climax, as is readily illustrated by the
archives from Ugarit – texts in Akkadian, local Ugaritic and in
Hurrian cheek by jowl, including literary works, besides Hittite and
Egyptian contacts. From the wealth of poetry that flourished in the
early biblical world during *c.* 1400–1200 BC, the single greatest
body of West-Semitic poetry so far known to us is the epic poetry
of Ugarit. Ugaritic itself is a language having numerous and quite
close affinities with biblical Hebrew, especially in vocabulary and
in poetic style and diction. It is our principal evidence for a rich
heritage of West-Semitic poetry, on which Ugaritic, Canaanite-
Phoenician and Hebrew all drew, having roots still further back in
time, as we have seen. Thus, not surprisingly, there are numerous
verbal parallels between Ugaritic poetic style and phraseology in
the Psalms, both Davidic and others. All the wealth of poetic
idioms – parallelism, etc. – known internationally since the third
millennium (and exemplified above) is present here, whether in
Ugaritic in the second millennium BC or in the Psalter in the tenth
century BC and onwards. Poems such as Exodus 15 or Judges 5
help to span the interval between *c.* 1200 and 1000 BC in the un-
folding of Hebrew poetry. There is, of course, no need to suppose
that the visible relationship between Hebrew ('South Canaanite')
and Ugaritic ('North Canaanite')[13] is anything other than a common West-Semitic linguistic and literary inheritance, just as
classical allusions in (e.g.) French, English, German, or Italian
writers (who may owe nothing to each other) are owed one and all
to the common classical inheritance from Greece and Rome in
European civilization. Certainly, the linguistic and literary affinities
are much closer altogether in the case of Hebrew, Canaanite-
Phoenician and Ugaritic. It is needless to exemplify here similarities
in incidental turns of speech in Hebrew and Ugaritic at any
length.[14] One well-known example from the Baal epic and a non-
Davidic psalm must here suffice as examples of closely analogous
phrasing and literary style.

Baal Epic:[15]

ht, 'ib-k B'l-m,	'Now your foe, O Baal,
ht, 'ib-k tmkhts,	Now, your foe you shall slay,
ht, ttsmt tsrt-k	Now, you shall destroy your enemy!'

Psalm 92:9 (Heb., 10):[16]

ky hn, 'ybyk YHWH	'For see, your foes, O LORD,
ky hn, 'yby-k y'bdw,	For see, your foes shall perish,
ytprdw kl-p'ly-'wn	Shall be scattered all evildoers!'

As can be seen, the use of the three-line unit (or tricolon) with 'expanded' parallelism is common to both. So too is the 'chiasmus' in the second and third lines of both – 'foe + verb (1)'; 'verb (2) + enemy/evildoer'. One may (if so inclined) contrast the literary similarity with the theological divergence. In the epic, we find Baal out for vengeance, be he right or wrong, so to speak; in the psalm, there abides a clear moral note, 'all evildoers shall be scattered' by a righteous God.

This simple example is but the tiniest sample from the rich literary backcloth to the psalms (and other biblical poetry) that Ugaritic can provide.[17] Even from David's time, Hebrew psalmody was heir to a tradition already centuries old; on these general grounds, there can be no objection to the existence of either Davidic or earlier psalms.

Finally, the titles of the psalms. Working in a vacuum, past generations of Old Testament scholars have imperiously dismissed the titles of the psalms as of no value, particularly as regards authorship. However, various factors (both inside and outside the Old Testament) point in the opposite direction. First, many of the headings were already obscure to, and not understood by, the Septuagint translators in the third/second centuries BC. Therefore, such headings must be dated to a previous period long enough before the Hellenistic age to have become traditional and so long traditional that their meaning could be lost even in part. The Septuagint both adds and omits headings, also. Second, the natural meaning of the narrative *context* of Psalm 18 in 2 Samuel 22:2–51 shows clearly that authorship *is* intended in this case – as it is of Hezekiah in Isaiah 38:9, and of Habbakuk in Hab. 3:1. If this is true of Psalm 18 within the Psalter, there is no intrinsic reason to dispute such attributions to David, or to his reign or initiative in other cases; contrary *proof* needs to be found first. This applies equally to the personal and musical elements in the headings.

Outside the Old Testament, the comparative evidence of the biblical world runs in parallel with the Old Testament evidence itself. For millennia, we have headings, sub-headings, colophons and even authors for ancient hymns. As for authors, the Hymn to the Nile in Middle-Kingdom Egypt was most likely written by that same (Dua)Khety who composed the 'Satire of the Trades' and was associated with the Instruction of Amenemhat I, in the twentieth century BC. To king Akhenaten may be credited the Hymn to the Aten (fourteenth century BC).[19] Much earlier than these was the famous priestess in Ur, Enheduanna, daughter of Sargon of Akkad, who lived on into the reign of her nephew Naram-Sin (*c.* 2300 BC). She is the world's earliest-known authoress.[20] To her credit belong two hymns to the goddess Inanna (Inanna and Ebih; Exaltation of Inanna), and the second, probably enlarged, edition of the Sumerian Temple Hymns. [21]

As for technical headings, sub-headings, colophons and classifications (including musical), these are abundantly represented in Mesopotamia. These are especially evident, for example, in the considerable amount of Sumerian hymnody published in recent years,[22] dating largely from the twenty-first/eighteenth centuries BC, as well as earlier and later. Music, too, was frequently used to accompany such hymns and psalms from over one thousand years before David and Solomon until the end of pre-classical antiquity.[23] Far from being strange or improbable, the picture of psalmody, both personal and institutional, seen in Samuel, Kings, Chronicles and the Psalter is essentially what one would be led to expect from the evidence of the outside world as well as from the biblical text itself.

SOLOMON, RULER, BUILDER, SAGE

1. *Politics*[24]

Solomon's reign saw both the peak and the decline of Israelite political power. At first, Solomon not only inherited but even enhanced David's empire. Remarkable was Solomon's receiving in marriage (early in his reign) a daughter of the pharaoh of Egypt (1 Kings 3:1). As dowry, he received Gezer, conquered by that king (1 Kings 9:16). Thus, it appears that the Egyptian king had raided south-west Palestine, probably defeating the Philistines right up to their neighbour, the old Canaanite city of Gezer. His defeat of so longstanding a foe as the Philistines was doubtless welcome to Solomon, but not an Egyptian presence just across his own border with Gezer. The two powers, therefore, came to some understanding and became allies, Solomon gaining Gezer as wedding-present. As a result, the Philistines ceased be a threat to Israel for a long time to come, even losing territory to Solomon. [25] The pharaoh concerned was most probably Siamun (*c.* 978–959 BC), the most dynamic ruler of Egypt's Twenty-first Dynasty. Historical records of any importance are almost totally lacking from the whole span of the Twenty-first Dynasty, particularly for foreign relations. Beyond private genealogies, local-affairs inscriptions in distant Thebes, and a handful of scattered minor stelae, we have next to nothing; and certainly no mention of *any* foreign ruler beyond Egypt, never mind David or Solomon. From Siamun's northern capital Tanis (biblical Zoan), we are fortunate to have *one* broken fragment of a triumph-scene showing the king slaying a fallen foe who grasps an axe of peculiar design, possibly of Aegean or West-Anatolian type. Such a derivation would well fit possible identification of this fallen foe as Philistine. Thus, Siamun may have conducted a 'police-action' to subdue the Philistines, to eliminate any threat to his own north-east border and any rivalry to his own trade-port of Tanis; agreement with Solomon could have been economically advantageous to both parties.

In his own far north-east, Solomon used his commanding position over Aram and Hamath to secure the routes to the Euphrates. He 'took' Hamath-Zobah, and built Tadmor (later Palmyra) in the wilderness and other store-cities in Hamathite territory (2 Chronicles 8:3–4). This suggests that some part of Zobah (assigned to Hamath by David?) had revolted and was promptly crushed by the new king (Solomon), who then proceeded to secure the Palmyra route to the Euphrates.[26]

To the south, aided by his father's old ally Hiram of Tyre, Solomon promoted trading and exploratory voyages down the Red Sea and beyond, to the mysterious Ophir. Ophir's location stubbornly remains unknown, but its reality as a source of gold is beyond any doubt, as is proven by a later ostracon (inscribed potsherd) from Tell Qasile that reads: 'Gold of Ophir, for Beth-Horon – 30 shekels'.[27] From South Arabia came the queen of Sheba (1 Kings 10:1–13) to visit Solomon, bringing a handsome present including 120 talents of gold.[28] A large sum, but not out-of-the-way – the still greater sum of 150 talents of gold was extracted from Metten II of Tyre by Tiglath-pileser III of Assyria *c.* 730 BC.[29] As others have suggested, probably much more was at stake in the queen's visit than just idle curiosity[30] – Solomon's seaborne enterprises stood to rival Sheba's prospects for overland trade, hence the need of some understanding between the two states.[31][2]

2. *More Economics and Ergonomics!*

Even more considerable were Solomon's revenues in gold from the triennial (1 Kings 10:22) expeditions to Ophir (1 Kings 9:28) at 420 talents, not to mention the total 'in one year'[32] of 666 talents of gold, about twenty tons (1 Kings 10:14). While some may be inclined to consider that the figure has suffered in textual recopying,[33] yet – when all is said and done – such an amount is neither impossible nor unparalleled. It may have derived from various external sources (such as the Ophir expeditions) as well as from heavy taxation within Israel.[34] Over a thousand years before Solomon's day, a defeated king of Mari paid tribute to Ebla of ten tons of silver and over a third of a ton of gold, a mere incidental in the economy of Ebla (cf. chapter 3, above). Five centuries after Solomon, the one province of 'India' (just the Indus basin) yielded an annual 360 talents of gold to the Persian emperors (Herodotus iii, 94). But these figures – and Solomon's 666 talents – are as nothing compared with the breathtaking munificence of Osorkon I of Egypt to the gods of Egypt barely ten years after Solomon's death. During Years 1 to 4 of his reign, this king presented a total of two million *deben* weight of silver (about 220 tons) and another 2,300,000 *deben* weight of silver and gold (some 250 tons) to the gods, largely in the form of precious objects (vessels, statuary, etc.). In other parts of the damaged inscription, many such objects are itemised, many by weight.[35] The grand total, *470 tons* of precious metal, outstrips twenty times over Solomon's reputed income of a mere twenty tons (the 666 talents) – yet, this record is detailed and first-hand. Not a little of that wealth may actually have been looted from Jerusalem by Osorkon's father Shishak (Shoshenq I), on his famous campaign (1 Kings 14:25–26). Needless to say, practically no scrap of that wealth has ever been recovered, apart from the silver coffin of Osorkon's son Shoshenq II; the gifts to the gods have all gone without trace, their very temples often but shapeless ruins.

To run his palace and seat of government (the 'Whitehall' of its day), Solomon required considerable revenues in kind – foodstuffs on a monthly rota from district governors (1 Kings 4:7, 22–23, 27–28). Large though these quantities seem, they are in fact directly comparable with the range of supplies for other royal courts in the ancient Near East as far apart as Mari and Egypt; and one month's supply of grain could be grown on about 424 acres of ground, an area some four-fifths of a mile square.[36] Hardly an excessive area out of any one province! There is no fantasy here.

As for the 'war-machine', Solomon's 1,400 chariots (1 Kings 10:26; 2 Chronicles 1:14) are notably fewer than the 2,000 chariots attributed to Ahab of Israel a century later by the Assyrian annals.[37] The figure of 4,000 stalls for chariot-horses in 2 Chronicles 9:25 should probably be preferred to that of 40,000 in 1 Kings 4:26. The Kings figure is probably nothing more than a tiny scribal copying-slip of one letter: *t* for *m*. The smaller figure would equip the 1,400 chariots with one span or pair of horses each, plus 600 'reserve' spans for nearly half the force, to cover against losses in war, replace older animals by younger, etc. Again, such figures are consistent with other ancient statistics. Three or four centuries before Solomon, the king of the small but wealthy state of Ugarit was negotiating for 2,000 horses on just one occasion[38] – doubtless in addition to what he already possessed. In the tenth century BC, one would expect the 12,000 'horsemen' (1 Kings 4:26; 2 Chron.

9:25) to have been charioteers, not cavalry.[39] This figure, at 3 men to a car, would cover 1 crew on duty and 2 crews in reserve for 1,-200 chariots, and 1 crew each on duty and in reserve for the other 200 chariots. Men not on active service simply lived their normal lives (e.g. on the land) and in their home towns, doing their stint of direct service in peacetime by rota. Precisely this procedure is well-known elsewhere in the biblical Near East, as at Ugarit, from where we have lists of towns with names of charioteers living in them.[40] To finish with economics, the changing price of decent horses is worth passing notice: 150 shekels in Solomon's time (1 Kings 10:29). While in and near horse-raising districts hacks came cheap, the prices internationally for good horses show a declining arc over the centuries as their use became more widespread and their numbers greater. Thus they fetched up to 300 shekels in the eighteenth century BC (Mari), went down to 200 shekels by the thirteenth century BC (Ugarit), and hence might well cost just about 150 shekels by the tenth century BC (Solomon).

3. *Solomon the Builder*

Solomon's most famous building was the Temple at Jerusalem. Of this, no stone remains – it was utterly devastated by the Babylonians in 586 BC, being replaced more modestly under the Persian rule (*c.* 538–521 BC), and more grandiosely by Herod whose efforts were demolished by Rome in hhe war of 68–70 AD. Hence, the descriptions in Kings and Chronicles are now our sole record. But, despite the problems posed by technical terms, these descriptions do reflect recognisable architectural features of the Levant in the second/first millennia BC, and beyond. The scheme of a pillared portico, vestibule and inner sanctuary (holy of holies) was current in Syria from at least the twenty-fourth/nineteenth centuries BC at Ebla (see chapter 3), is attested at thirteenth century Hazor in Canaan itself, and soon after Solomon's day again in Syria (at Tell Tayinat). The temple proper was of relatively modest size by Near-Eastern standards, hardly more than 120 feet long by 60 feet wide overall, of solid ashlar masonry.[41] The wealth of gold, etc., used in its decoration (1 Kings 6:21 ff.) is typical of the lavish ways of the ancient Near East. In Egypt, temples had silver and gold covered floors and stairways,[42] Queen Hatshepsut capped and plated her giant obelisks (97 feet high) with gold and electrum,[43] Ramesses II's skilled artisans cared for gold-covered temple-doors and sacred barques,[44] and Osorkon I's incredible largesse to Egyptian temples we have already seen. The temple itself, moreover, was not 'on its own'; it will have stood in a paved precinct, enclosed within surrounding walls, as most such temples did.[45]

To carry through the building of the temple in just seven years, Solomon levied two groups of people for lumbering, quarrying and transport of materials (stone and timber), in alliance with Hiram of Tyre. Again, the figures are large, therefore are frequently criticised as corrupt or just fanciful, and hence are little studied. Certainly, it is tempting to emend wholesale figures such as 70,000 to 7,000 or 700; but such procedures remain arbitrary unless textual or other evidence can be cited in support, as in the simple case of 4,000 or 40,000 stalls dealt with above. That example shows that careful textual criticism can help to a better understanding. However, no simple solution of that kind can be applied here. And first, one should ask whether the figures in fact *may* actually make sense, in themselves and in Near-Eastern context, before rushing headlong to jettison or emend them. Let us look at the figures, at their possible structure, and at the range of background evidence.

From 'all Israel', Solomon took, we are told, 30,000 men, in three divisions of 10,000 each, each division doing one month's service in Lebanon by rota (1 Kings 5:13–14). For the labouring work, the fetching, carrying and quarrying, Solomon further conscripted another 153,300 men (variant, 153,600), from the subsisting alien population, Canaanites and the like (1 Kings 5:15, 16; cf. 2 Chron. 2:2, 17–18). Unlike the Israelites, these people were to be put on perpetual levy for both the temple and other building-works (cf. 1 Kings 9:21). The 153,300 conscripts were divided into 70,000 labourers and 80,000 quarrymen, with 3,300 (or 3,600) [46] overseers. This would give a figure of 300 chief overseers over 3,000 foremen (1 chief to each 10 foremen), and 1 foreman per group of 50 labourers or quarrymen. These proportions make good enough sense, regardless of overall scale. Problems of textual transmission may have affected the variation between 550 Israelite officers in 1 Kings 9:22–23 and 250 such officers in 2 Chronicles 8:9–10. However, it is noteworthy that the 30,000 temporary levy of Israelites in 1 Kings 5:13–14 does not reappear in 2 Chronicles. Thus, it is conceivable that the 550 officers of 1 Kings 9:22 f. may include 300 officers to oversee the 30,000 (at 1 per 100?) [57] besides the 250 included in common with 2 Chron. 8:9–10, engaged on other duties and projects. In themselves, therefore, the Solomonic figures yield a sensible enough structure.

Have we any external scale by which to appraise such figures? The answer is yes; external data are limited but quite instructive, so far as they go. First of all, in terms of 'middle management', Solomon's 550 Israelite officers and 330 foremen and chiefs over conscripts, perhaps about a thousand administrators if one adds in an unknown number of palace officials, etc., are quite modest in number when compared with the great staff of 4,700 bureaucrats in the acropolis of Ebla city some thirteen centuries before Solomon (cf. chapter 3). Likewise 12 men to assure palace supplies (1 Kings 4:7 ff.) are trifling compared with the 103 leaders and their 210 aides that exercised similar functions at Ebla! Two separate authorities[48] have calculated the Israelite population of Solomon's kingdom (as distinct from the foreign 'empire' territories) at 700,000 or 800,000 people. With the alien population of Canaanites and others as well, Western Palestine may have supported then over a million altogether. These figures may, still, be a little on the modest side when one recalls that the 140-acre city of Ebla in the 24th century BC held over a quarter-million people, equal to more than a quarter of all of Solomon's Palestinian subjects as just reckoned above!

Second, the question of quarrying, etc., expeditions. A thousand years before Solomon, the short-lived pharaoh Mentuhotep IV dispatched 10,000 men into the dreary wilderness of Wadi Hammamat to fetch just *one* stone coffin and lid with a set of stone monuments. For the safe transport of the coffin-lid alone, 3,000 sailors were assigned.[49] Some fifty years later, Sesostris I of the 12th Dynasty sent an expedition of well over 18,000 men to the same narrow desert valley to fetch stone *not* for an entire temple (as Solomon did in Lebanon's easier setting) but just 60 sphinxes and 150 other statues. We are expressly told that 2,000 or 1,500 or 1,000 or 500 men were assigned to *individual* blocks of stone, perhaps depending on size.[50] About 200 years before Solomon, Ramesses IV sent over 9,000 men to Hammamat (of whom 900 died . . .), just to quarry blocks for a set of statues.[51] In the light of these statistics, it is perhaps not unreasonable to wonder if Solomon's larger numbers (employed in relays, and for seven years' minimum) who went to hew and to quarry, not just for groups of statues but for an entire temple, are less unrealistic than many have supposed hitherto, and may contain more than a modicum of truth.

Of Solomon's other buildings, nothing remains of the other ambitious structures at Jerusalem (1 Kings 7:1 ff.); like the palaces of many another potentate, they have been swept away long since. However, the unified building-works of Solomon and his levies in more modest projects are well illustrated by the finding of standard-size gateways[52] and casemate walls of the tenth century BC at Hazor, Megiddo and Gezer, all strategic centres within the kingdom (1 Kings 9:15).[53] Work at Gezer also confirmed a destruction there, just prior to Solomonic work on the fortifications – most probably visited upon Gezer by 'the pharaoh that smote

Gezer' (1 Kings 9:16), most likely Siamun as we have seen. Similarly, Ezion-Geber in the role of depot for Red Sea expeditions may be represented by the ruins at Tell el-Kheleifeh on the north end of the Gulf of Aqaba, as its main occupation began in the tenth century BC.[53a] In the Negeb or southland, Arad was rebuilt with a strong, towered citadel, and Beer-Sheba likewise became a royal strongpoint,[54] among various other works.

4. Solomon the Sage

In literature, the name of Solomon is traditionally linked with the book of Proverbs, rather as that of David is with the psalms. Here too, the ancient Near East offers a wealth of rich background material that helps to place Solomon's possible relationship to the book of Proverbs and 'wisdom' in a fuller and more factual perspective than is usually envisaged, not least in Old Testament studies.

The present book of Proverbs contains (as any reader may verify) at least four works, as follows:

>*Proverbs of Solomon* (1–24)
>*Proverbs of Solomon,* recopied under Hezekiah (25–29)
>*Words of Agur* (30)
>*Words for Lemuel* (31)

Of these, the first two are of some length; the last two, quite short. That for Lemuel by his mother includes also the poem on the good wife. The first work, 'Proverbs of Solomon' (1–24), incorporates 'words of the wise' – i.e., culled from earlier sages – explicitly in two closing sections (22:17 ff.; 24:23 ff.). Unlike the three other works with just title and main text, this first work has a fuller literary structure: title, prologue (1–9), sub-title (10:1), and then main text.

However, the immense wealth of ancient Near-Eastern wisdom literature enables us to go further. All four of the individual works in Proverbs belong to one particular branch of ancient wisdom literature: *'instructions'*, in which a named author sets forth what he deems to be wise and unwise conduct, in a long series of observations, admonitions and word-pictures of various kinds. Ancient Egypt, the Levant and Mesopotamia between them offer some forty such works (in varying states of preservation) from *c.* 2700 BC down to Roman times: nearly thirty from Egypt, a dozen from Syria, the Hittites, and above all Mesopotamia. From this rich array of literary works all belonging to one class, it is possible to write in outline the history of development of this entire group of writings, and to put the four works in Proverbs in their proper setting in that panorama.[55] Here, the most essential points must suffice.

During the whole twenty-seven centuries that such instructional works were composed, their authors habitually cast them in one or other of two basic formats. Both formats were used side by side by various authors, with no 'evolution' from one to the other. *Type A* was the simpler, The author would begin with a formal title to the work, identifying himself by name in the third person, and then proceeded directly with his work. In Egypt, such sages as Hardjedef, Merykare's father (third millennium BC), *Ancient Writings* and Hori (late second millennium BC), and Amenothes (first millennium BC) all belong to Type A. In Mesopotamia and the Levant, so do Shube-awilim (second millennium) and *Advice to a Prince* (first millennium). Here too belong three of the works in Proverbs: Solomon edited under Hezekiah (25–29), Agur (30), and Lemuel (31).

More interesting was *Type B*. After a formal title (as in Type A), the author would begin with a prologue, very often devoted to exhortations. Then, sometimes after a sub-title, comes the main body of the work. To this scheme belongs the basic work of the book of Proverbs, 1–24, the Proverbs of Solomon *par excellence*. This Type B format is abundantly attested at all periods in the biblical world. Examples are: Egyptian Ptahhotep and Old-Sumerian Shuruppak (third millennium BC); Egyptian (Dua)Khety, 'Sehetepibre', Man to his Son, and Amenemhat I, plus classical Sumerian and Akkadian versions of Shuruppak (all early second millennium); Egyptian Aniy, High Priest Amenemhat, Amenemope, Amennakht, and the Akkadian Counsels of Wisdom (late second millennium); Egyptian Ankh-sheshonqy and Levantine/Mesopotamian (Aramaic) Ahiqar (first millennium BC). Thus, the assertion so commonly found in Old Testament studies that Proverbs 1–9 was composed and prefixed to 10 ff. after the Babylonian exile (fifth century onwards) is totally contradicted by the entire literary evidence of the whole of the rest of the ancient Near East. As that evidence shows, a prologue such as 1–9 is *integral* to the complete work, 1–24. Other supposed reasons for a very late date, such as vocabulary, concepts (e.g., personification) are also totally false, as the concepts concerned reach back into the second and third millennia BC, as does the history of much of the vocabulary.

Thus, no-one can prove that Solomon personally collected, wrote or inspired the first two sections (1–24, 25–29) of Proverbs. But his possible authorship of one complete work (1–24), drawing on older wisdom,[56] and role of collector of material copied-up later (Hezekiah, 25–29) are entirely feasible suppositions in the context of the literary, linguistic and conceptual world of the forty or so other works of the kind known to us today.

7

Wars and Rumours of Wars

1. *End of an Empire*

In the last decade or so of his reign, Solomon's regime was beset with problems at home and abroad. On the south, prince Hadad of Edom returned from Egyptian exile to reclaim the independence of Edom (1 Kings 11:14–22). This must have endangered Solomon's hold on the Arabah rift valley (south from the Dead Sea) with its access to copper-deposits, and to Ezion-Geber and the Red Sea. His sources of wealth from the south, therefore, were probably curtailed. In the north, a certain Rezon gained control of Damascus and the former kingdom of Aram-Zobah (1 Kings 11:23–25). With this revolt, Solomon's northern foreign holdings fell away completely. An independent Aram cut him off both from Hamath (now also left independent) and from the routes to the Euphrates; northern trade would suffer.

Nearer home, one Jeroboam son of Nebat was heralded by a prophet as future ruler of the northern tribes of Israel as distinct from Judah and Benjamin. Solomon's attempts to eliminate him were frustrated by Jeroboam's flight into Egypt, he finding safe haven at the court of the new pharaoh Shishak (1 Kings 11:26–40), i.e. Shoshenq I, founder of the new, Libyan, Twenty-second Dynasty. Stripped of supporting revenues from both north and south, taxation now bore heavily upon the Hebrew people themselves – and perhaps more upon Israel than on Judah (possibly favoured by the royal house). Thus, at Solomon's death, his shrivelled domains were ripe for disruption, even at home, when Jeroboam returned from Egypt. When the new king Rehoboam refused to lighten the people's burdens, Israel broke away with Jeroboam as its king. So, even the heartland of Solomon's former 'empire' was now rent in twain, into two rival, petty states.

2. The First Oppressors: Shishak of Egypt

'United we stand, divided we fall!': a suitable epitaph for the Hebrew monarchy. In the 5th year of Rehoboam, *c.* 925 BC, Shoshenq I of Egypt launched his armies upon the two puny kingdoms.[1] His official reason was a border incident near the Bitter Lakes (on the line of the modern Suez Canal). 'My Majesty found that ... [they] were killing [my soldiers – and] my army-leaders. His Majesty was troubled about them .... Then His Majesty said to his courtiers, ... "[See,] these atrocities they have committed!" ... [Then His Majesty went forth ...], his chariotry accompanying him, without their (= the enemy's) realizing it ... His Majesty wreaked great slaughter among them ...' Thus far Shoshenq's damaged war-stela from Karnak. The Egyptian war-machine rolled into Philistia. Several detachments forked off to the right, south-eastwards, to strike at Judah's southern forts (Beer-Sheba, Arad, etc.), and subdue the Negeb and desert fringes. Shoshenq and the main army continued north-east, up the valley of Ajalon to Gibeon, where he encamped. Cooped up in Jerusalem itself nearby, Rehoboam was invited to submit and pay a massive tribute, or be crushed. Stripping Temple and palace alike of Solomon's wealth in gold (1 Kings 14:25–26), he paid up promptly, confronted by Shoshenq's huge force – 1,200 chariots, 60,000 main troops ('horsemen') and a horde of auxiliaries: Libyans, Sukkiim and Nubians (2 Chron. 12:2–9). The Sukkiim are mentioned only in the Chronicles account, and were the Tjuku or Tjukten scouts of Egyptian texts – an example of the original and independent value that can attach to items of information preserved only by Chronicles.

From Gibeon, Shoshenq struck northwards through the heart of Judah, up to Shechem, capital of his former protégé Jeroboam. But this wily character had already fled east across the Jordan and holed up in Penuel. Nothing daunted, Shoshenq dispatched a flying column to Penuel, to bring Jeroboam to heel, while he himself progressed grandly on through Israel north-westwards to Megiddo. There Shoshenq set up his field H.Q., sending raiding-parties into Galilee, and awaiting the return of his Penuel contingent. Meantime, the royal craftsmen set up a huge victory-stela in the king's

name at Megiddo itself – a 'jumbo' visiting-card![2] Then the
pharaoh returned south to Gaza (to be rejoined by the Negeb con-
tingents), and thence in triumph to his Delta capital at Tanis
(Zoan), laden with booty and doubtless leaving behind him two
very chastened Hebrew kings.

3. *The Dynasty of Ahab and Jezebel*

For the next two hundred years, *c.* 925–722 BC, the twin
kingdoms were caught up in a long series of petty rivalries with
each other and with such local neighbours as the Aramean rulers
of Damascus, the Transjordanian kingdoms of Ammon, Moab and
Edom, or with the Philistines, while the Assyrian colossus slowly
and inexorably loomed up on the horizon by 850 BC. It is a long
tale often told, and therefore a bird's eye view of a few interesting
details must suffice here.

In Judah, the dynasty of David continued on the Jerusalemite
throne in regular succession. But in Israel, a series of unstable
regimes followed one another swiftly in coup after coup.
Jeroboam's son was ousted by Baasha. Baasha's son fell to Zimri.
Zimri lasted a week, until the army strong man, Omri, besieged
him successfully in Tirzah, and then had to overcome a rival, Tibni.
Omri bought the hill of Shemer, and built there a royal citadel –
Samaria. This new capital was completed and adorned by his son
Ahab. Excavations at Samaria long ago revealed something of the
former splendour of the royal citadel, well laid out, and the main
buildings executed in fine masonry. One particular detail that has
often caught attention is the reference to the 'ivory house' of Ahab
(1 Kings 22:39). This appears to have been a pleasure-pavilion, in
which the walls and furnishings had been adorned with coloured
ivory-work, set with inlays, giving a brilliant decorative effect.[3]
Numerous fragments of the ivories were found during the excavations. They are similar in many respects to the Phoenician and
other ivories so avidly collected (as loot and tribute) by Assyrian
kings and hoarded in their great palaces in Calah and Nineveh (cf.
Amos 3:12b). This was then the mode, 'the way of the world', to
which Ahab eagerly conformed. Such fashions were doubtless encouraged by such notable characters as Jezebel, Ahab's Tyrian
queen, patroness of the cult of Tyrian Baal.

However, Ahab had more serious building to do. Excavations at
Hazor and Megiddo have vividly illustrated the drastic refortifica-
tion of these centres with the solid walls now deemed necessary as
defence against shifty neighbours (such as Damascus) or growing
major threats (Assyria). Water-supplies were assured by execution
of massive tunnelling-works down to springs, within the city-

perimeters – again, as at both Hazor and Megiddo. [4]At Megiddo in particular, Ahab's works were very extensive, including the large series of stables formerly assigned to Solomon's time. [5] Israel and Judah had learned to live with one another, the former subduing Moab (cf. 2 Kings 1:1; 3:4 f.) and the latter, Edom (1Kings 22:47). But the approach of Assyria inspired wider alliances. Osorkon II of Egypt had renewed his dynasty's alliance with Byblos, and he and the dynasty of Ahab also found it mutually convenient to become allies. The excavations at Samaria produced fragments of a royal alabaster presentation-vase marked with the titles of Osorkon II of Egypt and the note '81*hin*' as mark of capacity for the precious oil or unguent that it had once contained. The approach of Shalmaneser III of Assyria stimulated a coalition of practically all the Levantine states, encouraged also by Egypt's sending 1000 men,[6] to oppose him at the Battle of Qarqar in 853 BC At some cost, the coalition halted Assyria's advance for the time being, despite her claims of 'victory'.[7] The statistics are of interest: Hadadezer of Damascus fielded 1,200 chariots, 1,200 horsemen, 20,000 infantry; Ahab of Israel, 2,000 chariots and 10,000 infantry, etc. In fact, the allies mustered at least, 3,940 chariots, 2,900 horsemen and cameleers, and over 62,000 infantry. But hardly was the immediate threat repulsed, than the coalition broke up; Ahab died in conflict with the Arameans of Damascus.

4. From Jehu to the Fall of Israel

The short reigns of Ahab's sons saw the successful breakaway of Moab from vassalage under its king Mesha,[8] and finally a coup d'état by Jehu, founder of yet another new dynasty, in 841 BC. That very year, Jehu had promptly to pay tribute to Shalmaneser III of Assyria who was again pressing hard on the petty kings of the Levant. But it was the new king of Aram-Damascus, Hazael, who now wrought the greater havoc upon a weakened Israel (2 Kings 10:32–33; 13:22). Besides his appearances in the inscriptions of Shalmaneser III,[9] and as 'Mari' in those of Adad-nirari III, [10] two ivory fragments looted from Damascus bear the label-text . . *1-mrn Hz'l*, '. . . belonging to our lord Hazael',[11] using the same Aramaic title, *mari*, 'lord' by which he had become known to Adad-nirari's scribes. In 796 BC, Adad-nirari III extracted massive tribute from Hazael, including 2,000 talents – nearly 60 tons! – of silver. He likewise mulcted the kings of Tyre and Sidon, and 'Ia'asu (king) of Samaria', i.e. the newly-enthroned Joash of Israel, grandson of Jehu.[12] The Assyrian pressure weakened Aram so much that Hazael's successor Benhadad III was no match for his rivals Joash of Israel (2 Kings 13:24–25) and Zakur of Hamath.

For a brief span, c. 780–740 BC, both Israel (under Jeroboam II) and Judah (under Uzziah or Azariah) enjoyed a fragile outward prosperity. But not without social tensions and exploitation, as prophets like Amos make clear – condemning those that 'lie upon beds of ivory, but are not grieved for the affliction of Joseph' (i.e. the Israelite people), in the words of Amos 6:4–6. From Samaria at this general time we have the 'Samaria ostraca', a series of dockets apparently recording deliveries to the palace of oil and wine, possibly as revenue levied from crown estates. [13] Uzziah of Judah greatly restored his kingdom's power southwards (at Edom's expense), building a series of forts and re-establishing control of Elath (old Ezion-Geber) on the Red Sea Gulf of Aqaba (2 Kings 14:22; 2 Chron. 26:10). A series of forts of this period has been identified in the Negeb region, [14] and a sealstone optimistically attributed to the king's son and eventual virtual coregent, Jotham, was found at Tell el-Kheleifeh (Ezion-Geber), [15] perhaps confirming the presence of their rule in these southern reaches.

The ostraca and innumerable seals inscribed in ancient Hebrew script – intelligible only to those who could read – illustrate the wide use of alphabetic writing and of at least rudimentary literacy in Israel and Judah during the period of the kingdoms. [16] The production in this overall region of long inscriptions not only in Hebrew but in other West-Semitic dialects such as Moabite and Aramaic is shown by king Mesha's stela, as well as by the Aramaic inscriptions on plaster from Tell Deir Alla in the Jordan valley, mentioning the prophet or seer Balaam (cf. chapter 5). Kings and officials of the kingdom of Ammon are also becoming increasingly known from both seals and longer inscriptions. [17] Returning to Amos, his prophecies of judgement spanned the whole Levant, right across via Damascus (Amos 1:3–5) to the Euphrates, to 'him that holds the sceptre from Beth-Eden' (1:5). Coming in the mid-eighth century BC, this was a direct reference to Shamshi-ilu, the proudly-independent governor of Bit-Adini on the middle Euphrates, who for thirty years (c. 780–745 BC) was the virtually absolute ruler of his domain, not even troubling to mention his official masters, the Assyrian kings, in his inscriptions. His fall did come, from c. 745 BC, with the advent of a powerful new king, Tiglath-pileser III. [18]

But Shamshi-ilu was not alone in feeling the impact of renewed Assyrian might. During 743–732 BC, this descended like the proverbial wolf on the fold, subduing Uzziah of Judah and Menahem of Israel, and ending the kingdom of Damascus. Tiglath-pileser III devastated northern Israel, including Hazor (2 Kings 15:29) where have been found eloquent traces of the ferocity of that destruction in a layer of ashes a metre thick over the ruined buildings.[19] The Assyrian great king replaced Pekah on Israel's throne with a new king, Hoshea. When Tiglath-pileser died in 727 BC, Hoshea foolishly opted to rebel against Assyria. In 726/5 BC, he refused tribute to Shalmaneser V, and instead sent for aid from 'So, king of Egypt' (2 Kings 17:4). Not a whisper of help materialised from that quarter, and thus Shalmaneser V began the siege of Samaria without external interference (*c.* 725–722 BC). At its fall, the city's population was deported to Assyria by the new King, Sargon II. But who was the mysterious and unhelpful king So? By about 725 BC, Egypt had two lines of senior pharaohs reigning in the Delta – at that time, Osorkon IV in Tanis (Zoan) and Iuput II in Leontopolis further south. Neither king actually ruled effectively over anything more than his own local province. 'So' is most likely to have been an abbreviation for Osorkon IV of Tanis (Zoan), the recognised objective of Hebrew envoys to Egypt in the eighth and seventh centuries BC (cf. Isaiah 19:11, 13; 30:2, 4).[20]

The deportation of the Israelites to Assyria (2 Kings 18:9–12) spelt their kingdom's final eclipse, and was duly celebrated in the inscriptions of Sargon II: '27,290 of its inhabitants, I carried away as booty'.[21] In Assyria itself, one slight trace of some of the captive Hebrews appears to have been found. An ostracon from Calah (now Nimrud) of about 720/700 BC contains a list of names, often of a good 'biblical' stamp – 'Elinur son of Menahem; Nedabel son of Hanun; Elinur son of Michael', and so on.[22] But in the course of time, the exiled Hebrews were progressively assimilated into the Assyrian-Aramean amalgam of peoples inhabiting northern Mesopotamia.

JUDAH ALONE

1. *Hezekiah, Assyria and Egypt*

Escaping the rapacity of Sargon II, Hezekiah of Judah provoked his successor Sennacherib who campaigned in Syria-Palestine in 701 BC and unsuccessfully besieged Jerusalem (2 Kings 18:13 ff.; 19:1–36; Isaiah 36, 37). These episodes also feature in the inscriptions of Sennacherib himself, who greatly emphasises his capture of Lachish (shown in reliefs now in the British Museum), as he could not claim the outright capture of Jerusalem.[23] One factor that has often puzzled historical enquirers is the role of 'Tirhakah king of Kush' (2 Kings 19:9; Isaiah 37:9) – especially as Tirhakah was not king of Egypt and Kush (Nubia) until 690 BC and onwards. Ultimately the solution to this problem is a simple one. In 701 BC,

Tirhakah was but a prince at the side of his militant brother, the
new pharaoh Shebitku, who dispatched Tirhakah with an army to
assist Hezekiah in fending-off the Assyrian advance. But the
narrative in Kings and Isaiah does *not* end in 701 BC – it carries
right through to the death of Sennacherib in 681 BC (2 Kings
19:37; Isaiah 37:38), which is nine years *after* Tirhakah had
become king of Egypt and Kush. In other words, the biblical
narrative (from the standpoint of 681 BC) mentions Tirhakah by the
title he bore *at that time* (not as he was in 701) – as is universal
practice then and now. Unaware of the importance of these facts,
and badly misled by a wrong interpretation of some of Tirhakah's
inscriptions, Old Testament scholars have often tumbled over each
other in their eagerness to diagnose hopeless historical errors in
Kings and Isaiah, with multiple campaigns of Sennacherib and
what not – all needlessly. [24]

2. The Final Century

Assyria dominated the political scene down to the decade
630/620 BC, after which her foes steadily rose to engulf her. Only
under Hezekiah's third successor, Josiah, did Judah see hope of escaping the Assyrian yoke. He was able briefly to reclaim a large
measure of independence and to extend the area under his control.
His religious reforms (2 Kings 22–23; 2 Chron. 34–35) removed
the last vestige of subservience to Assyria, itself now hard-pressed
to survive the attacks of Babylon under Nabopolassar and his
allies the Medes. In 612 BC, Nineveh fell, and so the last Assyrian
king made his base at Harran, well west of Assyria proper. In 609,
Josiah lost his life trying to hinder the attempt by Necho II of
Egypt to aid the Assyrians (cf. 2 Kings 23:28–29; 2 Chron.
35:20–24). But he did not die in vain; in 609/8 BC, the Assyrian
state ceased to exist, and passed into history. Alongside the Old
Testament, our principal source of information on these stirring
times is the Babylonian chronicles, a compressed but relatively objective chronological summary of the principal events. [25]

Josiah's successors, however, may well have come to feel that
the end of Assyria meant a case of 'out of the frying-pan into the
fire'. In 609 BC, Necho II had appointed Jehoiakim as vassal-king
in Judah. The new king wasted his threatened country's assets in
short-sightedly building a lavish new palace with forced labour (cf.
Jeremiah 22:13–19), probably the citadel excavated at Ramat
Rahel, just south of Jerusalem. [26] In 605 BC, Nabopolassar's son
the crown prince of Babylon, Nebuchdrezzar, heavily defeated
Necho II of Egypt at the Battle of Carchemish, and so claimed
control of all Syria and Palestine, including Judah whence he took

hostages. That same year, Nebuchadrezzar II became king of Babylon. Three years Jehoiakim remained his vassal, then rebelled (2 Kings 24:1). The Babylonian chronicle gives us the background to this sudden change. In 601 BC, the Egyptian and Babylonian armies had clashed with mutually heavy losses, after which the Babylonian army at least needed a considerable refit. But Jehoiakim's fancied independence was not destined to last. Duly refitted, Nebuchadrezzar in 598/7 BC marched west, while Jehoiakim died, leaving the throne – and the crisis – to his son Jehoiachin. In March 597 BC Jerusalem and its new young king capitulated to the Babylonian emperor (2 Kings 24:8–17) who, as the chronicle states, having 'captured the king, he appointed there a king of his own choice, received it (Jerusalem's) heavy tribute, and sent them (dethroned king and tribute) to Babylon', along with many Judean notables. The new king was Jehoiachin's uncle, Zedekiah.

The end came swiftly. Zedekiah could not restrain the unruly faction in Judean politics, and got embroiled in anti-Babylonian intrigue, despite the prophet Jeremiah's warnings. In 589, Judah thus openly revolted, encouraged by the incautious new Egyptian king, Hophra (Apries of the Greek historians). Promptly, the Babylonians invaded Judah, taking cities such as Azekah and Lachish, and doggedly besieging Jerusalem until its final fall in 587/6 BC. This time, the fall was final – the Babylonians destroyed everything, leaving Jerusalem a desolation. Archaeological finds illustrate those dark, dramatic days. From the ruins of Lachish, a series of letters in Hebrew on ostraca (sherds) vividly reflect the oncoming Babylonian menace and the tensions in Judah. [27] Mention of people going down to Egypt in Ostracon III reminds one of the luckless prophet Uriah (Jeremiah 26:20 ff.). In Ostracon VI, the princes are accused of 'weakening our hands' (i.e. disheartening the writers), the very phraseology that the Judean princes used against Jeremiah (Jer. 38:4). The use of fire-beacons for signalling is found in both Ostracon IV and Jeremiah (6:1), both employing the same term. At Jerusalem, the Kenyon excavations revealed tumbled masses of destroyed and fallen walls and terracing, the bleak harvest of the Babylonian destruction. More recent work has found in the ruins arrowheads said to have been fired by the Babylonian attackers.

THUS SPOKE THE PROPHETS

One of the most remarkable features of Hebrew history, particularly for the five centuries or more from Samuel through to the Babylonian and Persian supremacies, was the role of those men and women commonly called 'prophets' (Hebrew *nabi*). Their most remarkable representatives were individuals who spoke out in the name of the God of Israel and Judah to recall their people to the basic norms and values of life as God's people under his covenant. Samuel proclaimed that 'to obey (God) is better than (formal) sacrifices' (1 Sa. 15:22), a theme pursued long afterwards by Hosea: 'I desire mercy and not (mere) sacrifice, the knowledge of God more than burnt offerings' (Hosea 6:6). So also, Micah:'What does the LORD require of you? But to do justly, to love mercy, and to walk humbly with your God' (Micah 6:8). Compassion for the oppressed, wrath against the exploiter, rooted in the character of their God and his covenant which, ever since Sinai, had bound Israel to the vision of a model community under their divine Sovereign – an obligation not relaxed in any way by the interposition of earthly kings as temporal leaders under that greater Sovereign.

The covenant (cf. chapter 5, above) was attended by promise of blessings for obedience and sanctions of curses (punishments) for disobedience. In this factor is rooted the judgements and blessings pronounced upon Israel and Judah by the prophets. In recalling the people to their supreme sovereign, the prophets in effect invoked sanctions on the people's unfaithfulness as the covenant laid down – and also the vision and promise of blessing on the contrite and returning prodigal. The old nineteenth-century theory claimed that the prophets were originally mere peddlers of unrelieved doom, to which meddling 'editors' added promises of blessing to soften the effect: this distortion takes no account of the basis from which the prophets took their cue, sometimes explicitly using the theme of the LORD's 'dispute' or 'controversy' with his people over their faithlessness (cf. Hosea 4:1–2; 12:2; Isaiah 34:8; Micah 6:1–3). Thus, the prophets spoke out on the basis of a covenant given *in the past*, in relating to it the condition and behaviour of their people *in the present*, appealing to a concern for the consequences dependent on a response marked by either obedience or disobedience *in the future*. All three time-zones belong to the prophets, not just any one of them.

1. Ancient Near Eastern Background

The origins of the biblical prophetic movement have been sought in many directions – but nowhere in the ancient biblical world do we find the equal of a Nathan or an Isaiah or a Jeremiah who, as single individuals (no legions at *their* command), stood up and boldly reproved kings and princes. All peoples have sought two-way communication between themselves and deity. Speaking *to* deity was, and is, expressed in prayer. To obtain responses *from* deity, the pagan nations of antiquity developed a series of techniques – principally divination, soothsaying or oracles, and magic (cf. Deut. 18:9–14). In Mesopotamia, for example, whole manuals and text-series are devoted to various classes of omens and their interpretation. In stark contrast, ancient Israel had her 'spokesmen' (probable meaning of *nabi*, the word so often translated 'prophet') who, under an inner conviction and inspiration, spoke out messages from Deity: for the true prophet, neither more nor less than God willed (Deut. 18:15 ff.). It is instructive to note the mutually-exclusive nature of the two forms of activity. Divination, oracles, etc., were the usual rule in Mesopotamia and the Near East, with very little 'prophecy' from spokesmen.[28] But spokesmen (prophets) held the central role in Israel, with divination, etc., dismissed to the sidelines as mere aberrations, false to normative Hebrew faith; magic had no role to play in Old Testament prophecy.

Thus, the amount and relevance of ancient Near-Eastern data on 'prophecy' is necessarily limited. But texts excavated at Ebla, Mari, in Egypt, Mesopotamia and Anatolia do provide some background, illuminating within its modest limits. From Ebla come mentions of two classes of 'prophets', the *mahhu*[29] and the *nabi'utum* related linguistically to Hebrew *nabi*, 'prophet, spokesman' (cf. chapter 3 above). Knowledge of the actual functions of the *nabi'utum* must await publication of the Ebla texts.

From Mari, some twenty-three documents attest 'prophetic' activity (eighteenth century BC), by *mahhu*, 'ecstatics', *apilu* 'respondents', and also prophetesses.[30] Usually they delivered a relatively short message about matters of concern to the king – his offerings to the gods, or funerary oblations to deceased predecessors, or about political events (friends and foes). The messages were sometimes received in dreams or during trances. Sometimes, they carried threat or promise, should the king respectively disregard or heed the messages. Thus, one may already see here – so early in history – the background to the concepts of the requirements of deity coming through spokesmen, enjoining obedience, and with appeal to blessing or sanctions (dependent on future response). But we have here no Nathan or Amos – no Mari prophet dares reprove the king for his personal sins, or to upbraid him because of social abuses and injustice, or to preach judgement on a nation, or blessings on the contrite. The contrast in essential content, therefore, is clearly marked. At best, Mari offers us part of the 'prehistory' of the concept of 'prophecy'.

From Egypt, a further dimension of that prehistory may be ad-

ded. During the twenty-second to thirteenth centuries BC, at least,
the Egyptians considered that sayings about the future should be
expected to be fulfilled. One finds occasional references to 'what
the ancestors foretold', now fulfilled, while the 'prophecy' of
Neferty is actually a pseudo-prophecy, modelled on the pre-
existing concept of prediction.[31] Also, several Egyptian literary
works of the early second millennium BC make their point *not* by
staccato oracles (as at Mari) but by long, even impassioned
speeches, including pleas for civil and royal justice – such works
include The Eloquent Peasant and the Admonitions of Ipuwer, for
example.[32] They are precursors of 'preaching'. Hence, one should
not imagine the Hebrew prophets of a millennium later as being
limited to a few stumbled ejaculations, but as men well able to
speak out at similar length centuries later.

The Hittites (fourteenth/thirteenth centuries BC) used a phrase –
literally, 'a man of God ' – for someone who might, by omen or
dream, give an answer from deity, rather as at Mari earlier on. [33] In
Syria-Palestine, legal texts from Ugarit mention 'seers' only in
passing.[34] But the Egyptian report of Wenamun mentions a youth
at the court of the king of Byblos, who fell into an ecstatic trance
and proclaimed that Wenamun was indeed the envoy of the Egyptian god Amun (*c.* 1075 BC).[35] In north Syria (*c.* 780 BC), king
Zakur of Hamath had his court seers who gave him messages of
deliverance from his god Baal-shamain,[36] rather like the Mari
'prophets' or the paid court 'prophets' of Ahab (1 Kings 22:6 ff.).
From first-millennium Mesopotamia, our evidence is limited. Some
texts that were once thought to be 'apocalyptic prophecies' are, in
fact, ancient attempts to base forecasts of the future upon the pattern of past history.[37] However, brief announcements as from the
gods – again, as at Mari long before – were still addressed to kings
and others; so in the time of Esarhaddon king of Assyria, for
example.[38]

2. *The Strands of Biblical Prophecy*

Thus, in overall context, the ancient biblical world in third,
second, and first millennia BC alike illustrates various features
associated with 'prophecy'. These include messages from deity (often in dream or trance), sometimes carrying future sanction or
blessing depending on response. Attempts at prediction, and
fulfilled predictions occur and (in Egypt) 'preaching' on social ills.
However, one finds practically nothing in terms of real personal
reproof for sin, no judgement on a nation; here, the Old Testament
prophets appear to stand out distinctively, transforming the whole
concept of 'prophecy'.

The strands of prophecy in the Old Testament are parallel and multiple. Besides the central role of spokesmen from God (Deuteronomy 18:15–20) from Moses's time, there is the feature of giving praise to God, often with, or by, music – compare Miriam 'the prophetess' (Exodus 15:20 f.), the elders with Moses (Numbers 11:16–17, 24–29), and Deborah who was both spokeswoman (Judges 4:6 ff.) and praise-leader (Judges 5:1 ff.). Alongside the famed spokesman Samuel, we see groups of prophets singing and music-making in 'prophesying' as Miriam had done (i.e., in praise), in 1 Samuel 10:5–6, 10–11. Obviously, one may speak in such cases of people being in an ecstasy of praise – but very far from being reduced to a mere dervish-like frenzy.[39] Besides those of spokesmen and leaders of praise, a further role of the Hebrew prophets was that of writers. Such was Samuel (1 Sa. 10:25), along with Gad, Nathan and others (cf. 1 Chron. 29:29; 2 Chron. 9:29). Their lineage as firm and fearless spokesmen continued during the rest of the Hebrew monarchy. In contrast stood the 'tied prophets', attached to the royal court as in Ahab's Israel, subservient to the king (1 Kings 22) – these could too easily be 'false prophets', rather than true. From the eighth century BC onwards, the prophets (or their assistants)[40] also wrote what they spoke, and so left a permanent record of their utterances – initially, perhaps, as witnesses for posterity, that their words might be seen to be justified in the outcome. So, we possess the works of that noble company from Amos, Hosea, Isaiah, via Jeremiah and Ezekiel, down to Haggai, Zechariah and Malachi, for example.

Finally, prophets and temple cult deserve passing mention. Once upon a time, it was fashionable in Old Testament studies to assume that prophets and priests were ever deadly rivals, always at loggerheads. Such views were based on mistaken interpretations of prophetic denunciations of *false* cult (e.g., hypocritical substitution of mere formal ceremonial for right living) as if they were condemnations of *all* cult. But as the ancient Near-Eastern data make clear, there was frequently – from Ebla and Mari to Assyrian imperial times – a close relation to temple-cult with prophets as well as priests. In ancient Israel, some prophets were themselves associated with the temple in Jerusalem, such as Jeremiah (1:1) or Ezekiel (1:3), while others – like Amos (1:1; 7:14–15) – were entirely laymen who had received a call to speak out.

8

Exile and Return

'... there we sat, indeed we wept as we remembered Zion'. Thus, the exiles in Psalm 137, bitter and melancholy, far from their homeland. That exile in distant Babylon varied for different members of the Hebrew community. Like Ezekiel 'by the river Chebar', most would be out in the villages and farms of the Babylonian plains, put to work on agriculture and irrigation, canal-cleaning and the like. Others would find employ for their various skills. The leaders were taken to Babylon itself. The royal family were kept at the court of Nebuchadrezzar II, and accounts of their food-allowances for the years 595–570 BC (in grain and oil) have been found in basement storerooms of the royal palace, possibly a building that had once supported the famous 'hanging gardens' of Babylon.[1] Jehoiachin and his sons were thus looked after well enough, but essentially under a form of house arrest. Such arrangements and allowances – under pleasanter circumstances – are mentioned again later for Jehoiachin in the reign of Awil-Marduk ('Evil-Merodach') about 560 BC, in 2 Kings 25:27–30. The Judaean elders in Babylon had been long since counselled by Jeremiah to make the best of their lot in that metropolis (Jeremiah 29).

1. The Concept of Exile

In modern histories of Israel and Judah, or of the Old Testament, the exile in Babylon tends to feature as *the* exile, and even on its own with initial capital-letter as 'the Exile', as though it were something unique. A drastic experience, at first totally unnerving and tending to induce despair, it undoubtedly was for those who actually were compelled to travel far eastwards to the hot Mesopotamian plains, and be paraded through Babylon as helpless captives of the victors. But once there, life had to continue somehow – and it did, despite the melancholy of Psalm 137. Before the calamitous crash of 586 BC, the Judaeans had stubbornly hoped on for deliverance from Babylonian capture, somehow – that hope, Jeremiah and Ezekiel had to condemn. But once the crash *had* come and the people were carried off into seeming despair, then both Jeremiah (30–31, etc.) and Ezekiel (36–37, etc.) had to proclaim that all was *not* finished, that in God's plan for the ages there was a future for his erring people. Thus, continuing life was not merely existence, but could have hope and purpose.

Thus *this* exile was only *one* instance of a custom of ancient Near Eastern warfare that had existed as a threat to *all* smaller nations and peoples in that area for untold centuries before. In the Old Testament itself, there had already been the Israelite exile in Assyria beginning from 734 and 722 BC, executed in two phases under Tiglath-pileser III (2 Kings 15:29) and by Shalmaneser V and Sargon II (cf. 2 Kings 17:6; 18:11). From the Assyrian vantage-point, indeed, these two deportations were merely incidents, part of a long series in the Levant and elsewhere. Away back in Moses's time, in the thirteenth century BC, Shalmaneser I deported young people of Urartu (Ararat) into Assyria, and likewise exiled some 14,400 prisoners from the middle Euphrates region (Hanigalbat).[2] In the late twelfth century BC, Tiglath-pileser I copied this practice, and from the ninth century BC onwards (beginning with Assur-nasir-pal II and Shalmaneser III), exile was an economic and political weapon exploited by every Assyrian monarch who waged foreign wars. Nor were the Assyrians the first or only state to impose exile on defeated foes. Again, in the thirteenth century BC, Ramesses II of Egypt is described as the one who removed southerners to the north, northerners to the south, easterners to the west, and westerners to the east, and in practice Ramesses III (*c.* 1180 BC) transported Libyans and Sherden into Egypt.[3] Still earlier, the Hittite king Mursil II repeatedly deported subject-populations on the grand scale – 15,300 one year, 66,000 another year, and so on.[4] Centuries before Moses, back in the eighteenth century BC (Mari), in the seventeenth century BC (Hattusil I of the Hittites), and the fifteenth century BC (Tuthmosis III and IV, Amenophis II, of Egypt), deportation of defeated peoples in upper Mesopotamia, Anatolia and Canaan itself recurs in the inscriptions of the victors in these periods and places. [5]

Therefore, the threat of exile far from home was *always* a reality that overshadowed the smaller nations or peoples like Israel, even from long before the days of a Moses or a David or a Solomon, right down to the eventual deportations of the Hebrews in the eighth century BC to Assyria and in the sixth to Babylon. Thus, threats of deportation among sanctions on disobedience in (e.g.) Leviticus 26:33, 39, 41, or Deuteronomy 28:36, 41, 64, are *not* reflections of the Babylonian exile written up afterwards (as 19th-century dogma has it), but are simply *one* of the *constant* potential fates that the 'small' nations had always to envisage at the hands of 'great powers', from one age to the next. Away back in the sanction-curses that end his 'law-code', Hammurabi of Babylon (*c.* 1750 BC) calls down upon any ruler who should offend against these laws 'the dispersion of his people', and that the goddess Inanna should 'deliver him into the hands of his enemies, and may they carry him away in bonds, to a land hostile to him'! [6] Here, formulated as early as the patriarchs, is the threat of exile *from* Babylon! The references in Leviticus and Deuteronomy are equally generalized, and hence cannot be used of themselves to date any part of these works so late as the Babylonian exile, or to any specific exile. In hindsight, of course, we can view the Assyrian and Babylonian exiles as 'fulfilments' of such sanctions, but not as actually historically present in the original writing of these passages. The generality of such sanctions in law, treaty and covenant is likewise illustrated by Esarhaddon's treaty with Baal, king of Tyre, in the curses of which we find: 'may (the Tyrian gods) Melqart and Eshmun deliver your land to destruction, and your people to be deported . . .', [7] which in fact had no final historical fulfilment.

Thus, the Babylonian exile must have affected the captive Judeans deeply; but it was not a unique event. And, as we have seen, the prophets Jeremiah and Ezekiel pointed forward to the future, saying that there was hope to come.

2. *The Significance of the Babylonian Exile*

It has sometimes been thought that this brief period of some fifty to seventy years was *the* creative period for Old Testament literature, when old traditions were either collected or simply 'invented', to be set down firmly in writing for perhaps the first time. The sixth century BC is characterized as a period when Egypt and Babylon both looked back to their ancient glories, reviving modes of one, even two, thousand years before. However, this picture is beset with logical fallacies and factual errors. Ancient glories were indeed harked back to, in both Egypt and Babylon. But only in a few outward trappings. Thus, in Babylon, archaic forms of signs and words might be used in a certain proportion of monumental or commemorative inscriptions – but the day-to-day administration was run (and recorded) on strictly contemporary lines and in current script. In Egypt, the officials (like their pharaohs) used ancient titles upon monuments, but in practice functioned within the reformed, fairly centralized administration of the vigorous Saite Dynasty 26 (*c.* 664–525 BC), with everyday texts written in increasingly flowing script – demotic, which took over steadily from the older hieratic. In literature in both civilizations, while new work was produced, the sixth century BC was definitely *not* a great 'creative' period, rather an age of conservation. In Mesopotamia, the scribes copied and recopied already long-extant classical Akkadian literature (even the long-outdated laws of Hammurabi) and adapted bilingual Sumero-Akkadian texts; little new was created (so far as we know), other than royal inscriptions, some hymns, and further rituals. In Egypt, similarly, there were rather fewer new works to set alongside the recopying of old, classical Middle Egyptian literature, and even the recopying of the Pyramid Texts for late funerary use from the originals of nearly two millennia before. It was, strikingly, an age of conservation, not creation. Therefore, if anything of the spirit of the age 'rubbed off' on the Hebrews in Babylonia, it would –again – be the recopying, conservation, of *already-existing older literature*, far more than the creation of numerous fresh new works. The opposite myth – that much of the Old Testament was essentially 'created' at this period – rests (1) on a gross misunderstanding of trends in the ancient Near East in the seventh-sixth centuries BC, and (2) upon now outdated nineteenth-century theories about the stitching-together of purely imaginary literary strands.[8] (J, E, P, D) into the present-day 'five books of Moses', plus analogous (and equally unrealistic) theories of the origins of much else in the Old Testament. On the basis of these modern myths, the supposed literary productivity of a cowed and conquered people within just fifty to seventy years was both phenomenal in scale and wholly anomalous in character. Instead, we should view Hebrew literary activity in the sixth century BC as, again, largely conservational – copying and preserving already existing works, with minimum of editing, far more than the writing of wholly new ones. Deliberately fashioned, archaic *literary* works were produced neither in Egypt nor in Babylon – nor, therefore, should they be assumed for the Hebrews. Instead, in the sixth century BC, original Hebrew writings were of limited number, if of memorable quality – the completion of Jeremiah's and Ezekiel's prophetical books, and the book of 1–2 Kings which derived most of its content from pre-existing first-hand sources. [9] Plus either the latter part of Isaiah or the book of Daniel, [10] depending on one's philosophical prejudices and attitude to the nature of biblical prophecy. Among pure poetry, we may include a few psalms like Ps. 137, and Lamentations (whether written by Jeremiah or not). The original Hebrew writings of the exilic period were thus of importance, but not nearly so numerous as has often been suggested. The period was seen as one of divine chastisement, with deliverance to come – a time for taking stock of basic values, and of retaining a heritage in hope of a better future.

THE SILVER AGE

During the reigns of Nebuchadrezzar's successors in Babylon, a formidable new power had arisen in neighbouring Iran. During the reign of Nabonidus (whose son Belshazzar was regent in Babylon), Cyrus of Persia took over the larger Median realm, becoming also king of the Medes, by 546 BC. [11] In autumn of 539 BC, after a battle at Opis for the province of Babylon, [12] Cyrus's troops quickly occupied Babylon itself, in which city Cyrus himself was hailed as liberator a few days later.

Cyrus instituted new policies, and decreed the return of subject peoples and their gods to their homelands, principally in and adjoining Mesopotamia. [13] Thus, his decree to the Judeans in Babylon allowing those who wished to return to Judea (Ezra 1:1 ff.) has long been recognised as being in line with the policy, acts and decrees of Cyrus and Darius I as known from other and first-hand sources. [14] Thus, the temple at Jerusalem was modestly rebuilt, despite delays, under Sheshbazzar and Zerubbabel, it being completed by 515 BC, focus for a restored Jewish community. Encouragement came from the prophets Haggai and Zechariah; later, perhaps, Malachi sought to stir up a disillusioned community that had lapsed into slack ways. They were the last of the preaching and writing prophets. Besides the restored community in Judea and Jerusalem, large communites of Jews continued to live and thrive in Babylonia. Others, likewise, in Egypt, as is evidenced by the archives (in Aramaic, sister tongue of Hebrew) of a body of Jewish mercenary soldiers and their families at the south end of Egypt, manning a garrison on Elephantine island (close to Aswan).

During the fifth century BC, the puny community in Judea still had its troubles. Ezra the scribe paid visits there from Babylonia in 458 BC and later, to regulate spiritual life and to fend off absorption of the Jews by their neighbours through injudicious intermarriages (book of Ezra). In 445 BC, Nehemiah (cupbearer to Artaxerxes I of

Persia) got permission to visit Jerusalem and rebuild its walls. In his efforts, Nehemiah was opposed by three jealous neighbours: Sanballat I, governor of Samaria just to the north; Tobiah, governor in Ammon, eastward across the Jordan; and Geshem or Gashmu, 'the Arabian', to the south (Nehemiah 2:19).

Each of these three has received some illumination from archaeological sources. Longest-known and most familiar is Sanballat of Samaria. He is named as father of two sons (one, Delaiah) in one of the Aramaic papyri from Egypt (Elephantine), of 408 BC, to whom the Jews there appealed for help. [15] Sanballat's family kept control of the Samaria governorship for about another century, down to the time of Alexander the Great – evidence for Sanballat II, Hananiah and Sanballat III is provided by a series of papyri (*c.* 350–330 BC) found not far from Samaria in recent decades. [16] A parallel family-line of governors of Ammon is also known to have succeeded Nehemiah's second foe for many generations – their tombs, including a once-splendid mausoleum or temple(?), are known at Araq el-Emir in Transjordan. [17] The most enigmatic of Nehemiah's opponents was the third – 'Geshem the Arabian'. He turns out to have been, in fact, the most powerful and dangerous of the trio. From the ruins of a small pagan shrine in the Egyptian east Delta came a set of eight fine silver vessels of the period of the Persian Empire, three being inscribed. One splendid dish is inscribed: 'What Qaynu son of Geshem, King of Qedar, brought (as offering) to (the goddess) Han-Ilat!' [18] The kings of Qedar had the confidence of the Persian kings, and a realm that stretched from North Arabia across Edom and Sinai to the borders of Egypt. Hence the seriousness of rumours spread by such a 'key man' against Nehemiah, and the sinister tone of the phrase 'and Gashmu says it . . .' (Nehemiah 6:6).

Thus the Old Testament closes with the biographical narratives of Ezra and Nehemiah in the fifth century BC. Also to that period belongs Chronicles. This is a history in part parallel with that represented by Genesis to Kings, with supplementary material, and notably different perspectives in time and in emphasis. 1 Chronicles spans primeval and early Hebrew history in the briefest form from Adam to David by a series of genealogies, some in Genesis-Kings, some from quite other, independent, sources, and devotes its main account to David's reign. 2 Chronicles covers the period from Solomon's accession to the fall of Jerusalem, ending with the same harbinger of hope – Cyrus's decree – that begins Ezra. The contrast in treatment of the earliest traditions and history in Chronicles and in Genesis is very striking, and shows the change in perspective across the centuries. In subject-matter, Chronicles is especially concerned with religious matters – the cult and temple under David and Solomon, and the history of faith and apostasy under their successors. Chronicles stands near the end of Old Testament history-writing, designed for the use of a religious community bereft of political independence, whose hope lay in its faith as the anchor also of its identity in the world. The religious traditions of the past were thus kept as a stimulus to present and future hopes. In these functions, Chronicles was not wholly alone in the outgoing ancient Near Eastern world. Beginning under Persian rule and especially under the regime of the foreign (Macedonian) Ptolemaic kings during the third to first centuries BC, the priests of Egypt's great temples also consigned their immemorial religious traditions to major compilations both on papyrus (mainly lost) and on temple-walls (in good measure preserved), these being the spiritual focus of a populace denied political freedom. In Mesopotamia during the fifth to first centuries BC, the gradually shrinking number of cuneiform scribes and scholars likewise kept alive their literature and traditions, often centred on the temples. In all of these terminal legacies – Chronicles included – is preserved a large amount of valuable information, often of very early origin, even when cast in later form.

9

In the Fullness of Time

When Alexander the Great vanquished Darius III in 331 BC and wrested from him the rule of the entire ancient Near East, a completely new era in world history opened up.[1] Following the Macedonian conqueror, there came east not only the Greek language which rapidly replaced Aramaic as the language of administration in his unwieldy new empire, stretching as it did from Athens to the Indus, but also the Greek or 'Hellenistic' culture, modes of thought and way of life. Alexander himself died within a decade (323 BC), with no true successor. His generals carved up the gargantuan empire among themselves, so that by 300 BC Ptolemy (I) held Egypt, and Seleucus (I) Syria and (initially) Mesopotamia, while others took over Anatolia and Greece itself. Palestine fell to the share of Ptolemy I of Egypt. A century later, in 198 BC, Antiochus III of Syria defeated the forces of Ptolemy V, and so Palestine (including Judea) came under a new master. Greek was everywhere the language of civilised intercourse, and Hellenistic culture the mode, attracting many Jews and weaning some away from the traditions of their forefathers.

However, a flashpoint came when Antiochus IV Epiphanes endeavoured to impose Hellenism more directly upon Judea, following upon intrigues over the high-priestly succession in Jerusalem. These moves culminated in 167 BC with the official proscription of normative Judaism, the conversion of the Jerusalem temple to the worship of Zeus – the 'abomination of desolation' announced in

Daniel (9:27, etc.). Persecution resulted in resistance, eventually led by Mattathias and his sons, notably Judas Maccabaeus. From repeated wars emerged an embattled but independent Jewish kingdom until, in the last century BC, Rome's power totally supplanted the collapsing realm of the Seleucids of Syria, and in time replaced the Maccabees by a new ruler over Judea – Herod the Idumean, 'Herod the Great', from 40/37 to 4 BC. Thereafter, Palestine was divided into fiefs among his sons into the first century AD, under the strict rule of Rome – a series of procurators ruled Judea in the emperor's name, the most notorious being Pontius Pilate. In the first decades AD, we are in the world of the New Testament.

THE DEAD SEA SCROLLS

1. *The World of the Dead Sea Scrolls*

Within the Jewish community in Judea, various internal religious groupings grew up, partly through the impact of Hellenism. Hebrew had largely been replaced by Aramaic in everyday use while, as we have seen, Greek was the language of government and international culture. So pervasive had the use of Greek become that, from the mid-third century BC, the Old Testament scriptures were translated into Greek by Jewish scholars in Alexandria, ending up with the Greek translation of the Hebrew text today known as the Septuagint.[2] The 'parties' that emerged within Palestinian Judaism included the Sadducees who accepted the ancient written Law, but not all the orally-transmitted interpretations and supplementary rulings that had grown up; they leaned also towards Hellenism in some measure. Their rivals were the Pharisees, from a more traditional devotional background, who were the expounders of the Law and of the growing mass of supplementary tradition that formed 'a fence about the Law'. Various other movements arose, notably the Essenes who maintained their own separate communities and groups. Such groups had the ideal of a purer, more 'spiritual' religious faith, and despised what they saw as the 'establishment' time-serving authorities of the Jerusalem temple.

One such group (Essene or otherwise) was the community that built itself a centre on the marl plateau overlooking the north-west corner of the Dead Sea in the second century BC. This lasted until the great earthquake of 31 BC, was deserted during Herod's reign (37–4 BC), after which the community re-established itself there into the first century AD. Then, with the crisis of the first Jewish revolt against Rome (66–70 AD), the sect hid its precious library of scrolls in the nearby caves and fled. The Roman Tenth Legion destroyed the place and the group never returned, leaving its scrolls unwittingly to posterity. For a time, the Romans kept a small military guard-post on the site (up to about 100 AD), and later it was briefly occupied by Bar-Kokhba's men during the second Jewish revolt (132–135 AD). Thereafter, the site fell into oblivion until modern times.

Then in 1947, after being stumbled on by a local goatherd, the scrolls came to public knowledge as the 'Dead Sea Scrolls', creating a sensation. They contain four classes of ancient writings, mainly in Hebrew, some in Aramaic. *First*, copies of the books of the Old Testament, every book being attested (even if only by scraps) except Esther. These MSS vary in preservation from one splendidly complete scroll of an entire biblical book down to the merest scraps. *Second*, copies of other known religious writings such as the Apocrypha – works like Tobit, Enoch, Jubilees and so on – besides similar works entirely new to us. *Third*, sectarian biblical commentaries, taking the form of verse-by-verse commentaries on Old Testament books (especially the prophets) from the community's own particular viewpoint. *Fourth*, writings that were composed by and about the community itself – its beliefs and rules – that inspired such works as the Manual of Discipline, Thanksgiving Hymns and the like.[3]

2. The Scrolls and the Old Testament

Ultimately, by far the most important contribution of the Dead Sea Scrolls for biblical study lies in their witness to the recopying and transmission of the Hebrew text of the books of the Old Testament. Until these manuscripts were discovered, our earliest *complete* copy of the Hebrew Old Testament text was the 'Leningrad Codex' of about 916 AD. As the scrolls date variously from the second century BC to the first century AD, they take us back virtually *a thousand years* in the history of the recopying of the Old Testament books. What is more, for the most part they very substantially support the traditional consonantal text of the Hebrew Bible, demonstrating the very high level of reliability with which it has been copied during that thousand years from (say) 100 BC to 900 AD. Occasionally, a minor improvement in reading is offered by the Scrolls; oftener, the traditional text is superior to the minor divergencies found in the Scrolls. Some scrolls provide what may be (a) form(s) of Hebrew text underlying some readings presupposed by the Greek (Septuagint) translation of the Old Testament, and perhaps even of the Samaritan version of the Pentateuch. However, the importance of these should not be exaggerated, particularly as – again – the traditional Hebrew text is in any case generally so greatly superior in its readings to these versions. A point of great importance is that the Dead Sea Scrolls represent a 'lay' text-tradition, distinct from the official text-tradition of the Jerusalem temple. It is the close agreement of the two separate and parallel traditions of text that strengthens our confidence in the basic text to which they both bear witness. [4] Furthermore, if the Hebrew text of the Old Testament books has been so well transmitted by successive generations of careful copyists for the last thousand years between 100 BC and 900 AD, then surely it is in order to suggest that comparable care was also probably exercised by copyists in the centuries between the actual composition of the various books and the Dead Sea Scroll copies of the second and first centuries BC. Certainly, in the ancient Near East within which the Old Testament books were first written, such scribal care is amply attested among the Hebrews' neighbours on all sides for many centuries.

3. *The Scrolls and the New Testament*

For the New Testament, the impact of the Scrolls is rather less direct. They certainly illustrate at first hand the currents of thought and of eager expectation of a messiah (or messiahs) in Judaism in the first centuries BC and AD into New Testament times. Just as such books as Deuteronomy, Isaiah and the Psalms are particularly quoted in the New Testament, so, too, the Scrolls community at Qumran turned most often to these same books. In the early years, various hasty comparisons were made with the New Testament that have not stood the test of time. There was the case of the 'Teacher of Righteousness' (more accurately and less cosmically, 'righteous teacher'), alleged to have been a kind of messiah, crucified and then raised to confound his foes, a 'first Jesus' so to speak. In reality, the 'righteous teacher' had been merely the devout scripture-expositor of the sect, and the manner of his death is unknown to us. Far from experiencing a sudden resurrection, the 'righteous teacher' was simply expected (like many another pious Jew) to rise again 'at the end of the days', at the general resurrection. He was never regarded as any kind of messiah. Various features of the Scrolls community can be compared with usage in the New Testament, but they often exhibit notable differences. For example, the practice of holding all goods in common occurs both in the Scrolls Manual of Discipline (vi:22) and in Acts (4:32 ff.). However, with the Scrolls community this practice was *compulsory* and *regular*; in the early church, it was a *voluntary* and *temporary* feature, later replaced by freewill offer-ings of a proportion of one's goods or income.[5]

ARCHAEOLOGY AND THE NEW TESTAMENT

The relation of archaeology to the New Testament is twofold. First, through the discovery of ancient manuscripts of New Testa-ment books, it gives us direct evidence on the reliability and preser-vation of the New Testament text (as do the Scrolls for the Old Testament). Second, as for the Old Testament, a whole variety of discoveries in Palestine, the Near East and the Roman Empire give us a rich background for the people, places and events of the New Testament.

Among works of classical (Greek and Latin) literature, the writings of the New Testament – 4 gospels, 21 letters, the history of Acts and visions of Revelation – have a manuscript attestation second to none, and superior to most. No one blinks an eyelid at depending for the Latin text of Julius Caesar's *Gallic War* (com-posed within 58/56 BC) upon manuscripts all of which are *900 years later* than Caesar's time, only nine or ten of the manuscripts being good textual copies. No-one doubts that we still read the real text of the works of Herodotus or Thucydides (450 BC), even though the oldest available full manuscripts (only eight or so) date from 1,300 years later![6] For the New Testament, how different and how vastly superior is the manuscript evidence. Some 5,000 Greek MSS (whole or fragmentary) are known, not a mere eight or ten. The most notable MSS are the Codexes Vaticanus and Sinaiticus of *c.* 350 AD – only 250 years after the end of the New Testament period (100 AD), not 900 or 1,300 years! Older still are the Chester Beatty and Bodmer biblical papyri, including six new Testament MSS of the second and third centuries AD, only 150 years after the New Testament period. Further back still, there is the Rylands fragment from a manuscript of John's gospel (18:31–33, 37 f.), datable by its script to about 130 AD – little more than a generation after the New Testament period itself. As this fragment came from Egypt, it is evident that John's gospel had been composed, recopied, and begun to circulate well beyond Palestine *before* 130 AD. Hence, on this evidence alone, it must have been composed (at latest) by 90/100 AD, and more probably earlier. Thus, the manuscript-attestation for the New Testament is of the highest quality in terms of date, and the sheer wealth of MSS also enables textual scholars to determine very closely indeed the correct readings of the New Testament's basic text – 'both the authenticity and the general integrity of the books of the New

Testament may be regarded as finally established', as Sir Frederic
Kenyon, an acknowledged master in this field, wrote some forty
years ago.[7] The continuing discoveries and work of the intervening
decades have not changed, merely enhanced, the truth of his
judgement.[8]

Turning from the text itself to its content, again, the general picture is a remarkably rich one. Ever since the Anatolian explora-
tions and discoveries of (Sir) William Ramsay earlier this century,
the accuracy of Luke as a historian and reporter has been upheld
by a multiplicity of details, particularly in the book of Acts. He
assigns the right titles to the proper officials at the correct periods
of time in question. Such are the proconsul in Cyprus (Acts 13:7)
and of Achaia (Acts 18:12), the Asiarchs at Ephesus (Acts 19:31),
among others. Back in Palestine, among Herod's heirs, Luke was
careful to entitle Herod Antipas the *Tetrarch* of Galilee, not loosely
'king' as many of his subjects flatteringly did (Luke 3:1, 19; cf.
Matthew 14:1, 9).

Luke's writings are not alone in being sober records of reality,
archaeologically speaking. The repute of Herod the Great as a
builder, at the stones of whose temple Jesus's disciples and others
marvelled (Luke 21:5; cf. John 2:20) has been fully borne out by
recent work at Jerusalem at the site of the temple enclosure,[9] and
by work at his fortress-palaces elsewhere,[10] as at Herodium[11] and
Masada.[12] From Corinth to Rome, Paul sent greetings in his letter
to the Romans, including from Erastus the treasurer (Romans
16:23). The selfsame individual was most probably the donor of a
pavement of the first century AD at Corinth, inscribed in the name
of one Erastus, curator of public buildings.[13] And so on. Not surprisingly, trained historians of the Graeco-Roman world have
repeatedly commented favourably upon the high historical value of
the New Testament writings, and of Luke-Acts especially.[14]
Needless to say, problems of interpretation in detail exist in this
field just as in any other, but are not necessarily insoluble.[15] Certainly the evidence derived from this field of study calls into question the groundless scepticism underlying much German New
Testament scholarship, based as it is (like its Old Testament counterpart) upon hypothetical theories of form criticism, redaction
'history' of the writings and so on, unrelated to observed literary
usage in the surrounding world. Even in a 'visionary' book like
Revelation, one may perceive the subtle undertones that relate the
letters to the seven churches (Revelation 2–3) to the local features
and background.[16] Thus, for example, Laodicea was a rich
banking-centre in a fertile countryside at an important junction of
routes in Roman Asia. It lacked, however, a direct water-supply.

Therefore its supplies had to be piped some distance from the hot springs, and were probably disappointingly lukewarm on arrival at the city-end, 'neither hot nor cold' (cf. Revelation 3:14–22, esp. 16).[17]

IN CONCLUSION

In the foregoing pages, we have travelled far in space and time – across hundreds of miles and through several thousands of years. We have visited not one, but half-a-dozen civilizations: Sumerian, Babylonian and Assyrian in Mesopotamia (Iraq), Hittite and Hurrian in Anatolia, Egyptian and Nubian in the Nile Valley, Eblaite, Ugaritic, Canaanite, Moabite, Philistine and others in Syria-Palestine. One and all, neighbours of the Hebrews and their ancestors.

Yet we have only touched on a sampling of the aspects and topics that might be surveyed under the broad heading of the Bible in its world – a world of archaeology and sites, of ancient objects and buildings, a world of texts and inscriptions that speaks eloquently of the hopes, fears, beliefs and doubts, joys and sorrows, loves and hates, of our distant precursors on history's stage. Whole realms of specialised study still await dedicated minds to explore them thoroughly and systematically. Even matters that have received full examination and technical publication cannot be more than sketched or outlined in brief works such as this present one.

Nevertheless, some salient points may be worth noticing in closing. The first is the immense revolution in our knowledge of the ancient past over the last two hundred years, and the growing precision and detail in that knowledge during the last thirty years or so in particular. A second is the fact that, just as texts on their own can be just disembodied voices speaking out in a vacuum, so also 'dirt-archaeology' of walls, pots and levels can often say remarkably little, and is often very incomplete, unless its evidence can be wedded to, and supplemented by, that of the texts and inscriptions. It may be undesirable (as well as uncomfortable!) to actually dig up the ancient East with Bible in one hand and spade in the other. But for any site dug which is thought to occur in written sources it is absolutely essential to do two things: to dig with the fullest care to recover all real evidence for the nature and history of occupation of a site – and to check up *all* the ancient sources for the places that the site might be supposed to represent, *including* the data in the biblical writings when they happen to be part of the available written record. Few ancient sites mentioned in the Bible are so perfectly known that one can afford to dispense with *any*

written data, biblical or otherwise. Thirdly, it is not the basic purpose of orientalists or archaeologists either to prove or disprove
any particular ancient document, the Bible included. It *is* their purpose to obtain the fullest and clearest possible picture of antiquity
(biblical and otherwise) for the common benefit of all, be they
biblical students or otherwise. If in the course of a fair and full in-
vestigation of the total available resources, the verdict is frequently
a high measure of agreement between the Bible and the world that
is its ancient and original context, then this result should not be
specially prized or despised, but used quietly and sanely to gain a
good understanding of both. When problems arise (as they do in all
fields of study, without exception), usually from incomplete or
defective information, then they should be treated alike in all cases
(biblical and otherwise) – critically, sympathetically, thoroughly,
drawing only provisional conclusions when lack of data makes
final ones impracticable. The biblical world has yet much treasure
to yield to us in times to come (Ebla is but one example), yet in
human experience, none to be compared with the Bible itself.

BC	EGYPT	PALESTINE	SYRIA	MESOPOTAMIA	BC
10,000	Predynastic cultures	Neolithic Pre-pottery, Pottery (Jericho), & Chalcolithic cultures	Neolithic and Chalcolithic cultures	Jarmo, Hassuna, etc., Halaf, Ubaid, Uruk cultures	10,000
3200				First writing	3200
3rd millennium	ARCHAIC PERIOD (Dyns. 1,2)	EARLY BRONZE AGE Local city-states	EARLY BRONZE AGE	EARLY DYNASTIC Sumerian city-states Gilgamesh, Enmebaragisi	3rd millennium
2500	OLD KINGDOM, or Pyramid Age (Dyns. 3–6)		Early-Syrian Dynasty, Ebla (*c.2400–2300*)	Empire of Akkad Sargon (2350) Naram-Sin (2300) Ur-III Empire (c.2113–2006)	2500
2000	1st Intermediate Period MIDDLE KINGDOM (Dyns.11–12)	Intermediate E.-Br.-Mid.-Br.			2000
2nd millennium	*Dyn.12*:1991–1786	MIDDLE BRONZE AGE ('Patriarchal age')	MIDDLE BRONZE AGE Ibbit-Lim, Ebla	OLD-BABYLONIAN PERIOD Mari archives, Amorite dynasties, Hammurabi of Babylon (1792–1750)	2nd millennium
	2nd Intermediate Period (1786–1552), incl. Hyksos kings	Invention of alphabet	Dynasties in Ugarit and Byblos		
1500	NEW KINGDOM, or 'Empire' *Dyn.18*: Tuthmosis III, Amenophis III, Akhenaten, Tutankhamun	LATE BRONZE AGE Egyptian rule	LATE BRONZE AGE Egyptian & Hittite rule	Kassite Dyn. in Babylon	1500
		El-Amarna tablets	Hittite power		

(BC)	(EGYPT)	(PALESTINE)	(SYRIA)	(MESOPOTAMIA)	(BC)
1300	*Dyn.19:* Sethos I, Ramesses II, Merenptah	Hebrews, exodus & into Canaan	Ugarit, state archives	Middle-Assyrian kings (Shalmaneser I) (Tukulti-Ninurta I)	1300
1200	*Dyn.20:* (1190–1069) Ramesses III, End of Empire. LATE PERIOD	Judges Saul	'Sea Peoples'		1200
1000:1st millennium					1000:1st millennium
925	*Dyn.21:* Siamun *Dyn.22:* Shoshenq I (Shishak), 945–924 Osorkon I, 924–889 Osorkon II, 874–850	David & Solomon *JUDAH & ISRAEL* Rehoboam Jeroboam I Jehoshaphat Ahab Jehu	'Neo-Hittite' & Aramean states *DAMASCUS:* Ben-Hadad I, Ben-Hadad II Hazael (Zakur, Hamath) Ben-Hadad III Fall of Damascus (734)	*Assyria:* Shalmaneser III (859–824)	925
800	Shoshenq III (*Dyn.23:* breaks away)	Jehoash Uzziah Jeroboam II Jotham Menahem Pekah		Adad-nirari III (811–783) Tiglath-pileser III (745–727)	800
750	Osorkon IV ("So")	Ahaz Hoshea Fall of Samaria, 722	. . . . Direct	Shalmaneser V (727–722) Sargon II (722–705)	750
700	*Dyn.25:*716–664 Shabako Shebitku Tirhakah (690–664) *Dyn.26:*664–525 Psammetichus I (664–610)	Hezekiah Manasseh	Assyrian Rule	Sennacherib (705–681) Esarhaddon (681–669) Assurbanipal (669–626) Fall of Assyria, 609	700
600	Necho II (610–595) Psam.II (595–589) Hophra (589–570) Amasis (570–526)	Josiah Jehoiakim Jehoiachin Zedekiah	Battle of Carchemish, 605	. . . . *Neo-Babylonian Empire:* Nebuchadrezzar II (605–562)	600

(BC)	(EGYPT)	(PALESTINE)	(SYRIA)	(MESOPOTAMIA)	(BC)
	Psam.III (526/5)	Fall of Jerusalem, 587/6		'Evil-Merodach' (562–560) Nabonidus (556–539) Fall of Babylon	
	. . . .	. . Exile in Babylon		. . . . Cyrus (539–530)	
			THE PERSIAN EMPIRE		
	Cambyses (525–521) Darius I (521–486)		The Province "Beyond the River"	Darius I (522–486) Xerxes I (486–465)	500
		Zerubbabel, 536 Temple finished, 516			
500	Xerxes I Artaxerxes I	Ezra visits Jerusalem, 458 Nehemiah there, 445–433		Artaxerxes I (464–424) Darius II (424–404) Darius III (335–331)	
	Dyns.28–30(400–341) 2nd Pers. Rule: (341–332)				
		ALEXANDER THE GREAT (331–323)			
300	The Ptolemies	(Ptolemaic rule to 198) Seleucids, 198ff. Maccabees, 165ff. Rome & Herod (37–4)	The Seleucids Antiochus IV Roman rule	Seleucids Arsacids, 129ff. (Parthia)	300
	Rome rule, 30				
AD to 100		NT Period			AD
0					0

Footnotes

CHAPTER ONE (pages 12–18)

1. References given in Kitchen, *Ancient Orient & Old Testament*, 1966, p. 65, nn. 29–31; cf. also the admirably cautious remarks by J. B. Pritchard, *Gibeon Where the Sun Stood Still*, 1962, pp. 157–158.
2. Published by Kitchen, *Journal of Egyptian Archaeology* 50(1964), pp. 63–70, cf. pp. 56, 53, Plate III.
3. For the three sites, see conveniently, K. M. Kenyon and others, in M. Avi-Yonah (ed), *Encyclopedia of Archaeological Excavations in the Holy Land*, II, 1976, pp. 550–575.
4. Cf. survey reported by L. T. Geraty, *American Schools of Oriental Research Newsletter*, No. 8 (January 1977), p. 12.
5. On this subject, cf. the salutary remarks by A. F. Rainey, 'Sites, Ancient, Identification of', in *The Interpreter's Dictionary of the Bible, Supplementary Volume*, 1976, pp. 825–827.
6. On the alphabet in ancient Israel and beyond, see respectively A. R. Millard, *Biblical Archaeologist* 35 (1972), pp. 97–111, and P. K. McCarter, *Bibl. Archeol.* 37 (1974), pp. 54–68.

CHAPTER TWO (pages 21–26)

1. The two phases of this early Jericho are usually termed 'Pre-Pottery Neolithic A and B' in archaeological works.
2. On religion in Chalcolithic Palestine, cf. C. Elliott, *Palestine Exploration Quarterly* 109 (1977), pp. 3–25.
3. Cf. the reports by S. W. Helms in *Levant* 7 (1975), 8 (1976), and 9 (1977).
4. So, 'Dumuzi and Enkimdu' (Kramer, in Pritchard, *Ancient Near Eastern Texts*, 1950/69, pp. 41–42), and the 'Dispute of Cattle and Grain' (cf. Kramer, *The Sumerians*, 1963, pp. 220–222).
5. The former is a book (1876), the latter, a lecture (Dec. 2nd, 1872; in *Transactions of the Society of Biblical Archaeology* 2 (1873), pp. 213–234).

6. A Heidel, *The Babylonian Genesis*, 2nd ed., 1951 (& reprs.); A. Heidel, *The Gilgamesh Epic and Old Testament Parallels*, 2nd ed., 1949 (& reprs.); E. A. Speiser, in Pritchard (ed.), *Ancient Near Eastern Texts*, pp. 60–99, and A. K. Grayson, in 3rd ed., pp. 501–507.

7. Cf. Pettinato, *Biblical Archaeologist* 39 (1976), p. 50, corresponding to Sumerian *a-ab*, 'waters'.

8. Cf. Heidel, *Babylonian Genesis*, pp. 101 f., 129 f., and his whole discussion, pp. 82–140.

9. So, W.G. Lambert, *Journal of Theological Studies* 16 (1965), p. 291.

10. Heidel, *Babylonian Genesis*, pp. 82–140; J. V. Kinnier-Wilson, in D. W. Thomas (ed.), *Documents of Old Testament Times*, 1958, p. 14 ('no connections of any kind'); Lambert, *Journ. Theol. Studies* 16 (1965), pp. 287–300, esp. pp. 289, 291, 293–9; A. R. Millard, *Tyndale Bulletin* 18 (1967), pp. 3–4, 7, 16–18.

11. Translation, Heidel, *Babyl. Genesis*, pp. 68–71 (not in Pritchard).

12. In Heidel, *op. cit.*, p. 64 (not in Pritchard).

13. In Heidel, *op. cit.*, pp. 61–63 (not in Pritchard).

14. In Heidel, *op. cit.*, pp. 72–73; Speiser in Pritchard, *Anc. Near Eastern Texts*, pp. 100–1.

15. W. G. Lambert & P. Walcott, *Kadmos* 4 (1965), pp. 64–72; Pritchard, *op. cit.*, 3rd ed./*Supplement*, p. 517 f./81 f.

16. See (e.g.) M. E. L. Mallowan, *Iraq* 26 (1964), pp. 62–82; R. Raikes, *Iraq* 28 (1966), pp. 52–63; W. W. Hallo in Hallo & Simpson, *The Ancient Near East, A History*, 1971, pp. 28 ff., 35 ff.

17. Cf. the remarks of Lambert & Millard, *Atrahasis*, pp. 16, 25 (with refs.). A 'king list' of the city of Lagash (*c.* 1700 BC) also began with the flood, cf. E. Sollberger, *Journal of Cuneiform Studies* 21 (1967), pp. 279 ff.

18. Fully edited by W. G. Lambert & A. R. Millard, *Atra-hasis, The Babylonian Story of the Flood*, 1969.

19. See M. Civil in Lambert & Millard, pp. 138 ff.

20. Lambert & Millard, *Atrahasis*, pp. 131–133.

21. Press reports of creation and flood stories among the literary tablets found at Ebla (*c.* 2350 BC) have not yet been officially confirmed; any such would be of the greatest interest. At the end of Mesopotamian history, one should also remember the summary of the flood by Berossus (given in Lambert & Millard, *op. cit.*, pp. 134–137).

22. Contradictions have often been alleged, by attributing various numbers in the narrative to different 'documents'; the contradictions (like the 'documents') are purely imaginary and have been repeatedly exposed as such; cf. (e.g.) Heidel, *The Gilgamesh Epic and Old Testament Parallels*, pp. 245–8.

23. The 'difference' between Gen. 6:19, 20 and 7:2, 3 is sometimes imagined to indicate multiple sources. In 6:19–20, 'pairs' is general (and one cannot have a plural of a Hebrew dual), while the command in 7:2–3 is more specific – pairs only of unclean, and seven pairs of clean, species. Cf. Kitchen, *Ancient Orient & OT*, 1966, p. 120 and references; W. J. Martin, in J. H. Skilton et al. (eds.), *The Law and the Prophets*, 1974, pp. 92 f.

24. Owing to the peculiar nature of the Sumerian King List (discontinuous dynasties; large regnal figures), one cannot, of course, use it to calculate the date of the flood.

25. Cf. J. J. Finkelstein, *Journal of Cuneiform Studies* 17 (1963), p. 46, Table II.

26. For summary and evaluation, cf. A. R. Millard, *Tyndale Bulletin* 18 (1967), pp. 4 ff., besides Lambert & Millard, *Atrahasis*, pp. 8 ff.

27. Note Mallowan's remarks on the Mesopotamian (not Palestinian) features of the flood phenomena (*Iraq* 26 (1964), p. 64).

28. And much earlier by others to Ebla; if press reports of a flood-story there are confirmed later. Other literature was certainly so transmitted.

29. Cf. the interesting treatment of the headings (or colophons?) by P. J. Wiseman (ed. D. J. Wiseman), *Clues to Creation in Genesis*, 1977, pp. 34 ff., revised from P. J. Wiseman, *New Discoveries in Babylonia about Genesis*, 1936, pp. 45 ff.

30. Within later biblical tradition, this usage is securely attested down to New Testament times; cf. the three series of 14 generations (Matt. 1:1–17), standing for a much longer series as the Old Testament books make clear.

31. Such as all the dynasties of Lagash, hence perhaps that city's 'anti-establishment' king-list (Sollberger, *Journ. Cuneiform Stud.* 21 (1967), pp. 279 ff.).
32. See Jacobsen, *The Sumerian King List*, 1939, pp. 2–4 (following on early over-optimism).
33. Thus, so careful and critical a scholar as the late Adam Falkenstein considered Gilgamesh not only to have been a real ruler, but to have been the contemporary (if not the builder) of Early-Dynastic II structures at Uruk (in *Reallexikon der Assyriologie*, III/5 (1968), p. 359).
34. The Sumerian title *en*, 'lord', was prefixed to the king's name in later times.
35. In *Zeitschrift für Assyriologie* 53/NF. 19 (1959), pp. 9–26.
36. Cf. remarks by Jacobsen, *Sumerian King List*, p. 153, n. 40, and p. 166 f. with n. 3 (citing also Sidney Smith).
37. Published by J. J. Finkelstein, *Journal of Cuneiform Studies* 20 (1966), pp. 95–118.
38. Published by I. J. Gelb, *Journal of Near Eastern Studies* 13 (1954), pp. 222 ff.; also Oppenheim in Pritchard, *Anc. N. E. Texts*, 3rd ed., 1969, p. 564, or *Supplement*, p. 128.
39. Cf. also A. Malamat, *Journal of the American Oriental Society* 88 (1968), Speiser Memorial Volume, pp. 163–173, with Table, p. 172.
40. For Sumerian, cf. remarks and table by W. W. Hallo in S. J. Lieberman (ed.), *Sumerological Studies in Honor of Thorkild Jacobsen*, 1976, pp. 197 ff., 200; for Babylonian, cf. table before p. 1, in W. G. Lambert, *Babylonian Wisdom Literature*, 1960.
41. Cf. Chronicle 18 in A. K. Grayson, *Assyrian and Babylonian Chronicles, (Texts from Cuneiform Sources*, V), 1975, pp. 40 ff., 139 ff.
42. Lambert, *Journ. Theol. Studies* 16 (1965), p. 299.
43. Lambert proceeds to suggest that even the period of the judges is far 'too late', and favours the Amarna period (14th century BC). However, Hebrew contact with Mesopotamia (during the Egyptian sojourn) was not likely to be very close then, and the factors considered here point more realistically to the early 2nd millennium BC.

CHAPTER THREE

1. The account given in this chapter is based exclusively upon the official, first-hand reports by Profs Matthiae and Pettinato themselves, not upon the flurry of press reports (of very variable quality). To assure the authenticity of this sketch, running references are given to the Matthiae and Pettinato reports. For abbreviations used, see Bibliography.
2. For this phase, see Matthiae, *OR-44*, pp. 337 ff.; *CRAIBL-76*, pp. 190 ff.
3. For what follows, see Pettinato, *OR-44*, pp. 361 ff.
4. Following Matthiae, *CRAIBL-76*, pp. 203 ff.
5. Tablet TM. 75, G. 336 (*c.* 2300 BC), transcribed and discussed by Pettinato and Matthiae, *RSO-50*, pp. 1–30, and briefly by Pettinato, *BA-39*, p. 47.
6. A figure quoted by Pettinato, *BA-39*, p. 47, from a further text.
7. Mentioned by Pettinato, *RSO-50*, p. 13, n. 29. Wider services required 11,700 men, Matthiae, *BA-39*, 107.
8. This paragraph depends on Pettinato, *BA-39*, p. 47 and n. 8 (text cited).
9. Compare our modern use of 'the city' for innermost London, or the 'inner city' for the central part of any of our large cities.
10. Gate of the sun-god.
11. Cf. Pettinato, *BA-39*, p. 45, § A, I; Pettinato, *OR-44*, p. 365; Matthiae, *CRAIBL-76*, p. 205.
12. Excellent account by C. J. Gadd, in *Cambridge Ancient History*,[3] I/2, 1971, pp. 417–463 (Ch. IX).
13. I.e., *Sharru-ken*, 'legitimate king', probably a surname that replaced his personal name.
14. Contrast the accounts given in the best histories published before 1975, e.g., Gadd, *Cambs. Anc. History*, cited just above.
15. Or, Reshi-Ennum (Pettinato, *RLA*, V, p. 12).
16. On him, cf. Matthiae, *CRAIBL-76*, p. 209, n. 53, who suggests that he may have

reigned just before or after Igrish-Halam. For all that follows, see Pettinato, *BA-39*, pp. 47–48, and Matthiae, *CRAIBL-76*, pp. 209–214.

17. Cited by Pettinato, *BA-39*, p. 48. & n. 14. According to latest indications, the king Irkab-Damu should not be last of his line, but be placed between Igrish-Halam and Ar-Ennum,. Dubuhu-Ada may not have had chance to succeed his long-lived father Ibbi-Sipish whose reign may have been that actually ended by Naram-Sin. Cf. P. Matthiae, *Comptes rendus de l'Academie des inscriptions & belles-lettres*, 1977, pp. 164 ff.

18. Cf. Matthiae, *CRAIBL-76*, p. 210, n. 54.

19. So, Pettinato, *BA-39*, p. 47, and *OR-44*, p. 367. Matthiae, *CRAIBL-76*, p. 210, & n. 54, p. 211, n. 65, envisages the new victory over Mari as occurring under Ebrum's successor, Ibbi-Sipish.

20. See summary, Pettinato, *BA-39*, p. 48.

21. Seemingly called Armi at this early period.

22. Matthiae, *CRAIBL-76*, p. 213 & n. 71; Pettinato, *BA-39*, p. 46.

23. Pettinato, *OR-44*, p. 365.

24. mentioned in the epithet, 'Dagan of Canaan', Pettinato, *BA-39*, p. 48.

25. Cf. (e.g.) Pettinato, *BA-39*, p. 46 & n. 7.

26. Ibdati king of Byblos is mentioned in Ur-III documents, cf. J. Bottéro, *Cambs. Anc. History*,[3] I/2, 1971, p. 560.

27. Cf. Matthiae, *CRAIBL-76*, p. 209, n. 52 (numbers of tablets), and Pettinato, *BA-39*, p. 45, § A, II & V.

28. Press reports of creation and flood stories have so far received no official confirmation.

29. Cf. Pettinato, *BA-39*, p. 45, IV; Matthiae, *CRAIBL-76*, p. 209.

30. Cf. Pettinato, *BA-39*, pp. 48–50.

31. On this pair, cf. E. Laroche, *Recherches sur les noms des dieux hittites*, 1947, p. 46; E. von Schuler, in W. Haussig (ed.), *Wörterbuch der Mythologie*, I, 1965, p. 177. Ashtabi or Ashtapi was the equivalent of the Mesopotamian gods Ninurta and Zababa.

32. On temples discovered, cf. briefly Matthiae, *OR-44*, pp. 344–346, fig. 3, pls. 31–34, with ref to earlier publications.

33. Cf. his guarded remarks, *BA-39*, p. 48.

34. Cf. (e.g.) F. R. Kraus, *Könige, die in Zelten wohnten*, 1965, p. 4/124.

35. One must, of course, make full allowance for differences in meaning that can occur in different West Semitic dialects, and in different periods of time.

36. Cf. long since, S. R. Driver, *Literature of the Old Testament*, 1913, p. 134:38/39.

37. As (for example) in Brown, Driver & Briggs, *A Hebrew & English Lexicon of the Old Testament*, 1907 (& reprints), p. 508*b*.

38. Attested in Great Papyrus Harris I, under Ramesses III/IV; see refs., Kitchen, *Ancient Orient & OT*, 1966, p. 144 & n. 13.

39. Cited by Pettinato, *OR-44*, p. 369 & n. 44, p. 371 & n. 83.

40. As Brown, Driver, Briggs, *Lexicon*, p. 960*a, b*, would have it.

41. Pettinato, *OR-44*, p. 372 & n. 98.

42. Brown, Driver, Briggs, *Lexicon*, p. 979*a*.

43. Pettinato, *OR-44*, p. 372 top; *RSO-50*, p. 11 & n. 17: 'gate of (*shi*) the city'.

44. Cf. list, Pettinato, *BA-39*, p. 50.

45. C. H. Gordon, *Ugaritic Textbook*, 1965, p. 367, No. 379.

46. Pettinato, *BA-39*, p. 50.

47. 'Late' (Brown, Driver, Briggs, p. 293*b*, f.); in Ugaritic, Gordon, *Ugaritic Textbook*, 1965, p. 395, No. 843 (esp. 3 Aqhat 9); Eblaite, Pettinato, *OR-44*, p. 372 & n. 92.

48. Cf. long since, A. T. Olmstead, *Assyrian Historiography*, 1916, pp. 7–8, 42 & n. 2.

49. Pettinato, *BA-39*, 47 & n. 11.

50. Cf. also H. W. F. Saggs, *The Greatness that was Babylon*, 1962, pp. 255–257, and in chapter 6 below.

51. *BA-39*, p. 47.

52. As is exemplified below, from the text edited by Pettinato, *RSO-50*, pp. 1 ff., esp. pp. 3–8.

53. Cited by Pettinato, *BA-39*, pp. 48, 50, etc.
54. Sundry unconfirmed reports suggest that such names as Esau, Saul, David, etc., also occur in the Ebla tablets. If so, exactly the same applies to them as to Ishmael and Israel considered here.
55. Matthiae, *OR-44*, pp. 345–6 and fig. 3 (p. 347); for the Hazor temple, cf. Y. Yadin, *Hazor, the Rediscovery of a Great Citadel of the Bible*, 1975, pp. 96 ff.
56. Pettinato, *BA-39*, p. 49.
57. A study of prophetism at Ebla is promised by Pettinato (cf. *BA-39*, p. 52, n. 17).

CHAPTER FOUR

1. So in the Encyclopaedia article, reprinted in J. Wellhausen, *Prolegomena to the History of Ancient Israel*, 1885 (repr. 1957), pp. 429–431.
2. Wellhausen, *Prolegomena zur Geschichte Israels*, 6th ed., 1927, p. 316 (transl. by KAK), cf. *Prolegomena to the History . . .*, p. 318 f. Cited in part also by T. L. Thompson, *The Historicity of the Patriarchal Narratives*, 1974, p. 7, to whose work it is the ultimate key.
3. See H. Gunkel, *The Legends of Genesis*, 1901 (repr. 1964), pp. 1 ff., 19 ff., where – again – rationalism reigns, uncontrolled by any proper external criteria from the biblical Near East.
4. *The Old Testament, An Introduction*, 1965, p. 42; cf. G. Fohrer, *Introduction to the Old Testament*, 1970, pp. 121–4.
5. E.g., Fohrer, *History of Israelite Religion*, 1973, p. 32 and n. 15, following his *Introduction to the OT*, 1970, pp. 121–122.
6. E.g., W. F. Albright, *From the Stone Age to Christianity*, 1940 (cf. 1957 ed., pp. 236 ff.), and *The Biblical Period*, 1949, pp. 1 ff.
7. J. Bright, *A History of Israel*, 2nd ed., 1972, pp. 76 ff.
8. References given in my *Ancient Orient & OT*, 1966, p. 42 and n. 36.
9. In *Bulletin of the American Schools of Oriental Research*, No. 163 (1961), pp. 36 ff., esp. pp. 40 ff.
10. E. A. Speiser, *Genesis, Anchor Bible*, 1964, pp. xxxix ff., 86 ff., and intermittently.
11. The principal works are: T. L. Thompson, *The Historicity of the Patriarchal Narratives*, 1974; J. van Seters, *Abraham in History and Tradition*, 1975; earlier, D. B. Redford, *A Study of the Biblical Story of Joseph, Vetus Testamentum Supplements* 20, 1970.
12. *Abraham in History & Tradition*, p. 39.
13. *Op. cit.*, p. 16.
14. Translations, (e.g.) M. Lichtheim, *Ancient Egyptian Literature, a Book of Readings*, I, 1973, pp. 227, 228; Wilson, in Pritchard, *Ancient Near Eastern Texts*, p. 20 (in line 110, read 'tent' for 'camp').
15. If one adopts the lower date advocated by van Seters, *The Hyksos*, 1966, pp. 103–120 (possible but not proven); otherwise a still earlier date will apply.
16. Admonitions, 10:1–2; cf. Lichtheim, *op. cit.*, p. 158; A. H. Gardiner, *The Admonitions of an Egyptian Sage*, 1909, p. 71; this passage was omitted in Pritchard, *Anc. Near E. Texts*, p. 443.
17. Translated by S. N. Kramer, *Genava* 8 (1960), p. 281; cited also by G. Bucellati, *The Amorites of the Ur III Period*, 1966, pp. 92, 330.
18. In 2nd-millennium Ugaritic, for example; C. H. Gordon, *Ugaritic Textbook*, 1965, p. 353, No. 106. On tents and early date, cf. D. J. Wiseman, 'They lived in Tents', in G. Tuttle (ed.), *Biblical and Near Eastern Studies*, 1977/78, in press.
19. Sufficient references in my *Anc. Orient & OT*, pp. 79–80; dismissal of such evidence by van Seters, *Abraham*, p. 17, is simply special pleading for apologetic purposes (i.e., to support an artificially-late date).
20. *Historicity of the Patriarchal Narratives*, 1974, pp. 14–15.
21. Cf. Abraham's wealth in livestock (besides precious metal), Gen. 12:6; 13:2, 5 ff.; 24:35.
22. Note Gen. 12:5 ('the people that they had gotten in Harran'); 13:7–8 (Abraham's herdsmen); 14:14 (muster of 318 armed retainers); 17:23, 27 (all the men of the household, born or bought); 23:6; 24:35, 59.

23. Seismic activity (loss of Sodom and Gomorrah) is not unknown; the firepot and torch perhaps came in vision (Gen. 15:17) in Abraham's sleep, cf. Gen. 15:1, 12.
24. 'Poem', lines 122 ff., Ramesses quotes Amun's reply to him; translated, Sir A. H. Gardiner *The Kadesh Inscriptions of Ramesses II*, 1960, p. 10; omitted in Pritchard, *Anc. Near E. Texts*, pp. 255–6.
25. It is of interest to note that 'the Lord appeared' to people usually in dreams, as in Gen. 28:12, 16 (cf. 35:7), or 31:11.
26. Leaving aside works of pure mythology exclusively concerned with the gods, in which humans do not appear.
27. Good random examples of such are those of Uni (Lichtheim, *Anc. Egyptian Literature*, I, 1973, pp. 18–22; extract only, in Pritchard, *op. cit.*, 227–8), Harkhuf (Lichtheim, *op. cit.*, pp. 23–27; omitted in Pritchard); Sebek-khu (Wilson in Pritchard, *Anc. Near E. Texts*, p. 230) and Ikhernofret (Wilson in Pritchard, *op. cit.*, pp. 329–330; Lichtheim, *op. cit.*, pp. 123–5); Amenemhab (Breasted, *Ancient Records of Egypt*, II, 1906, pp. 227–234 (§§ 574–592), and pp. 318–9 (§§ 807–9), and Bakenkhons (Breasted, *op. cit.*, III, pp. 234–7 (§§ 561–8). These range in date from 2300 BC, via 1850 BC, to 1450 and *c.* 1225 BC.
28. Sinuhe, cf. Lichtheim, *Anc. Eg. Literature*, I, 1973, pp. 222–233; Wilson in Pritchard, *Anc. Near E. Texts*, pp. 18–22. Wenamun, cf. Lichtheim, II, 1976, pp. 224–230, and Wilson in Pritchard, pp. 25–29. Providential is the ecstatic youth in Wenamun (Lichtheim, II, p. 225; Wilson/Pritchard, p. 26); as for deity, Sinuhe praises Montu for success in combat, and prays for return home (Lichtheim, I, pp. 228; 228–9; Wilson/Pritchard, p. 20 (Montu), but omitting the prayer-section).
29. Papyrus Westcar, cf. Lichtheim, *Anc. Eg. Literature*, I, 1973, pp. 215–222 (animals, p. 219); entirely omitted from Pritchard. Still later, the Demotic tales of Setne-Khamuas celebrate Prince Khaemwaset, famous fourth son of Ramesses II, a thousand years after his death (13th century BC) in fanciful fashion (F. Ll. Griffith, *Stories of the High Priests of Memphis*, 1900).
30. The names Anup and Bata are divine names in the Tale of the Two Brothers; Shipwrecked Sailor and Foredoomed Prince have no specific proper names. Sailor, cf. Lichtheim, *Anc. Eg. Lit.*, I, pp. 211–215; omitted from Pritchard. Prince, Lichtheim, II, pp. 200–203; omitted from Pritchard. Two Brothers, Lichtheim, II, pp. 203–211; heavily abbreviated in Pritchard, pp. 23–25.
31. Egypt and Naharin (Prince); Egypt and Syria, 'Cedar Valley' (Two Brothers), etc.
32. Leaving aside here, most royal inscriptions (hieroglyphic texts of princes of Byblos, 2nd millennium BC; Phoenician and Aramaic texts, 1st millennium BC).
33. Royal, but narrates the king's fortunes as a displaced fugitive in very graphic, 'non-royal' circumstances. S. Smith, *The Statue of Idrimi*, 1949; Oppenheim in Pritchard, *Anc. Near E. Texts*, 3rd ed., pp. 557–8, or *Supplement*, pp. 121–2.
34. See J. C. de Moor in *Zeitschrift für alttestamentliche Wissenschaft* 88 (1976), pp. 324, 335 f., and K. A. Kitchen, 'The King List of Ugarit', in *Ugarit-Forschungen* 9 (1977/78), in press.
35. As pointed out by the French scholars A. Caquot, M. Sznycer, A. Herdner, *Textes Ougaritiques*, I, 1974, pp. 409 ff., esp. pp. 413–5.
36. References collected in W. Schramm, *Einleitung in die Assyrischen Königsinschriften*, II, 1973, pp. 120–122. Translated, Luckenbill, *Ancient Records of Assyria*, I, 1926, pp. 295–6 (§§ 823–7).
37. Namely Bel-harran-beli-usur and Shamash-resha-usur, cf. Schramm, *op. cit.*, II, pp. 122–3, for references.
38. Cf. Gadd in *Cambridge Ancient History*, 3rd ed., I/2, 1971, pp. 426–7.
39. Gadd, *op. cit.*, pp. 442–3; cf. Grayson and Sollberger, *Revue d'Assyriologie* 70 (1976), pp. 103–128 (in French).
40. Cf. J. M. Munn-Rankin, in *Cambr. Anc. History*, 3rd ed., II/2, 1975, p. 286 f. and n. 5.
41. The former, summarized (in French) by J. J. A. van Dijk, *Sagesse Sumero-akkadienne* , 1953, pp. 11–12; the latter, translated by B. Alster, *Studies in Sumerian Proverbs*, 1975, pp. 90 f., 92 ff.
42. Translated, respectively, by O. R. Gurney, *Anatolian Studies* 6 (1956), pp. 145 ff.,

and by C. J. Gadd, *Iraq* 25 (1963), pp. 181ff.
43. All references for Hittite literature are in E. Laroche, *Catalogue des textes hittites*, 1971, and 1st supplement, *Revue Hittite et Asianique* 30 (1972/74), pp. 94–133.
44. Cf. (e.g.) the 'foundation-inscription' of Iahdun-Lim, king of Mari (*c.* 1800 BC), entirely in the 3rd person; Oppenheim, in Pritchard, *Anc. Near E. Texts*, 3rd ed., pp. 556–7, or *Supplement*, pp. 120–1.
45. These external criteria give the lie completely to the fairy-tale nonsense enunciated by Gunkel (*Die Sagen der Genesis*, 1901; in English, *The Legends of Genesis*, 1901, repr. 1964), which takes no serious account whatsoever of the ancient Near-Eastern literary background.
46. Depending on whether the accession of Ramesses II occurred in 1290 or 1279 BC (1304 is now excluded). The 'Israel Stela' of Merenptah (tacitly supported by other texts of his) sets Israel in Canaan by his 5th year; therefore any members of that group who had come from Egypt must have left Egypt well before that date.
47. The classic view of 100 years ago, promoted in even more extreme form by T. L. Thompson, J. van Seters, etc.
48. In his *The Historicity of the Patriarchal Narratives*, 1974, p. 8.
49. References for Anittas, cf. my *Ancient Orient & OT*, p. 46 and n. 53; and in *Tyndale Bulletin* 17 (1966), p. 78 and nn. 48, 52–53; also now, E. Neu, *Der Anitta-Text*, 1974 (*Studien zu den Boghazköy-Texten*, 18).
50. Cf. Kitchen, 'The King List of Ugarit', *Ugarit-Forschungen* 9 (1977/78), in press.
51. The famous legal text of the official Mose, now republished by G. A. Gaballa, *The Memphite Tomb Chapel of Mose*, 1977.
52. Most of what was said by the present writer in *Tyndale Bulletin*, 17 (1966), pp. 63–97, and in *Anc. Orient & OT*, 1966, pp. 41–56, etc., still retains full validity (only some Nuzi references should be dropped, such as the 'Dilbat' Abram). The panicky judgements expressed (e.g.) by S. M. Warner and J. M. Miller, *Journal for the Study of the Old Testament* 2 (1977), pp. 50 ff. and 62 ff., betray muddled thinking on methodology and a failure to understand the nature of evidence. They fail totally to grapple with the fallacies in Thompson and van Seters.
53. Elements Abu-, rama, in H. B. Huffmon, *Amorite Personal Names in the Mari Texts*, 1965, pp. 154, 262, refs. Similar type of name, Ab(u)-shar(ru), 'the father is king', in the Beni-Hasan scene (19th century BC) of 37 Asiatics visiting Egypt.
54. As in the forms Naharin, Nahrima, equivalents of Naharaim, in mid 2nd millennium BC. Van Seter's South-Arabian parallel is rather uncertain (wrong h?), on his own admission (*Abraham* ..., p. 42, n. 7).
55. References, see my *Anc. Orient & OT*, p. 48, n. 64; in his desperate efforts to get 'late' material, T. L. Thompson is forced to go for non- 'Imperfective' names on the root *'aqab*, hence not proper parallels to Jacob.
56. See *Ancient Orient & OT*, pp. 48–49 with nn. 63–68; Kitchen, *Tyndale Bulletin* 17 (1966), pp. 68–69 and refs.
57. Gen. 29:25 ff.; Lipit-Ishtar, cf. Kramer in Pritchard, *Anc. Near E. Texts*, p. 160. Cf. also Hammurabi's laws, § 148 (Meek/Pritchard, p. 172).
58. E.g., the texts in Speiser, *Annual, American Schools of Oriental Research*, 10 (1930), pp. 8, 30, 32, 35, 39. This double share can occur as early as the 18th century BC (as at Mari, text, n. 63 below).
59. In § 15 (Meek, in Pritchard, *Anc. Near E. Texts*, p. 198). Of course, if there is but one son by the first wife, the result is the same as in the preceding thousand years (examples of 1st-millennium documents, cf. van Seters, *Abraham* ..., pp. 91–92, who deliberately refuses to acknowledge the closer Mari parallel in order to overplay the late data).
60. Cf. also Lipit-Ishtar, § 25; Abraham's sending the lesser offspring away duly provided-for implies their having their freedom, as here.
61. A situation still true in Nuzi (cf. Speiser, *Annual, American Schools of Oriental Research*, 10 (1930), p. 32. Contrast Assyrian usage, both early (Finkelstein in Pritchard, *Anc. N. E. Texts*, 3rd ed., p. 543:4, or *Supplement*, p. 107:4) and late (example, J. N. Postgate, *Fifty Neo-Assyrian Legal Documents*, 1976, p. 106), perhaps showing regional differentiation.
62. But not definitely, as seen by van Seters, *Abraham*..., pp. 18–19, who compares

Akkadian *mar-biti*, misleadingly defining this as Late Babylonian, whereas it is attested as early as Old Babylonian (early 2nd millennium) and Middle Babylonian (later 2nd millennium), in references given by W. von Soden, *Akkadisches Handwörterbuch*, p. 616a, § 10b, and by M. David, *Die Adoption im altbabylonischen Recht*, 1927, p. 101, VAT 8947:21. The constant refusal by van Seters, Thompson, etc., to deal fairly with the *full* data – early as well as late – is a serious distortion of the evidence, and emphasises the weakness of their basic case.

63. Examples from the early 2nd millennium BC range from Sippar and Babylon (M. Schorr, *Urkunden des altbabylonischen Zivil - und Prozessrechts*, 1913, Nos. 8, 9, 17, 22) far northwest to Mari (*ARMT*, VIII, No. 1; Finkelstein in Pritchard, *Anc. Near E. Texts*, 3rd ed., p. 545:*13*, or *Supplement*, p. 109:*13*). Slaves could also be freed by adoption, cf. Schorr, *op. cit.*, Nos. 23–29, and remarks by David, *Die Adoption . . .*, pp. 68–69. In a Middle Assyrian adoption (David, *op. cit.*, p. 101), the adoptee is also safeguarded, but with lesser share.

64. Duly criticised and dismissed by van Seters, *Abraham*, pp. 71 ff. and refs., following D. Freedman, *Journal of Anc. Near Eastern Society, Univ. Columbia*, 2 (1970), pp. 77–85.

65. On this, cf. M. Greenberg, *Journal of Biblical Literature* 81 (1962), pp. 239–248; followed by van Seters, *op. cit.*, pp. 93 f.

66. For a critical reassessment of Nuzi data (better balanced than van Seters or Thompson), see M. J. Selman, *Tyndale Bulletin* 27 (1976), in press.

67. *Journal of Biblical Literature* 87 (1968), pp. 401–8; *Abraham in History & Tradition*, 1975, pp. 68 ff.; with A. K. Grayson, in *Orientalia* 44 (1975), 485 f.

68. See the original publication by Gardiner and De Zulueta, *Journal of Egyptian Archaeology* 26 (1940/1), pp. 23–29. This document is exceptional, not a sample of 'normality'.

69. See J. N. Postgate, *Fifty Neo-Assyrian Legal Documents*, 1976, p. 106.

70. First propounded by M. R. Lehmann, *Bulletin, American Schools of Oriental Research* No. 129 (1953), pp. 15–18; cf. my *Ancient Orient & OT*, pp. 154–5.

71. As pointed out by H. A. Hoffner, *Tyndale Bulletin* 20 (1969), pp. 33–35, who would discount the Hittite parallel completely.

72. So, G. M. Tucker, *Journal of Biblical Literature* 85 (1966), pp. 77–84, followed by van Seters, *Abraham*, pp. 98–100.

73. Points clearly set out by me, *Ancient Orient & OT*, pp. 155–6, as seen by (e.g.) Bright, *A History of Israel*, 2nd ed., 1972, p. 79, n. 84; but deliberately ignored (hence, suppressed) by van Seters, *Abraham*, pp. 98–100.

74. Pointed out by D. J. Wiseman, *Bibliotheca Sacra* 134 (1977), p. 130, n. 29, with reference to the tablet British Museum, *Cuneiform Texts*, 45, 1964, No. 60.

75. References, see my *Ancient Orient & OT*, pp. 50–51 with notes.

76. Full references, *op. cit.*, pp. 45–46, with nn. 48–52.

77. Refs., see *op. cit.*, p. 47 with nn. 55–58, to which add Iahdun-Lim of Mari, cf. Oppenheim in Pritchard, *Anc. Near E. Texts*, 3rd ed., pp. 556–7, or *Supplement*, pp. 120–1.

78. As by van Seters, *Abraham . . .*, p. 300 and n. 13, and in *Bibliotheca Orientalis* 33 (1976), p. 220.

79. See n. 77, end, above.

80. Important here is the critical reassessment of the Mari evidence on pastoralism and 'nomadism' by J. T. Luke, *Pastoralism and Politics in the Mari Period*, (University Microfilms), 1965, a work available, but totally ignored by van Seters.

81. The attempt by D. B. Redford, *A Study of the Biblical Story of Joseph*, 1970, to date that narrative to the 7th/5th centuries BC is simply wishful thinking based on special pleading (e.g., *paqad* called 'late', but known from the 18th century BC at least); sufficiently refuted by me, *Oriens Antiquus* 12 (1973), pp. 233–242.

82. On slave-prices, cf. already *Ancient Orient & OT*, pp. 52–53; on *saris*, Kitchen, *Journal of Egyptian Archaeology* 47 (1961), p. 160, completing *Anc. Orient & OT*, pp. 165–6.

83. Papyrus Brooklyn 35. 1446, W. C. Hayes, *A Papyrus of the Late Middle Kingdom*, 1955 (cf. Wilson-Pritchard, 3rd ed., p. 553 f.); Posener, *Syria* 34 (1957), pp. 145–163.

84. As did a king 'Ameny the Asiatic', and perhaps the king Khendjer, if his name is related to Ugaritic *hnzr*, with strong *h*.
85. Papyrus Chester Beatty III, in Gardiner, *Hieratic Papyri in the British Museum, Third Series*, I, 1935, pp. 9–23; A. L. Oppenheim, *The Interpretation of Dreams in the Ancient Near East*, 1956.

CHAPTER FIVE

1. In their tomb-chapels, 13th-century Egyptian officials sometimes honoured great men of two or three centuries earlier, whom they looked back to as 'ancestors' (real or moral) – so Userhat, to a vizier and two high-priests (Tomb 51), N. de G. Davies, *Two Ramesside Tombs at Thebes*, 1927, pp. 20–22, pl. XV.
2. Cf. already Kitchen *Anc. Orient & OT*, p. 55.
3. The geographical and topographical evidence has been ably gathered up (in German) by M. Bietak, *Tell el-Dab'a II*, 1975; cf. Kitchen, *The Egyptian Nineteenth Dynasty*, (forthcoming).
4. Contexts, cf. translations, R. A. Caminos, *Late-Egyptian Miscellanies,* 1954, pp. 106, 188 (omitted from Pritchard, *Anc. Near E. Texts*).
5. On this document and bricks in Egypt, see Kitchen, 'From the Brickfields of Egypt', *Tyndale Bulletin* 27 (1976), forthcoming.
6. *Ibid.*, and my *Anc. Orient & OT*, pp. 156–7.
7. Stela of the officer Ramose (in French: Yoyotte, *Bulletin de la Société Française d'Egyptologie* 6 (1951), pp. 11–14), cf. great stela of the viceroy Setau, Kitchen, *Orientalia Lovaniensia Periodica* 6/7 (1975/76), pp. 295–302.
8. Translated, Caminos, *Late-Egyptian Miscellanies*, p. 491; omitted in Pritchard, *Anc. N. E. Texts*. Apiru includes, of course, much more than just the biblical Hebrews.
9. Papyrus Anastasi V, 19:2 ff.; Caminos, p. 255; Wilson in Pritchard, p. 259.
10. For these figures, see Sir A. H. Gardiner, *The Kadesh Inscriptions of Ramesses II*, 1960, p. 10, and Wilson in Pritchard, *Anc. N. E. Texts*, pp. 237, 246, 247, 279 (top).
11. Ali Shafei Bey, 'Historical Notes on . . . Exodus', *Bulletin de la Société Royale de Géographie d'Egypte* 21 (1946), pp. 231–287, esp. pp. 278 ff.
12. A proceeding repeated at Shechem, Joshua 24.
13. Lipit-Ishtar and Hammurabi of Babylon; translations by Kramer and Meek, in Pritchard, *Anc. Near Eastern Texts*, pp. 159–161 and 163–180.
14. Ur-Nammu, title and latter parts lost; translation, cf. Finkelstein in Pritchard, *op. cit.*, 3rd ed., pp. 523–5, or *Supplement*, pp. 87–89.
15. Laws from Eshnunna, lacking formal frame to the laws proper; translation, cf. Goetze, in Pritchard, *op. cit.*, pp. 161–3. For some laws copied as a student exercise, cf. Finkelstein (above), pp. 525–6/89–90.
16. Six in bilingual versions.
17. Which also prefixes an oath-formula to each of its stipulations.
18. Excluding merest fragments, but including the parity treaty between Ramesses II and Hattusil III.
19. A formal analysis first established clearly by the cuneiform legal scholar, Viktor Korosec, *Hethitische Staatsverträge*, 1931.
20. So, Sfire I; the treaty of Assur-nirari V of Assyria with the Syrian ruler Matiel has its own peculiar arrangement of curses added to each paragraph of stipulations, and the witnesses added at the end.
21. See already, my *Anc. Orient & OT*, 1966, pp. 90–102, which remains valid with only the slightest changes.
22. Cf. retrospect, Deut. 10:1–5.
23. Cf. Josh. 24:27.
24. Cf. references in *Anc. Orient & OT*, p. 98, nn. 44, 45.
25. Naturally, distinctions in emphasis, etc., also exist; cf. *Anc. Orient & OT*, p. 148 f.
26. In *The Biblical Archaeologist* 17 (1954), pp. 26–46, 50–76, esp. pp. 53–70, reprinted separately as G. E. Mendenhall, *Law and Covenant in Israel and the Ancient Near East*, 1955.

27. In 1955, the present writer first made a complete analysis of all available treaties, applying the results to Deuteronomy; publication has not been possible.

28. *Treaty of the Great King*, 1963, following-up articles in the *Westminster Theological Journal* in 1959–61.

29. *Treaty and Covenant*, 1963, pp. 82, etc. Similarly, Whitley, *Journal of Near Eastern Studies* 22 (1963), pp. 37–48, aptly censured by D. R. Hillers, *Treaty-Curses and the Old Testament Prophets*, 1964, p. 83, for attempting 'to make the facts fit a preconceived notion'.

30. *The Ancient Near Eastern Treaties and the Old Testament*, 1964, pp. 14–15; cf. *Anc. Orient & OT*, p. 95, n. 34.

31. Only *one* tiny fragment from a 1st-millennium treaty could (so far) possibly be construed as part of a historical prologue (so, A. F. Campbell, *Biblica* 50 (1969), pp. 534–5). Unfortunately for this much-heralded and miniscule exception, there is every probability that the section concerned is the end of the witness-paragraph followed by a brief introduction to the stipulations. It bears little resemblance to the often extensive historical prologues of the late 2nd millennium.

32. *Journal of Biblical Literature* 84 (1965), pp. 38–51.

33. R. Frankena, in Oudtestament. Studien 14 (1965), pp. 122–154; M. Weinfeld, *Biblica* 46 (1965), pp. 417–427.

34. Weinfeld himself had noted Old-Babylonian evidence that illustrates this fact (*op. cit.*, pp. 422, 423), but learned nothing from it.

35. Weinfeld, *Deuteronomy and the Deuteronomic School*, 1972, pp. 59–61: 'this traditional formulation remained substantially unchanged from the time of the Hittite Empire down through the neo-Assyrian period. There is no justification, then, for regarding the formulation of the Hittite treaties as being unique, nor . . . any basis for (the) supposition that only Hittite treaties served as the model . . . of the Biblical covenant.' Except for the laws-element, nothing could be further from the truth than the statement just quoted.

36. Cf. briefly, Kitchen, *A Review of Bright's History of Israel*, 3rd ed., Theol. Students' Fellowship, Leicester, 1976, pp. 5–6; P. C. Craigie, *The Book of Deuteronomy*, New International Commentary on OT, 1976, pp. 79 ff.

37. The 14 'additional' versions being 6 bilingual Hittite treaties and 8 additional duplicates of the Esarhaddon/Medes treaty, one per prince.

38. Kitchen, *Tyndale (House) Bulletin* 5/6 (1960), pp. 7–13.

39. References for these and other rituals, cf. Kitchen, *The OT in its Context*, 1973, pp. 17–18; an extract, Goetze in Pritchard, *Anc. N. E. T.* , p. 347.

40. References, in J. Douglas et al., eds., *New Bible Dictionary*, 1962, pp. 1328–1330; Kitchen, *Old Testament in its Context*, 1973, p. 18.

41. C. -M. Bennett, *Levant* 5 (1973), pp. 1–11 (esp. 1, n. 6); 6 (1974), pp. 1–24 (esp. 19); 7 (1975), pp. 1–19 (esp. 15); 9 (1977), pp. 1–10 (esp. 9).

42. Gen. 36:33 alone mentions Bozra any earlier, not explicitly as a city (contrast verses 32, 35, of other places); it may then have been simply a district like Teman in verse 34.

43. Edomite shepherds watering their flocks in the east Delta, cf. Wilson in Pritchard, *Anc. Near Eastern Texts*, p. 259 (for Beduin, read Shosu). A little later, Ramesses III mentions destroying the tents of Seir (*ibid.*, p. 262 top), using the Hebrew-Canaanite word *'ohel*. On Edom, cf. D. Baly, *The Geography of the Bible*, 1974, pp. 233–240.

44. Cf. Y. Aharoni, *Biblical Archaeologist* 39 (1976), pp. 63, 71.

45. Aharoni, *op. cit.*, pp. 71 ff.

46. Particularly as the precise identifications of Tell Milh, Tell Masos, Tell Ira and their sub-sites with Zephath, one or more Hormahs, and Arad of Yeroham remain disputed and cannot be settled finally at present.

47. Aharoni, p. 70.

48. See summary of the 1968–71 dig by S. H. Horn in M. Avi-Yonah (ed.), *Encyclopaedia of Archaeological Excavations in the Holy Land*, II, 1976, pp. 510–514 and references.

49. L. T. Geraty, in *American Schools of Oriental Research, Newsletter*, No. 8 (Jan. 1977), p. 12.

50. Cf. latest summary by A. D. Tushingham, in Avi-Yonah (ed.), *Encyclopedia of Archaeol. Excavations in the Holy Land*, I, 1975, pp. 332–3.
51. Kitchen, *Journal of Egyptian Archaeology* 50 (1964), pp. 50–70.
52. See J. Hoftijzer, *Biblical Archaeologist* 39 (1976), pp. 11–17 (and 87); full publication, J. Hoftijzer and G. van der Kooij, *Aramaic Texts from Deir 'Alla*, 1976.
53. Cf. (e.g.) J. M. Houston in J. D. Douglas et al., eds., *New Bible Dictionary*, 1962, p. 656.
54. Leaving only one wall-foundation-fragment (north-west corner) on the full height of the glacis; cf. Kenyon in Avi-Yonah (ed.), *Encyclopedia of . . . Excavations . . .*, II, 1976, pp. 561–3.
55. Cf. Kenyon, *op. cit.*, pp. 563–4.
56. See survey of areas dug, J. A. Callaway in Avi-Yonah (ed.), *Encyclopedia of . . . Excavations*, I, 1975, pp. 36–52.
57. Long ago, it was pointed out that Et-Tell's 'history' better suited that of Beth-Aven than Ai, by J. M. Grintz, *Biblica* 42 (1961), pp. 201–16.
58. Cf. Y. Yadin, *Hazor, Rediscovery of a Great Citadel . . .*, 1975, esp. ch. 9.
59. See Albright, in Avi-Yonah (ed.), *Ecyclopedia of . . . Excavations . .* I, pp. 171 ff.; contrast M. Kochavi, *Tel Aviv* 1 (1974), pp. 2–33 (favouring Khirbet Rabud).
60. See Kelso, in Avi-Yonah, *op. cit.*, pp. 190–3.
61. References, Kitchen, *Anc. Orient & OT*, p. 67, n. 39.
62. Cf. Kelso, *op. cit.*, p. 192, on Bethel.
63. Long ago refuted by G. E. Wright, *Journal of Near Eastern Studies* 5 (1946), pp. 105–114; even with the growth of archaeological knowledge in the interim, his main points hold.
64. Cf. (e.g.), J. T. Milik and F. M. Cross, *Bulletin of the American Schools of Oriental Research*, No. 134 (1954), pp. 5 ff.

CHAPTER SIX

1. Well shown long since by I. Mendelsohn, *Bulletin of the American Schools of Oriental Research*, No. 143 (1956), pp. 17–22.
2. That is, walls built in two parallel lengths, linked by cross-walls, forming interior compartments. These could either be filled in to give greater solidity, or kept free (and entered from the inside face) to provide storage space, according to need.
3. See the useful outline by L. A. Sinclair, in Avi-Yonah (ed.), *Encyclopedia of Archaeol. Excavations in the Holy Land*, II, 1976, pp. 444–446 and references; cf. N. Lapp, *Bulletin, American Schools, Oriental Research* 223 (1976), pp. 25–42.
4. Cf. A. Malamat, *Journal of Near Eastern Studies* 22 (1963), pp. 6–8; Mazar, *Biblical Archaeologist* 25 (1962), pp. 102 f.; in graphic form, Y. Aharoni, *The Land of the Bible*, 1966, Map 21 with pp. 263–4.
5. After Siegfried Schott, *Hieroglyphen*, 1950, pp. 19–21, pl.3 (German).
6. Various translations, e.g. Wilson in Pritchard, *Ancient Near Eastern Texts*, p. 228.
7. *Pyr. Texts*, §§ 393–414; translation, R. O. Faulkner, *The Ancient Egyptian Pyramid Texts*, I, 1969, pp. 80–83.
8. *Pyr. Texts*, § 343, cf. §§ 352, 359; Faulkner, *op. cit.*, pp. 73, 74, 75.
9. Cf. (e.g.) S. N. Kramer, *The Sacred Marriage Rite*, 1969, p. 33 end.
10. Cf. Kramer, *op. cit.*, p. 32 end.
11. For the chronology of Sumerian and Akkadian literatures, cf. in outline respectively, W. W. Hallo in *Sumerological Studies in Honour of Thorkild Jacobsen*, 1976, pp. 181–203 with table, p. 200, and W. G. Lambert, *Babylonian Wisdom Literature*, 1960, pp. 1–20 and table before p. 1. On Sumerian stylistics, cf. C. Wilcke (in German), *Studies . . . Jacobsen*, pp. 205–316.
12. Cf. briefly W. F. Albright in H. H. Rowley (ed.), *The Old Testament and Modern Study*, 1951, pp. 31–32, and *Bulletin, American Schools of Oriental Research*, No. 150 (1958), pp. 36, 38; and esp. M. Held, *Journal of the American Oriental Society* 79 (1959), pp. 171 f., n. 49, and 174–5.
13. Using these terms in a broad linguistic/cultural sense, not in the more limited political

sense; as pointed out by Rainey, *Israel Exploration Journal* 13 (1963), pp. 43–45, Canaan proper in the 2nd millennium BC is essentially Western Palestine, the Egyptian province of 'Canaan', well south of Ugarit.

14. Many are collected in L. R. Fisher (ed.), *Ras Shamra Parallels*, I, 1972, II, 1975, III (forthcoming), with which should be compared the cautionary review by J. C. de Moor and P. van der Hugt, *Bibliotheca Orientalis* 31 (1974), pp. 3–26.

15. Translated (e.g.) by Ginsberg, in Pritchard, *Anc. Near Eastern Texts*, p. 131 top; Ugaritic text is Herdner, *Corpus des tablettes en cunéiformes alphabetiques . . . 1929 à 1939*, 1963, p. 11, Text 2, 'IV', lines 8–9.

16. The Hebrew is here transliterated with consonants only, to put it in a form directly comparable with the Ugaritic, for clarity.

17. A very far-reaching application of Ugaritic to the psalter is that by M. J. Dahood, *Psalms I*, 1966, *II*, 1968, *III*, 1970, in the *Anchor Bible* series; however, the numerous suggested correlations and 'solutions' require careful sifting to separate real gains from chaff.

18. In passing, one may note Amos's allusion (6:5) to David's musical repute, only two centuries after the united monarchy.

19. Translation of Aten-Hymn, Wilson in Pritchard, *Anc. N. E. Texts*, pp. 369–371. On (Dua)Khety's virtuosity, cf. (in French) G. Posener, *Littérature et Politique dans L'Egypte de la XIIe Dynastie*, 1956, p. 19, and n. 7 with references. The Aten-Hymn, incidentally, is a source neither of monotheism nor of Ps. 104.

20. For an appreciation of her work, cf. W. W. Hallo and J. J. A. van Dijk, *The Exaltation of Inanna*, 1968, pp. 1 ff.

21. Cf. A. W. Sjöberg and E. Bergmann, *The Collection of the Sumerian Temple Hymns*, (*Texts from Cuneiform Sources*, III), 1969, p. 5.

22. Cf. such notations as *sagidda, irshemma, balbale*, and labelled 'antiphons' in texts such as those translated by Kramer in Pritchard, *Anc. N. E. Texts*, 3rd ed., pp. 576–8, 582–4, or *Supplement*, pp. 140–2, 146–8.

23. For Mesopotamia, cf. (e.g.) the numerous allusions cited in I. J. Gelb et al. (eds.), *The Chicago Assyrian Dictionary*, Vol. 21/Z, 1961, pp. 36–38, with summary p. 38.

24. For this section (esp. Egypt), cf. Kitchen, *Third Intermediate Period in Egypt*, 1972, pp. 279–283.

25. On this point, cf. Malamat, *Journal of Near Eastern Studies* 22 (1963), pp. 15 ff.; on the Philistines' later history, cf. Kitchen in D. J. Wiseman (ed.), *Peoples of Old Testament Times*, 1973, pp. 64–67.

26. Cf. Malamat, *op. cit.*, pp. 7–8, preferable to Bright, *History of Israel*, 2nd ed., 1972, p. 209, needlessly emending Tadmor to Tamar.

27. Illustrated, A. R. Millard, *The Bible BC*, 1977, p. 27.

28. The same amount was paid to Solomon by Hiram of Tyre (1 Kings 9:14), in respect of territory in Galilee.

29. Translation, Oppenheim in Pritchard, *Anc. N. E. Texts*, p. 282 (66).

30. Not to mention the silly, frivolous legends of amorous relations built upon an arbitrary interpretation of 1 Kings 10:13; these are sufficiently reviewed in J. B. Pritchard (ed.), *Solomon and Sheba*, 1974, and are of no value whatever to the serious historian. The essay in that volume on Solomon's reign is needlessly negative, erring in method and heedless of background data.

31. Cf. (e.g.) J. Bright, *History of Israel*, 1972, p. 211.

32. It is uncertain whether this really means 'every year', 'annually', as is sometimes thought (for which *kol-shanah* would be a more precise expression). Our passage may mean that this figure was the maximum in a twelvemonth, not necessarily every twelvemonth.

33. In 2 Chronicles 8:18, we find 450 talents for 420; this illustrates the problem of variants in figures in ancient sources.

34. Cf. the calculations made by H. W. F. Saggs, *The Greatness that was Babylon*, 1962, pp. 255–257.

35. Translated, Breasted, *Ancient Records of Egypt*, IV, 1906, pp. 362–6, §§ 729–737.

36. More details, cf. Kitchen in J. D. Douglas et al. (eds.), *New Bible Dictionary*, 1962, pp. 431–2.

37. Oppenheim in Pritchard, *Anc. N. E. Texts*, p. 279 top.
38. Text translated by Albright, *Bulletin of the American Schools of Oriental Research*, No. 150 (1958), pp. 37–38, from Virolleaud, *Palais Royal d'Ugarit*, II, 1957, pp. 27–28.
39. Already in the 14th century BC, Amenophis III of Egypt is described as 'upon horse' in the text relating to a scene of him riding *in* a chariot (Petrie, *Six Temples at Thebes*, 1897, pl. 10); terminology must be understood with reference to actual practice.
40. Edited (in French), Nougayrol, *Palais Royal d'Ugarit*, III, 1955, p. 192f.
41. For size, contrast (e.g.) the personal temples of Ramesses II and III at Thebes in Egypt, each some 500 feet long, 200 feet wide, within still vaster precincts; nor are these the largest of ancient temples.
42. Examples, cf. C. F. Nims, *Journal of Near Eastern Studies* 14 (1955), p. 116; R. A. Parker, *A Saite Oracle Papyrus*, 1962, pp. 7, 8; Breasted, *Ancient Records of Egypt*, II, 1906, p. 156, § 375:23, 25.
43. Cf. translations, Breasted, *op. cit.*, II, pp. 133 (§ 319), 156 (§ 376:28), 157–8 (§§ 377:37–8).
44. Texts of Nakht-Thuty, Kitchen, *Journal of Egyptian Archaeology* 60 (1974), pp. 168–172.
45. Cf. the outer courts, etc., in the later vision of Ezekiel, 40–44.
46. Simple omission of an *l* in *sh-l-sh* (leaving *sh-sh*) would turn 300 into 600.
47. The Israelites being less intensively supervised than the squads of alien conscripts?
48. Cf. W. F. Albright, *The Biblical Period from Abraham to Ezra*, 1963, pp. 55–56 with n. 118 (pp. 105/6), and H. W. F. Saggs, *The Greatness that was Babylon*, 1962, p. 256.
49. Translation, cf. M. Lichtheim, *Ancient Egyptian Literature*, I, 1973, pp. 113–115 (Montet No. 192).
50. Edited as No. 61 (in French) in G. Goyon, *Nouvelles Inscriptions Rupestres du Wadi Hammamat*, 1957, pp. 81–85, with useful remarks by W. K. Simpson, *Journal of Near Eastern Studies* 18 (1959), pp. 28–32, who mentions the closely-related text Montet No. 87.
51. Translation, cf. Breasted, *Ancient Records of Egypt*, IV, 1906, pp. 223–7, §§ 461–8.
52. At each site, almost precisely 4.2 metres wide.
53. See (e.g.) Y. Yadin, *Hazor, Rediscovery of a Great Citadel . . .*, 1975, pp. 200–231, and 193 ff. (Hazor itself); on Gezer, W. G. Dever, in M. Avi-Yonah (ed.), *Encyclopedia of . . . Excavations . . .*, II, 1976, p. 441.
53a. See B. Rothenberg, *Palestine Exploration Quarterly* 94 (1962), pp. 44–56, and N. Glueck, *The Other Side of the Jordan*, 1970 ed., pp. 111–118.
54. See the summaries in Avi-Yonah, *op. cit.*, I, 1975, pp. 82–84, 86 (Arad) and pp. 162, 168 (Beer-Sheba, level V).
55. Done in condensed form in Kitchen, 'Proverbs and Wisdom Books of the Ancient Near East – the Factual History of a Literary Form', to appear in *Tyndale Bulletin* 28 (1977/78); fuller presentation has been prevented so far.
56. Among which, the Egyptian work of Amenemope might well have been included, although the common assertion that Proverbs 22:17 ff. is directly derived from Amenemope is mistaken in precisely that simple form.

CHAPTER SEVEN

1. For full details of Shoshenq's campaign, see Kitchen, *Third Intermediate Period in Egypt*, 1972, pp. 293–302, and 432–447.
2. The surviving fragment (with Shoshenq's names) is illustrated (e.g.) in Y. Yadin, *Hazor, Rediscovery of a Great Citadel . . .*, 1975, p. 216.
3. Published by J. W. & G. M. Crowfoot, *Samaria-Sebaste II, Early Ivories from Samaria*, 1938.
4. See generally Yadin, *Hazor, Rediscovery . . .*, 1975, e.g. chapters 10, 11, 14.

5. Provided with mangers in such a way that these buildings cannot well be just stores, as are the pillared buildings at Arad for example.
6. Cf. H. Tadmor, *Israel Exploration Journal* 11 (1961), pp. 145–7.
7. Cf. Oppenheim in Pritchard, *Anc. Near Eastern Texts*, pp. 278/9 (where one should now read 'Egypt' for 'Musri').
8. Famous for his stela, the 'Moabite Stone' (cf. translation, Albright in Pritchard, *op. cit.*, pp. 320–1), which supplements 2 Kings 3.
9. Oppenheim in Pritchard, *op. cit.*, pp. 280–1.
10. *Idem.*, pp. 281–2.
11. Cf. Kitchen in J. D. Douglas et al. (eds.), *New Bible Dictionary*, 1962, pp. 506–7 with references, plus D. J. Wiseman, *Reallexikon der Assyriologie*, IV, 2/3, 1973, p. 238 f.
12. Text edited by S. Page, *Iraq* 30 (1968), p. 143; cf. further, Kitchen, *Old Testament in its Context*, 1973, p. 29 and nn. 21, 22.
13. Cf. Y. Aharoni, *Land of the Bible*, 1967, pp. 315–327.
14. Aharoni, *op. cit.*, pp. 313–4, and in *Israel Exploration Journal* 17 (1967), pp. 1–17.
15. Cf. latterly, N. Avigad, *Bulletin, American Schools of Oriental Research* , No. 163 (1961), pp. 18–22.
16. Cf. A. R. Millard, *Biblical Archaeologist* 35 (1972), pp. 97–111.
17. Among other studies, cf. (e.g.) S. H. Horn & F. M. Cross, *Bulletin of the American Schools of Oriental Research*, No. 193 (1969), pp. 2–19, and by H. O. Thompson & F. Zayadine, and F. M. Cross, *Bulletin, American School of Oriental Research*, No. 212 (1973), pp. 5–15; G. Garbini, *Journal of Semitic Studies* 19 (1974), pp. 159–168.
18. A. Malamat, *Bulletin of the American Schools of Oriental Research*, No. 129 (1953), pp. 25–26.
19. Cf. Yadin, *Hazor, Rediscovery of a Great Citadel . . .*, 1975, pp. 147–8, 175–183.
20. See Kitchen, *Third Intermediate Period in Egypt*, 1972, pp. 182, 372–5, for So.
21. Oppenheim, in Pritchard, *Anc. Near Eastern Texts*, pp. 284–5.
22. Published by M. H. Segal, *Iraq* 19 (1957), pp. 139–145; cf. Albright, *Bulletin, American Schools of Oriental Research*, No. 149 (1958), pp. 33–36.
23. Oppenheim, in Pritchard, *Anc. Near Eastern Texts*, pp. 287–8.
24. See the full treatment in Kitchen, *Third Intermediate Period in Egypt*, 1972, pp. 154–172, and 383–386 (disposing of Macadam's imaginary co-regency between Tirhakah and his predecessor), refuting the false claims of Bright, *History of Israel*, 2nd ed., 1972, p. 298 and n. 9.
25. Of this period, ed. D. J. Wiseman, *Chronicles of Chaldaean Kings*, 1956; this period and others, now in A. K. Grayson, *Assyrian and Babylonian Chronicles*, 1975, *(Texts from Cuneiform Sources*, V).
26. On which, see Aharoni, in D. W. Thomas (ed.), *Archaeology and Old Testament Study*, 1967, pp. 178–183.
27. Some translations, cf. Albright in Pritchard, *Anc. N. E. Texts*, pp. 321–2, and D. W. Thomas in Thomas (ed.), *Documents from Old Testament Times*, 1958, pp. 212–217; both with further references.
28. A point also observed by Hallo in W. W. Hallo & W. K. Simpson, *The Ancient Near East, A History*, 1971, p. 158 (cf. pp. 158 ff., for Mesopotamian divination).
29. Sometimes translated 'ecstatic', although the known contexts do not so far bear out the correctness of such a rendering.
30. Translations and notes, cf. (e.g.) H. B. Huffmon, *Biblical Archaeologist* 31 (1968), pp. 101–124; W. L. Moran, *Biblica* 50 (1969), pp. 15–56, and in Pritchard, *Anc. N. E. Texts*, pp. 623–5, 629–32, or *Supplement*, pp. 187–9, 193–6.
31. Cf. mentions, Kitchen, *Tyndale (House) Bulletin*, Nos. 5/6 (1960), pp. 6–7.
32. Translations, Wilson, in Pritchard, *Anc. N. E. Texts*, pp. 407–10, 441–6.
33. Cf. Kitchen, *Old Testament in its Context*, 1973, p. 32, *c*, references.
34. Cf. Rainey, *Biblical Archaeologist* 28(1965), p. 123.
35. Translation, Wilson, in Pritchard, *Anc. N. E. Texts*, p. 26b.
36. Rosenthal in Pritchard, *op. cit.*, 2nd & 3rd eds., p. 501/655, or *Supplement*, p. 219.
37. Cf. R. Drews, *Iraq* 37 (1975), pp. 39–55, esp. pp. 48–50.

38. R. D. Biggs and Moran in Pritchard, *op. cit.*, 3rd ed. pp. 605 f., 625 f., or *Supplement*, pp. 169 f., 189 f.
39. Contrast Saul (1 Samuel 18:10; 19:23–24) who probably did go into a frenzy.
40. Cf. Baruch as scribe for Jeremiah, Jer. 36:4, 18, 27–28, 32.

CHAPTER EIGHT

1. Ration-tablets translated by Oppenheim in Pritchard, *Ancient Near Eastern Texts*, p. 308, and by W. J. Martin in D. W. Thomas (ed.), *Documents of Old Testament Times*, 1958, pp. 84–86. Cf. study by W. F. Albright, *Biblical Archaeologist* 5 (1942), pp. 49–55.
2. Translated, D. D. Luckenbill, *Ancient Records of Assyria*, I, 1926, pp. 39–40 (§§ 114, 116), 57, 59–60 (§§ 164, 171); A. K. Grayson, *Assyrian Royal Inscriptions*, I, 1973, pp. 81, 82 (§§ 527, 530).
3. References, Kitchen in J. B. Payne (ed.), *New Perspectives on the Old Testament*, 1970, pp. 6, 20, n. 42.
4. References, *ibid.*, nn. 37–41.
5. *Ibid.*, nn. 28–36.
6. Stela, cols. (reverse) xxvi:75, and xxviii:15–25, cf. translation by Meek in Pritchard, *Ancient Near Eastern Texts*, pp. 179, 179–180.
7. Translation, cf. E. Reiner in Pritchard, *op. cit.*, 3rd ed., p. 534, (iv), or *Supplement*, p. 98.
8. On which matter, cf. Kitchen, *Ancient Orient & OT*, pp. 112 ff.
9. Among 'minor prophets', Nahum, Zephaniah, Habbakuk and perhaps Obadiah functioned during the half-century before the fall of Jerusalem.
10. Much of the criticism of the book of Daniel rests on mistaken views long since outdated. The language of the book, especially the Aramaic, is best datable to the 6th–4th centuries BC, less easily later. Its historical allusions (not merely to the Maccabean age) are of a quality far superior to Judith and related works, for example. Cf. Wiseman, Mitchell & Joyce, Martin, Kitchen, *Notes on Some Problems in the Book of Daniel*, 1965; more recently, A. R. Millard, *Evangelical Quarterly* 49/2 (1977), pp. 67–73.
11. Text published by Gadd, *Anatolian Studies* 8 (1958), p. 77; cf. Oppenheim in Pritchard, *Ancient Near Eastern Texts*, 3rd ed., p. 562 f. (*Supplement*, 126 f.); Wiseman in Thomas (ed.), *Documents of Old Testament Times*, 1958, p. 83, and in *Notes on . . . Problems . . . Daniel*, p. 13.
12. For the sequence of events, see S. Smith, *Isaiah XL-LV*, 1944. (*Schweich Lectures*), pp. 45–7, cf. p. 152, n. 142.
13. E.g., Cyrus Cylinder text, cf. Oppenheim, Pritchard, *Ancient Near Eastern Texts*, p. 316.
14. Examples and references, Kitchen, *Old Testament in its Context*, 1973, pp. 37–8, and nn. 26–29.
15. Cowley series, Nos. 30/31; translated, Ginsberg in Pritchard, *Ancient Near Eastern Texts*, p. 492.
16. See F. M. Cross, *Biblical Archaeologist* 26 (1963), pp. 110–121, and in D. N. Freedman and J. C. Greenfield, (eds.), *New Directions in Biblical Archaeology*, 1971, pp. 45–69, and references, Bright, *History of Israel*, 1972, p. 412, n. 10. Governors of Judah, cf. N. Avigad, *Bullae and Seals from a Post-Exilic Judean Archive*, (Qedem 4) 1976, esp. pp. 30–36.
17. On the family, cf. Mazar, *Israel Exploration Journal* 7 (1957), pp. 137–145, 229–238; tombs at Araq el-Emir and general history, cf. McCown, *Biblical Archaeologist* 20 (1957), pp. 63–76. Latterly, cf. P. W. Lapp, *Bulletin, American Schools of Oriental Research* 165 (1962), pp. 16–34, *ibid.*, 171 (1963), pp. 9–39, and in Avi-Yonah (ed.), *Encyclopedia, Archaeol. Excs., Holy Land*, II, pp. 527–531.
18. Full publication, I. Rabinowitz, *Journal of Near Eastern Studies* 15 (1956), pp. 1 ff. and plates 6–7; unaccountably omitted from later editions of Pritchard, *Ancient Near Eastern Texts*, and *Ancient Near East in Pictures*.

CHAPTER NINE

1. Among treatments of the Hellenistic period, cf. W. F. Albright, *From the Stone Age to Christianity,* 1957 ed., pp. 334 ff.; J. Bright, *A History of Israel,* 1972, ed., pp. 414 ff.; F. F. Bruce, *Israel and the Nations,* 1969 ed., pp. 120 ff.; C. F. Pfeiffer, *Between the Testaments,* 1959 & reprs.
2. From the legend that seventy scholars were responsible for the translation.
3. For a convenient survey in outline, see F. F. Bruce, *Second Thoughts on the Dead Sea Scrolls,* 3rd ed., 1966.
4. Cf. W. J. Martin, *The Dead Sea Scroll of Isaiah,* 1954, (*Sixth Campbell Morgan Memorial Lecture*), pp. 19–21 on this point, plus A. R. Millard, 'Text and Comment', in G. Tuttle (ed.), *Biblical and Near Eastern Studies,* 1977/78, in press.
5. Cf. Bruce, *Second Thoughts . . .,* 1969, ed., pp. 136 ff.; E. Yamauchi, *The Stones and the Scriptures,* 1973, pp. 138–147.
6. For these examples (among others), cf. F. F. Bruce, *The New Testament Documents, are they Reliable?,* 5th ed., 1960, p. 16 f.
7. Sir F. G. Kenyon, *The Bible and Archaeology,* 1940, p. 288 f.
8. Only an extremely ill-informed tyro speaking from a position of invincible ignorance could possibly allege these days that 'the Gospel texts . . . are pretty corrupt', unless the wish be father to the thought (*Radio Times,* 9th/15th April, 1977, p. 4).
9. Cf. account in M. Avi-Yonah (ed.), *Encyclopedia of Archaeological Excavations in the Holy Land,* II, 1976, pp. 604 ff.
10. On the Herods and their works, cf. the readable accounts by Stewart Perowne, *The Life and Times of Herod the Great,* 1957, and *The Later Herods,* 1958.
11. Cf. G. Foerster in M. Avi-Yonah, (ed.), *Encyclopedia of . . . Excavations . . .,* II, 1976, pp. 502–510.
12. Cf. Y. Yadin, *Masada,* 1966.
13. Cf. (e.g.) F. F. Bruce, *The New Testament Documents, are they Reliable?,* 1960 ed., p. 95.
14. Cf. the sample citations given by E. Yamauchi, *The Stones and the Scriptures,* 1973, pp. 94–97.
15. E.g., the celebrated problem of the role and dating of Cyrenius (Quirinius) as governor of Syria in Luke 2:2; cf. Bruce, *The New Testament Documents . . .,* pp. 86–87, and Yamauchi, *op. cit.,* pp. 97–98.
16. In outline, cf. J. A. Thompson, *The Bible and Archaeology,* 1965, pp. 413–420; and in J. D. Douglas et. al. (eds.), *New Bible Dictionary,* 1962, under each city.
17. Cf. M. Rudwick in *New Bible Dictionary,* 1962, pp. 716–717.

Select Bibliography

A. GENERAL WORKS

1. *Geographical Background:*

Aharoni, Y., *The Land of the Bible*, 1967; Burns & Oates, London.

Baly, D., *The Geography of the Bible*, 2nd ed., 1974; Lutterworth Press, Guildford & London.

May, H. G., Hamilton, R. W., Hunt, G. N. S., *Oxford Bible Atlas*, 1962; Oxford University Press, London.

2. *Surveys, Palestinian Archaeology:*

Albright, W. F., *The Archaeology of Palestine*, 4th ed., 1960; Penguin Books, Harmondsworth.

Amiran, R., *Ancient Pottery of the Holy Land,* 1970; Rutgers University Press, New Brunswick, USA.

Avi-Yonah, M., (ed.), *Encyclopedia of Archaeological Excavations in the Holy Land*, I-IV, 1975–77; Oxford University Press, London.

Kenyon, K. M., *Archaeology in the Holy Land*, 1960 (& reprs.); Ernest Benn Ltd., London.

Thomas, D. W., (ed.), *Archaeology and Old Testament Study*, 1967; Oxford University Press, London.

3. *Surveys, Ancient Near-Eastern Civilization and the Old Testament:*

Douglas, J. D. et al., (eds.), *The New Bible Dictionary*, 1962 (& reprs.); Inter-Varsity Press, Leicester.

Kitchen, K. A., *Ancient Orient and Old Testament,* 1966; Inter-Varsity Press, Leicester.

Millard, A.R., *The Bible BC,* 1977; Inter-Varsity Press, Leicester.

Pritchard, J. B., *The Ancient Near East in Pictures relating to the Old Testament,* 1954, 2nd ed. 1969; Princeton University Press, Princeton, New Jersey, USA.

Thompson, J. A., *The Bible and Archaeology,* 1965; Paternoster Press, Exeter.

Yamauchi, E., *The Stones and the Scriptures,* 1973; Inter-Varsity Press, Leicester.

4. *Historical Background:*
(*a*) *General*:

Edwards, I. E. S., Gadd, C. J., Hammond., N. G. L., *The Cambridge Ancient History,* 3rd ed., Volumes I/1–2, II/1–2, 1970–75; Cambridge University Press, Cambridge.

Hallo, W. W., Simpson, W. K., *The Ancient Near East, A History,* 1971; Harcourt, Brace, Jovanovitch Inc., New York, USA.

(*b*) *Biblical*:

Bright, J., *A History of Israel,* 2nd ed., 1972; SCM Press, London. Cf. Kitchen, K. A., *A Review of Bright's History of Israel,* 3rd ed., 1976; Theological Students' Fellowship, Leicester.

Bruce, F. F., *Israel and the Nations,* 3rd ed., 1969; Paternoster Press, Exeter.

Wiseman, D. J., (ed.), *Peoples of Old Testament Times,* 1973; Oxford University Press, London.

5. *Collections of Translated Texts*:

Breasted, J. H., *Ancient Records of Egypt,* I–V, 1906–7; Chicago University Press, Chicago, USA.

Grayson, A. K., *Assyrian Royal Inscriptions,* I-II, 1972, 1976; Harrassowitz, Wiesbaden, Germany.

Lichtheim, M., *Ancient Egyptian Literature,* I–II, 1973–76; University of California Press, Berkeley & Los Angeles, USA.

Luckenbill, D.D., *Ancient Records of Assyria and Babylonia,* I–II, 1926; Chicago University Press, Chicago, USA.

Pritchard, J. B., (ed.), *Ancient Near Eastern Texts relating to the Old Testament,* 1950, 2nd ed. 1955, 3rd ed. 1969. *Supplement,* 1968; Princeton University Press, New Jersey, USA.

Cf. handy abridgements from *Pictures . . .* and *Texts . . .,* hardback and paperback:–

Pritchard, J. B. (ed.), *The Ancient Near East,* I, II, 1958–75; Princeton University Press, New Jersey, USA.

Thomas, D. W., *Documents of Old Testament Times*, 1958 (& reprs.); Nelson, London.

B. BASIC STUDIES ON EBLA

Matthiae, *BA-39* = Matthiae, P., 'Ebla in the Late Early Syrian Period: the Royal Palace and the State Archives', *Biblical Archaeologist* 39/3 (Sept. 1976), pp. 94–113.

Pettinato, *BA-39* = Pettinato, G., 'The Royal Archives of Tell Mardikh-Ebla', *Biblical Archaeologist* 39/2 (May 1976), pp. 44–52.

Matthiae, *CRAIBL-76* = Matthiae, P., 'Ebla à l'Époque d'Akkad: archéologie et histoire', *Comptes rendus de l'Académie des inscriptions et belles-lettres, Avril-Juin 1976*, pp. 190–215.

Matthiae, *OR-44* = Matthiae, P., 'Ebla nel periodo delle dinastie amorree e della dinastia di Akkad: Scoperte archeologiche recenti a Tell Mardikh', *Orientalia NS* 44 (1975), pp. 337–360.

[To appear in English as: Matthiae, P., 'Ebla in the Period of the Amorite Dynasty and the Dynasty of Agade: Recent Archaeological Discoveries of Tell Mardikh', being *Monographs on the Ancient Near East*, Vol 1/5 (1977); Undena Publications, Malibu, California, USA]

Pettinato, *OR-44* = Pettinato, G., 'Testi cuneiformi del 3. millennio in paleo-cananeo rinvenuti nella campagna 1974 a Tell Mardikh = Ebla', *Orientalia NS* 44 (1975), pp. 361–374.

[To appear in English as: Pettinato, G., 'Cuneiform Texts of the 3rd Millennium in Old-Canaanite from the 1974 Season at Tell Mardikh=Ebla', being *Monographs on the Ancient Near East*, Vol. 1/6 (1977); Undena Publications, Malibu, California, USA.]

Pettinato/Matthiae, *RSO-50* = Pettinato, G., Matthiae, P., 'Aspetti amministrativi e topografici di Ebla nel III millennio Av. Cr.', *Rivista degli Studi Orientali* 50 (1976), pp. 1–30.

Pettinato, *RLA-V* = Pettinato, G., Matthiae, P., 'Ibla', in Edzard, D. O., et al. (eds.), *Reallexikon der Assyriologie und vorderasiatischen Archäologie*, V/1–2 (1976), pp. 9–20, with lists of pre-1974 publications of the dig; W. de Gruyter, Berlin/New York.

de Maigret, A., 'Due punte di lancia iscritte da Tell Mardikh-Ebla', *Rivista degli Studi Orientali* 50 (1976), pp. 31–41.

(A series of technical studies by both Matthiae and Pettinato, in Italian, French, German and English is due to appear in such specialised periodicals as *Oriens Antiquus, Archiv für Orientforschung,* and *Revue d'Assyriologie*).

C. SUPPLEMENT TO OTHER PERIODS AND TOPICS

1. *Archaeological Methods:* (cf. Chapter 1):
Franken, H. J., and Franken-Battershill, C. A., *A Primer of Old Testament Archaeology*, 1963; E. J. Brill, Leiden.
Kenyon, K. M., *Beginning in Archaeology*, 1952 (& reprs.); Phoenix House Ltd., London.
Lloyd, S., *Mounds of the Near East*, 1963; Edinburgh University Press.

2. *Archaeology of Early Near East*: (cf. Chapter 2):
Oates, D. & J., *The Rise of Civilization*, 1976; Elsevier-Phaidon, Oxford/London.
Postgate, J. N., *The First Empires*, 1977; Elsevier-Phaidon, Oxford/London.
Mellaart, J., *The Neolithic of the Near East*, 1975; Thames & Hudson, London.
Ruffle, J., *Heritage of the Pharaohs*, 1977; Elsevier-Phaidon, Oxford/London.

3. *First Half of 1st Millennium BC:* (cf. Chapters 6–8):
Avi-Yonah, M., *The Holy Land from the Persian to the Arab Conquest*, 1966; Baker Book House, Grand Rapids, Michigan, USA.
Gray, J., *Archaeology and the Old Testament World*, 1962; Nelson, London.
Kenyon, K. M., *Digging up Jerusalem*, 1974; Ernest Benn Ltd., London.
Kenyon, K. M., *Royal Cities of the Old Testament*, 1971; Barrie & Jenkins, London.
Kitchen, K. A., *The Third Intermediate Period in Egypt (1100–650 BC)*, 1972 [misprinted as 1973]; Aris & Phillips Warminster.
Yadin, Y., *Hazor, the Rediscovery of a Great Citadel of the Bible*, 1975; Weidenfeld & Nicholson, London.
Yadin, Y., *Hazor (The Schweich Lectures, 1970)*, 1972; Oxford University Press, London.

4. *Intertestamental (Dead Sea Scrolls) and New Testament Periods:* (Chapter 9):
Bruce, F. F., *The New Testament Documents, are they Reliable?*, 1960, 5th ed.; Inter-Varsity Press, Leicester.
Bruce, F. F. *Second Thoughts on the Dead Sea Scrolls*, 3rd ed., 1969; Paternoster Press, Exeter.

Burrows, M., *The Dead Sea Scrolls*, 1956; *More Light on the Dead Sea Scrolls*, 1958; Secker & Warburg, London.

Cross, F. M., *The Ancient Library of Qumran and Modern Biblical Studies,* 1958; Duckworths, London.

Finegan, J., *Archaeology of the New Testament*, 1969; Princeton University Press, New Jersey, USA.

Cf. Kane, J. P., 'Palestinian Archaeology and the New Testament', *Religion* 2 (1972), pp. 57–75.

Metzger, B. M., *The Text of the New Testament*, 2nd ed., 1968.

Pfeiffer, C. F., *Between the Testaments*, 1959 (& reprs.); Baker Book House, Grand Rapids, Michigan, USA.

Sherwin-White, A. N., *Roman Society and Roman Law in the New Testament*, 1963; Oxford University Press, London.

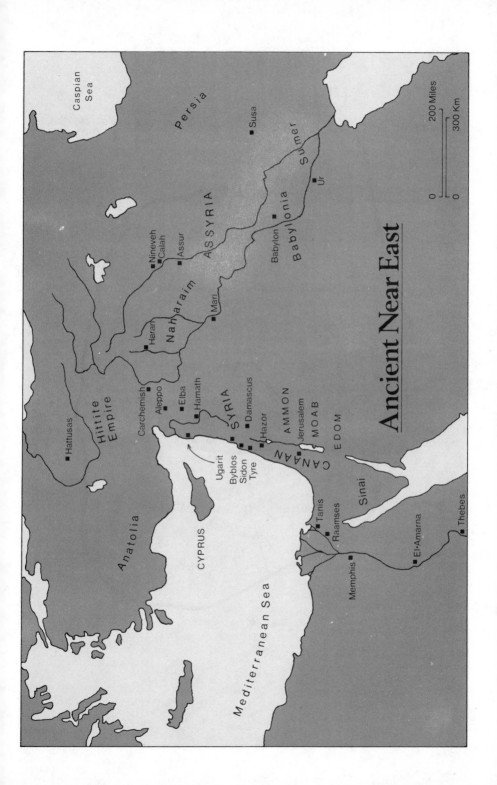

Ancient Near East

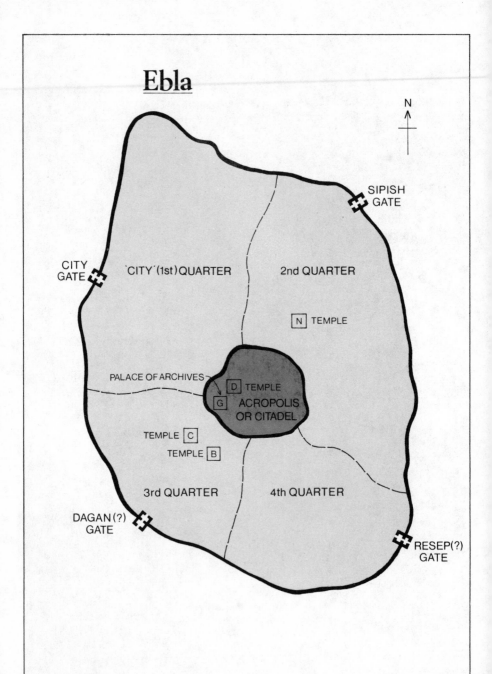

Ebla

N

SIPISH GATE

CITY GATE

'CITY' (1st) QUARTER

2nd QUARTER

N TEMPLE

PALACE OF ARCHIVES

D TEMPLE

G

ACROPOLIS OR CITADEL

TEMPLE C

TEMPLE B

3rd QUARTER

4th QUARTER

DAGAN (?) GATE

RESEP (?) GATE

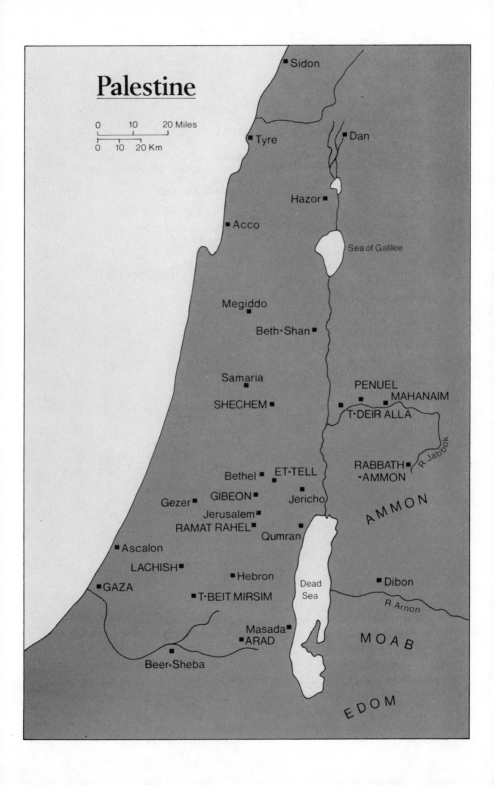

Index

A. GENERAL

B. BIBLICAL REFERENCES